JavaScript

Second Edition

ABSOLUTE
BEGINNER'S
GUIDE

Kirupa Chinnathambi

JavaScript Absolute Beginner's Guide, 2nd Edition

ISBN-13: 978-0-13-650289-0
ISBN-10: 0-13-650289-X

Library of Congress Control Number: 2019951999

1 2019

For information about buying this title in bulk quantities, or for special sales opportunities (which may include electronic versions; custom cover designs; and content particular to your business, training goals, marketing focus, or branding interests), please contact our corporate sales department at corpsales@pearson.com or (800) 382-3419.

For government sales inquiries, please contact governmentsales@pearsoned.com.

For questions about sales outside the U.S., please contact intlcs@pearsoned.com.

Editor-in-Chief
Mark L. Taub

Executive Editor
Kim Spenceley

Development Editor
Chris Zahn

Technical Editor
Trevor McCauley

Managing Editor
Sandra Schroeder

Senior Project Editor
Lori Lyons

Production Manager
Gayathri Umashankaran/
codeMantra

Indexer
Cheryl Lenser

Proofreader
Abigail Manheim

Cover Designer
Chuti Prasertsith

Compositor
codeMantra

Contents at a Glance

Register Your Book

Register your copy of **JavaScript Absolute Beginner's Guide, Second Edition**, at informit.com for convenient access to downloads, updates, and corrections as they become available. To start the registration process, go to www.informit.com/register and log in or create an account.* Enter the product ISBN, **9780136502890**, and click Submit. Once the process is complete, you will find any available bonus content under Registered Products.

*Be sure to check the box that you would like to hear from us in order to receive exclusive discounts on future editions of this product.

Table of Contents

Dedication

To Meena!

(Who still laughs at the jokes found in these pages despite having read them a bazillion times!)

Acknowledgments

As I found out, getting a book like this out the door is no small feat. It involves a bunch of people in front of (and behind) the camera who work tirelessly to turn my ramblings into the beautiful pages that you are about see. To everyone at Pearson who made this possible, thank you!

With that said, there are a few people I'd like to explicitly call out. First, I'd like to thank Mark Taber for giving me this opportunity, Kim Spenceley for carrying forward Mark's work in the second edition, Chris Zahn for meticulously ensuring everything is human-readable, and Loretta Yates for helping make the connections that made all of this happen. The technical content of this book has been reviewed in great detail by my long-time friends and online collaborators, Kyle Murray (1st edition) and Trevor McCauley (1st and 2nd editions). I can't thank them enough for their thorough (and frequently, humorous!) feedback.

Lastly, I'd like to thank my parents for having always encouraged me to pursue creative hobbies like painting, writing, playing video games, and writing code. I wouldn't be half the rugged indoorsman I am today without their support ☺

About the Author

Kirupa Chinnathambi has spent most of his life trying to teach others to love web development as much as he does.

In 1999, before blogging was even a word, he started posting tutorials on **kirupa.com**. In the years since then, he has written hundreds of articles, written a few books (none as good as this one, of course!), and recorded a bunch of videos you can find on YouTube. When he isn't writing or talking about web development, he spends his waking hours helping make the Web more awesome as a Product Manager for the Lightning Design System at Salesforce. In his non-waking hours, he is probably sleeping, joining Meena in running after their toddler daughter Akira, protecting himself from Pixel (aka a T-rex in an unassuming cat's body)...or writing about himself in the third person.

You can find him on Twitter, Facebook, LinkedIn, and the interwebs at large. Just search for his name in your favorite search engine.

Figure Credits

Figure	Attribution
Cover	© rozdesign/Shutterstock.com
chick images	© rozdesign/Shutterstock.com
FIG01-02a	Screenshot of google play ©2019 Google
FIG01-02b	Screenshot of twitter © 2019 Twitter, Inc
FIG01-02c	Screenshot of instagram © 2019 Instagram, Inc
FIG01-02d	Screenshot of Microsoft Edge © Microsoft 2019
FIG01-02e	Screenshot of google maps © 2019 Google
FIG01-03	Screenshot of Visual Studio Code © Microsoft 2019
FIG01-04	Screenshot of Google Chrome © 2019 Google
FIG01-05	Screenshot of an HTML pop-up © 2018 WHATWG
FIG01-06	Screenshot of an HTML pop-up © 2018 WHATWG
FIG03-08	Screenshot of an HTML pop-up © 2018 WHATWG
FIG04-03	Screenshot of an HTML pop-up © 2018 WHATWG
FIG04-04	Screenshot of an HTML pop-up © 2018 WHATWG
FIG04-06	Screenshot of an HTML pop-up © 2018 WHATWG
FIG05-01	Screenshot of Google Chrome © 2019 Google
FIG09-04	Screenshot of Dialog Box © Microsoft 2019
FIG09-06	Screenshot of Dialog Box © Microsoft 2019
FIG09-07	Screenshot of Google Chrome © 2019 Google
UNFIG11-01	Cartoon by Randall Munroe. Used with Permission from xkcd
FIG11-01	Screenshot of Google Chrome © 2019 Google
FIG11-02	Screenshot of Google Chrome © 2019 Google
FIG11-03	Screenshot of Safari © 2019 Apple Inc.
FIG11-04	Screenshot of Firefox © 2019 Mozilla Foundation
FIG11-05	Screenshot of Microsoft Edge © Microsoft 2019

FIG11-06 to FIG11-10	Screenshots of Google Chrome © 2019 Google
UNFIG11-02	Rozdesign/Shutterstock
UNPH16-01	DebbiSmirnoff/iStock/Getty images
FIG26-05	Screenshot of Google Chrome © 2019 Google
UNFIG29-01	Screenshot of Google Chrome © 2019 Google
UNFIG29-02	Screenshot of Google Chrome © 2019 Google
UNFIG29-03	Screenshot of Google Chrome © 2019 Google
FIG30-01	Screenshot of Kirupa.com © 'My Unconfigured Forum Ltd
UNFIG30-02	Screenshot of Internet explorer © 'Microsoft 2019
UNFIG30-03	Screenshot of Internet explorer © 'Microsoft 2019
UNFIG30-04 to UNFIG30-15	Screenshots of Google Chrome © 2019 Google
UNFIG31-01	Screenshot of Excel sheet © 'Microsoft 2019
FIG31-01	Screenshot of Google Chrome © 2019 Google
FIG31-02	Screenshot of Google Chrome © 2019 Google
FIG33-01	Audrius Merfeldas/123RF
FIG34-01	Dmitry Rukhlenko/Shutterstock

INTRODUCTION

Have you ever tried learning to read, speak, or write in a language different from the one you grew up with? If you were anything like me, your early attempts probably looked something like the following:

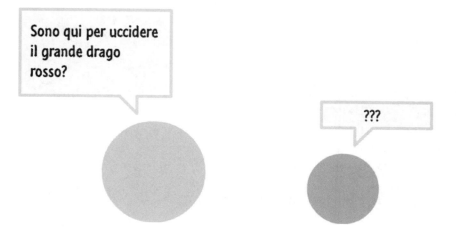

Unless you are Jason Bourne (or Roger Federer), you barely survived learning your first language. This is because learning languages is hard. It doesn't matter if you are learning your first language or a second or third. Being good at a language to a point where you are useful in a non-comical way takes a whole lotta time and effort.

It requires starting with the basics. It requires a boatload of practice and patience. It's one of those few areas where there really aren't any shortcuts for becoming proficient.

Parlez-vous JavaScript?

Successfully learning a *programming* language is very similar to how you would approach learning a *real world* language. You start off with the basics. Once you've gotten good at that, you move on to something a bit more advanced. This whole process just keeps repeating itself, and it never really ends. None of us ever truly stop learning. It just requires starting somewhere. To help you with the "starting somewhere" part is where this book comes in. This book is filled from beginning to end with all sorts of good (and hilarious—I hope!) stuff to help you learn JavaScript.

Now, I hate to say anything bad about a programming language behind its back, but JavaScript is pretty dull and boring:

Why won't you answer my calls???!!

```javascript
var count = 0;

function doingSomethingBoring() {
    count++;

    if (count > 10) {
        alert("Yaaaaaawwwnnnnnnnnn!");
    } else {
        alert("This one time, at band camp....");
    }
}
```

← Dull

Boring!

There is no other way to describe it. Despite how boring JavaScript might most certainly be, it doesn't mean that learning it has to be boring as well. (FYI: All grammatical snafus are carefully and deliberately placed—most of the time!) As you make your way through the book, hopefully you will find the very casual language and illustrations both informative as well as entertaining (infotaining!).

All this casualness and fun is balanced out by deep coverage of all the interesting things you need to know about JavaScript to become better at using it.

By the time you reach the last chapter, you will be prepared to face almost any JavaScript-related challenge head-on without breaking a sweat.

Contacting Me/Getting Help

If you ever get stuck at any point or just want to contact me, post in the forums at:

forum.kirupa.com.

For non-technical questions, you can also send e-mail to kirupa@kirupa.com, tweet to @kirupa, or message me on Facebook (facebook.com/kirupa). I love hearing from readers like you, and I make it a point to personally respond to every message I receive.

And with that, flip the page—it's time to get started!

IN THIS CHAPTER

- Learn why JavaScript is awesome
- Get your feet wet by creating a simple example
- Preview what to expect in subsequent chapters

1

HELLO, WORLD!

HTML is all about displaying things. CSS is all about making things look good. Between the both of them, you can create some pretty nifty-looking stuff like the weather example you can see in at **http://bit.ly/kirupaWeather**. Figure 1.1 shows what this weather example looks like.

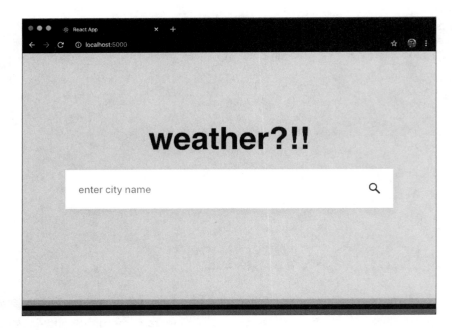

FIGURE 1.1

A colorful weather example highlighting a layout designed entirely using only CSS.

Despite how nifty sites built using only CSS and HTML look, they will be pretty static. They don't adapt or react to what you are doing. With those two, it's almost like watching a rerun of a great Seinfeld episode over and over again. It's fun for a while, but it gets boring eventually. The web today isn't static. The sites you use often (such as those in Figure 1.2) have a certain level of interactivity and personalization that goes well beyond what HTML and CSS by themselves can provide.

FIGURE 1.2

Examples of various web sites that rely heavily on JavaScript for their proper functioning.

To make your content come alive, you will need some outside help. What you need is JavaScript!

What Is JavaScript?

JavaScript is a modern-day programming language that is a peer of HTML and CSS. In a nutshell, it allows you to add interactivity to your document. A short list of things you can do with JavaScript include:

- Listen to events like a mouse click and do something.
- Modify the HTML and CSS of your page after the page has loaded.
- Make things move around the screen in interesting ways.
- Create awesome games that work in the browser like Cut the Rope.
- Communicate data between the server and the browser.
- Allow you to interact with a webcam, microphone, and other devices

....and much more! The way you write JavaScript is pretty simple—sort of. You put together words that often resemble everyday English to tell your browser what to do. The following example shows some old-fashioned, fresh outta-the-oven JavaScript:

```javascript
let defaultName = "JavaScript";

function sayHello(name) {
  if (name == null) {
    alert("Hello, " + defaultName + "!");
  } else {
    alert("Hello, " + name + "!");
  }
}
```

Don't worry if you don't know what any of that means. Just pay attention to what the code looks like. Notice that you see a lot of English words such as `function`, `if`, `else`, `alert`, `name`. In addition to the English words, you also have a lot of bizarre symbols and characters from the parts of your keyboard that you probably never notice. You'll be noticing them plenty really soon, and you'll also fully understand what everything in this code does as well.

Anyway, that's enough background information for now. While you would expect me to now provide a history of JavaScript and the people and companies behind making it work, I'm not going to bore you with stuff like that. Instead, I want you to get your hands dirty by writing some JavaScript. By the end of this tutorial, I want you to have created something sweet and simple that displays some text in your browser.

Hello, World!

Right now, you may feel a bit unprepared to start writing some code. This is especially true if you aren't all that familiar with programming in general. As you'll soon find out, JavaScript isn't nearly as annoying and complicated as it often pretends to be. Let's get started.

 TIP Basic Web Development Familiarity Needed
To start writing JavaScript, you need to have basic familiarity with building a web page, using a code editor, and adding some HTML and CSS. If you aren't too familiar with the basics around this, I encourage you to first read the **Building Your First Web Page** chapter. That will set you up nicely for what you'll be seeing next.

The HTML Document

The first thing you need is an HTML document. This document will host the JavaScript that you will be writing. Launch your favorite code editor. If you don't have one, I encourage you to use Visual Studio Code. After you've launched your favorite code editor, go ahead and create a new file. In Visual Studio Code, you will see a tab that says **Untitled** similar to the screenshot in Figure 1.3.

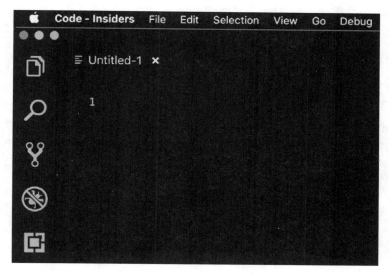

FIGURE 1.3

Untitled-1 tab in Visual Studio Code.

Save this newly created file by going to File | Save. You will be asked to give this file a name and specify where you would like to save it. Give this file the name **hello_world.htm** and save it to your **Desktop**. After you have saved this file, add the following HTML into it:

```
<!DOCTYPE html>
<html>

<head>
  <meta charset="utf-8">
  <title>An Interesting Title Goes Here</title>

  <style>

  </style>
</head>

<body>
  <script>

  </script>
```

```
</body>

</html>
```

After you've added this HTML, save your document to confirm these changes. It's time to take a look at what our page looks like in our browser.

In either File Explorer or Finder, navigate to your Desktop folder and double-click on **hello_world.htm**. You will see your default browser appearing and displaying the name of this file. You should see something that looks like what is shown in Figure 1.4.

FIGURE 1.4

Titled tab in Visual Studio Code.

If everything worked out well, you should see a blank page! No, there isn't anything wrong here. While our page has content, there is nothing visible going on. That's fine, for we'll fix that shortly. The key to making this fix is to go back to your code editor and focus on the `<script>` tag that you see toward the bottom of your HTML:

```
<script>

</script>
```

The `script` tag acts as a container where you can place any JavaScript you want to run inside it. What we want to do is display the words **hello, world!** in a dialog that appears when you load your HTML page. To make this happen, inside your script region, add the following line:

```
<script>
  alert("hello, world!");
</script>
```

Save your HTML file and run it in your browser. Notice what you will see once your page has loaded. You should see a dialog appear that looks like Figure 1.5.

> hello, world!
>
> Close

FIGURE 1.5

Your hello world dialog box should look like this.

If this is your first attempt at writing JavaScript, congratulations! Now, let's look at what you just did.

Looking at the Code: Statements and Functions

You just wrote a very simple JavaScript **statement**. A statement is a logical set of instructions that tell your browser what to do. A typical application will have many MANY statements. In our case, we just have one:

```
alert("hello, world!");
```

You can tell something is a statement by looking at the last character in it. It is usually a semicolon (`;`) just like what you see here.

Inside a statement, you will see all sorts of funky JavaScript jargon. Our code, despite being just one line, is no exception. You have this weird thing called `alert` that makes an appearance. This is an example of a common English word that behaves similarly in the JavaScript world. It is responsible for getting your attention by displaying some text.

To be more precise, the word `alert` is something known as a **function**. You will use functions all the time; a function is basically a reusable chunk of code that does something. The "something" it does could be defined by you, defined by some third-party library you are using, or it could be defined by the JavaScript framework itself. In our case, the code that gives your `alert` function the magical ability to display a dialog with a message you pass to it lives deep inside the browser. All you really need to know is that if you want to use the `alert` function, simply call it and pass in the text you want it to display. Everything else is taken care of for you.

Getting back to our example, the text you want to display is **hello, world!**, and notice how I am specifying it. I wrap the words inside quote marks:

```
<script>
  alert("hello, world!");
</script>
```

Whenever you are dealing with text (more commonly known as **strings**) you will always wrap them inside a single quote or a double quote. I know that seems weird, but every programming language has its own quirks. This is one of the many quirks you will see as you further explore JavaScript. We'll look at strings in greater detail shortly; for now, just enjoy the view.

Let's go one step further. Instead of displaying **hello, world!**, change the text you are displaying to say your first and last name instead. Here is an example of what my code looks like when I use my name:

```
<script>
  alert("Kirupa Chinnathambi!");
</script>
```

If you run your application, you will see your name appear in the dialog (Figure 1.6).

Kirupa Chinnathambi
Close

FIGURE 1.6

The dialog box now displays your name.

Pretty straightforward, right? You can replace the contents of your string with all sorts of stuff: the name of your pet, your favorite TV show, and so on—JavaScript will display it.

THE ABSOLUTE MINIMUM

In this tutorial, you created a simple example that helped get you familiar with writing some JavaScript code. As part of getting you familiar, I threw a lot of concepts and terms at you. I certainly don't expect you to know or remember all of them now. In future tutorials, we are going to pick each interesting part of what you've seen so far and elaborate on it in more detail. After all, I'm pretty sure you want to eventually do things in JavaScript that go beyond displaying some text in a ridiculously annoying way using a dialog box.

Going forward, at the end of each chapter, you may even see a set of links to external resources written by me or others. These resources will give you more details or a different perspective on what you learned, along with opportunities to put your learning into practice with more involved examples. Think of what you see in this book as a jumping-off point for greater and more awesome things.

If you have any questions on the content here, post on the forums at **https://forum.kirupa.com** for really quick help from both me as well as some of the web's coolest developers.

IN THIS CHAPTER

- Learn how to use values to store data
- Organize your code with variables
- Get a brief look at variable naming conventions

2

VALUES AND VARIABLES

In JavaScript, every piece of data that we provide or use is considered to contain a value. In the example we saw from our introduction, the words **hello, world!** might just be some words that we pass in to the `alert` function:

```
alert("hello, world!");
```

To JavaScript, these words have a specific representation under the covers. They are considered **values**. We may not have thought much about that when we were typing those words in, but when we are in JavaScript-country, every piece of data you touch is considered a value.

Now, why is knowing this important? It is important because we will be working with values a whole lot. Working with them in a way that doesn't drive you insane is a good thing. There are just two things we need to simplify our life working with values. We need to:

- Easily identify them
- Reuse them throughout your application without unnecessarily duplicating the value itself

Those two things are provided by what we are going to be spending the rest of our time on: **_variables_**. Let's learn all about them here.

Using Variables

A variable is an identifier for a value. Instead of typing **hello, world!**, every time you want to use that phrase in your application, you can assign that phrase to a variable and use that variable whenever you need to use **hello, world!** again. This will make more sense in a few moments—I promise!

There are several ways to use variables. For most cases, the best way is by relying on the `let` keyword followed by the name you want to give your variable:

```
let myText
```

In this line of code, we declare a variable called `myText`. Right now, our variable has simply been **declared**. It doesn't contain anything of value. It is merely an empty shell.

Let's fix that by **initializing** our variable to a value like...let's say...**_hello, world!_**:

```
let myText = "hello, world!";
```

At this point, when this code runs, our `myText` variable will have the value **_hello, world!_** associated with it. Let's put all of this together as part of a full example. If you still have **hello_world.htm** open from earlier, replace the contents of your `script` tag with the following...or create a new HTML file and add the following contents into it:

```
<!DOCTYPE html>
<html>

<head>
  <meta charset="utf-8">
  <title>An Interesting Title Goes Here</title>

  <style>

  </style>
</head>

<body>
  <script>
    let myText = "hello, world!";
    alert(myText);
  </script>
```

```
</body>

</html>
```

Notice that we are no longer passing in the **hello, world!** text to the `alert` function directly. Instead, we are now passing in the variable name `myText` instead. The end result is the same. When this script runs, an alert with **hello, world!** will be shown. What this change allows us to do is have one place in our code where **hello, world!** is being specified. If we wanted to change **hello, world!** to **The dog ate my homework!**, all we would have to do is just make one change to the phrase specified by the `myText` variable:

```
let myText = "The dog ate my homework!";
alert(myText);
```

Throughout our code, wherever we referenced the `myText` variable, we will now see the new text appear. While this is hard to imagine for something as simple as what we have right now, for larger applications, this convenience with having just one location where we can make a change that gets reflected everywhere is a major time saver. You'll see more, less trivial cases of the value variables provide in subsequent examples.

More Variable Stuff

What we learned in the previous section will take us far in life. At least, it will in the parts of our life that involve getting familiar with JavaScript. We won't dive too much further into variables here, for we'll do all of that as part of future chapters where the code is more complex and the importance of variables is more obvious. With that said, there are a few odds and ends that we should cover before calling it a day.

Naming Variables

We have a lot of freedom in naming our variables however we see fit. Ignoring what names we should give things based on philosophical / cultural / stylistic preferences, from a technical point of view, JavaScript is very lenient on what characters can go into a variable name.

This leniency isn't infinite, so we should keep the following things in mind when naming our variables:

- Variables can be as short as one character, or they can be as long as you want—think thousands and thousands of characters.

- Variables can start with a letter, underscore, or the $ character. They can't start with a number.

- Outside of the first character, our variables can be made up of any combination of letters, underscores, numbers, and $ characters. We can also mix and match lowercase and uppercase to our heart's content.

- Spaces are not allowed.

Below are some examples of valid variable names:

```
let myText;
let $;
let r8;
let _counter;
let $field;
let thisIsALongVariableName_butItCouldBeLonger;
let __$abc;
let OldSchoolNamingScheme;
```

To see if a variable name is valid, check out the really awesome and simple **JavaScript Variable Name Validator.**

Outside of valid names, there are other things to focus on as well, such as naming conventions and how many people commonly name variables and other things that you identify with a name. We will touch on these things in other chapters.

More on Declaring and Initializing Variables

One of the things you will learn about JavaScript is that it is a very forgiving and easy-to-work-with language.

Declaring a Variable Is Optional

For example, we don't have to use the `let` keyword to declare a variable. We could just do something as follows:

```
myText = "hello, world!";
alert(myText);
```

Notice the `myText` variable is being used without formally being declared with the `let` keyword. While not recommended, this is completely fine. The end result is that we have a variable called `myText`. The only thing is that, by declaring a variable this way, we are declaring it globally. Don't worry if the last sentence makes no sense. We'll look at what *globally* means when talking about variable scope later.

Declaring and Initializing on Separate Lines is Cool

There is one more thing to call out, and that is this: The declaration and initialization of a variable does not have to be part of the same statement. We can break it up across multiple statements:

```
let myText;
myText = "hello, world!";
alert(myText);
```

In practice, we will find ourselves breaking up our declaration and initialization of variables all the time.

Changing Variable Values and the const Keyword

Lastly, we can change the value of a variable declared via `let` to whatever we want whenever we want:

```
let myText;
myText = "hello, world!";
myText = 99;
myText = 4 * 10;
myText = true;
myText = undefined;
alert(myText);
```

If you have experience working with languages that are more strict and don't allow variables to store a variety of data types, this leniency is one of the features people both love and hate about JavaScript. With that said, JavaScript does provide a way for you to restrict the value of a variable from being changed after you initialize it. That restriction comes in the form of the `const` keyword that we can declare and initialize our variables with:

```
const siteURL = "https://www.google.com";
alert(siteURL);
```

By relying on `const`, we can't change the value of `siteURL` to something other than **https://www.google.com**. JavaScript will complain if we try to do that. There are some gotchas with using the `const` keyword, but it does a great job overall in preventing accidental modifications of a variable. For those pesky gotchas, we'll cover those in bits and pieces when the time is right.

TIP   Jump Ahead—Variable Scoping

Now that you know how to declare and initialize variables, a very important topic is that of visibility. You need to know when and where a variable you declared can actually be used in your code. The catch-all phrase for this is known as *variable scope*. If you are curious to know more about it, you can jump ahead and read Chapter 8, "Variable Scope."

THE ABSOLUTE MINIMUM

Values store data, and variables act as an easy way to refer to that data. There are a lot of interesting details about values, but those are details that you do not need to learn right now. Just know that JavaScript enables you to represent a variety of values such as text and numbers without a lot of fuss.

To make your values more memorable and reusable, you declare variables. You declare variables using the `let` keyword and a **variable name**. If you want to initialize the variable to a default value, you follow all of that up with an equal sign (=) and the value you want to initialize your variable with.

IN THIS CHAPTER

- Learn how functions help you better organize and group your code
- Understand how functions make your code reusable
- Discover the importance of function arguments and how to use them

FUNCTIONS

So far, all the code we've written really contained no structure. It was just… there:

```
alert("hello, world!");
```

There is nothing wrong with having code like this. This is especially true if our code is made up of a single statement. Most of the time, though, that will never be the case. Our code will rarely be this simple when we are using JavaScript in the real world for real-worldy things.

To highlight this, let's say we want to display the distance something has traveled (Figure 3.1).

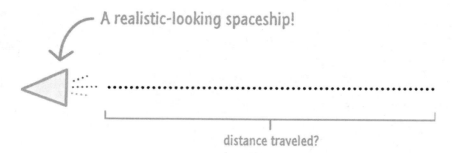

A realistic-looking spaceship!

distance traveled?

FIGURE 3.1

Distance traveled.

If you remember from school, the distance is calculated by multiplying the speed something has traveled by how long it took (Figure 3.2).

distance = speed × time

FIGURE 3.2

Calculating distance.

The JavaScript version of that will sort of look as follows:

```
let speed = 10;
let time = 5;
alert(speed * time);
```

We have two variables named `speed` and `time`, and they each store a number. The `alert` function displays the result of multiplying the values stored by the `speed` and `time` variables. This is a pretty literal translation of the distance equation we just saw.

Let's say we want to calculate the distance for more values. Using only what we've seen so far, our code would look as follows:

```
let speed = 10;
let time = 5;
alert(speed * time);


let speed1 = 85;
let time1 = 1.5;
alert(speed1 * time1);
```

```
let speed2 = 12;
let time2 = 9;
alert(speed2 * time2);


let speed3 = 42;
let time3 = 21;
alert(speed3 * time3);
```

I don't know about you, but this just looks **turrible**. Our code is unnecessarily verbose and repetitive. Like we saw earlier when we were learning about **variables**, repetition makes our code harder to maintain, and it also wastes our time.

This entire problem can be solved very easily by using what we'll be seeing a lot of here, **functions**:

```
function showDistance(speed, time) {
   alert(speed * time);
}


showDistance(10, 5);
showDistance(85, 1.5);
showDistance(12, 9);
showDistance(42, 21);
```

Don't worry too much about what this code does just yet. Just know that this smaller chunk of code does everything all those many lines of code did earlier without all the negative side effects. We'll learn all about functions and how they do all the sweet things that they do starting...right...now!

Onwards!

What Is a Function?

At a very basic level, a function is nothing more than a wrapper for some code. A function basically:

- Groups statements together
- Makes your code reusable

You will rarely write or use code that doesn't involve functions, so it's important that you get familiar with them and learn all about how well they work.

A Simple Function

The best way to learn about functions is to just dive right in and start using them, so let's start off by creating a very simple function. Creating a function isn't very exciting. It just requires understanding some little syntactical quirks like using weird parenthesis and brackets.

Below is an example of what a very simple function looks like:

```
function sayHello() {
  alert("hello!");
}
```

Just having a function defined isn't enough, though. Our function needs to be called, and we can do that by adding the following line afterwards:

```
function sayHello() {
  alert("hello!");
}
sayHello();
```

To see all this for yourself, create a new HTML document (call it **functions_sayhello.htm**) and add the following into it:

```
<!DOCTYPE html>
<html>

<head>
  <meta charset="utf-8">
  <title>Say Hello!</title>

  <style>

  </style>
</head>

<body>
  <script>
    function sayHello() {
      alert("hello!");
    }
```

```
    sayHello();
  </script>
</body>

</html>
```

If you typed all this in and previewed your page in your browser, you will see **hello!** displayed. The only thing that you need to know right now is that our code works. Let's look at why the code works next by breaking the `sayHello` function into individual chunks and looking at each in greater detail.

First, we see the `function` keyword leading things off as in Figure 3.3.

```
function sayHello() {

    alert("hello!");

}
```

FIGURE 3.3

The function keyword.

This keyword tells the JavaScript engine that lives deep inside your browser to treat this entire block of code as something having to do with functions.

After the `function` keyword, we specify the actual name of the function followed by some opening and closing parentheses, ( ) as in Figure 3.4.

```
function sayHello() {

    alert("hello!");

}
```

FIGURE 3.4

The function name and parentheses.

Rounding out our function declaration are the opening and closing brackets that enclose any statements that we may have inside (Figure 3.5).

```
function sayHello() {

    alert("hello!");

}
```

FIGURE 3.5

The opening and closing brackets.

The final thing is the contents of our function—the statements that make our function actually functional (Figure 3.6).

```
function sayHello() {

    alert("hello!");

}
```

FIGURE 3.6

The function content.

In our case, the content is the `alert` function that displays a dialog with the word **hello!** displayed.

The last thing to look at is the function call (Figure 3.7).

The function call is typically the name of the function we want to **call** (aka **invoke**) followed again by the parentheses. Without our function call, the function we created doesn't do anything. It is the function call that wakes our function up and makes it do things.

```
function sayHello() {

    alert("hello!");

}

sayHello();
```

FIGURE 3.7

The function call.

Now, what we have just seen is a look at a very simple function. In the next couple of sections, we are going to build on what we've just learned and look at increasingly more realistic examples of functions.

Creating a Function that Takes Arguments

The previous sayHello example was quite simple:

```
function sayHello() {
    alert("hello!");
}
sayHello();
```

We call a function, and the function does something. That simplification by itself is not out of the ordinary. All functions work just like that. What is different is the details on how functions get invoked, where they get their data from, and so on. The first such detail we are going to look at involves functions that take **arguments**.

Let's start with a simple and familiar example:

```
alert("my argument");
```

What we have here is our `alert` function. We've probably seen it a few (or a few dozen) times already. What this function does is take what is known as an **argument** for figuring out what to actually display when it gets called. Calling the alert function with an argument of ***my argument*** results in the display shown in Figure 3.8.

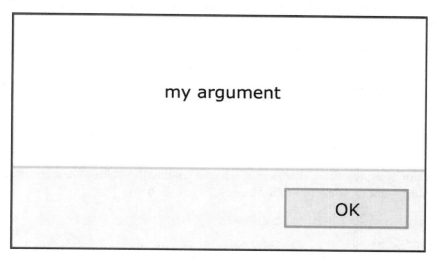

FIGURE 3.8

Displaying the argument.

The argument is the stuff between your opening and closing parentheses when calling the `alert` function. The `alert` function is just one of many functions available to you that take arguments, and many functions you create will take arguments as well.

To stay local, just from this chapter itself, another function that we briefly looked at that takes arguments is our `showDistance` function:

```
function showDistance(speed, time) {
    alert(speed * time);
}
```

See, you can tell when a function takes arguments by looking at the function declaration itself:

```
function showDistance(speed, time) {
    alert(speed * time);
}
```

What used to be empty parenthesis following the function name will now contain some information about the quantity of arguments your function needs along with some hints on what values your arguments will take.

For showDistance, we can infer that this function takes two arguments. The first argument corresponds to the speed and the second argument corresponds to the time.

We specify your arguments to the function as part of the function call:

```
function showDistance (speed, time) {
    alert (speed * time);
}


showDistance(10, 5);
```

In our case, we call showDistance and specify the values we want to pass to your function inside the parentheses (Figure 3.9).

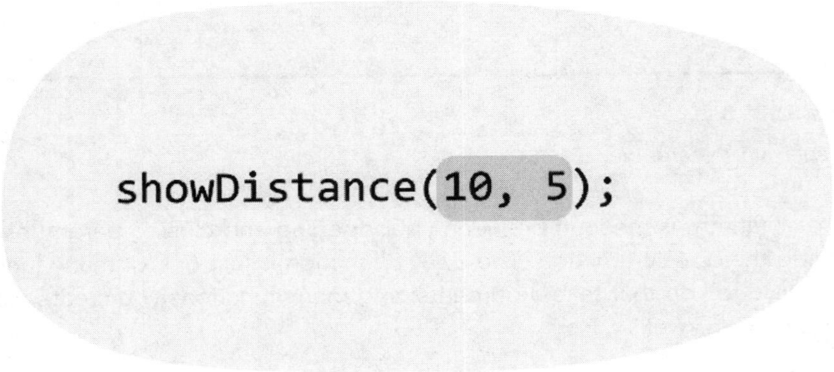

showDistance(10, 5);

FIGURE 3.9

Values we want to pass to the function.

Because we are providing more than one argument, we can separate the individual arguments by a comma. Oh, and before I forget to call this out, the order in which you specify your arguments matters.

Let's look at all of this in greater detail starting with the diagram in Figure 3.10.

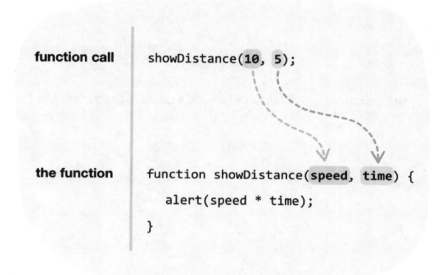

FIGURE 3.10

A diagram of the function call.

When the showDistance function gets called, it passes in a **10** for the speed argument, and it passes in a **5** for the distance argument. That mapping, as shown in the previous diagram, is entirely based on order.

Once the values you pass in as arguments reach our function, the names we specified for the arguments are treated just like variable names as shown in Figure 3.11.

We can use these variable names to easily reference the values stored by the arguments inside our function without any worry in the world.

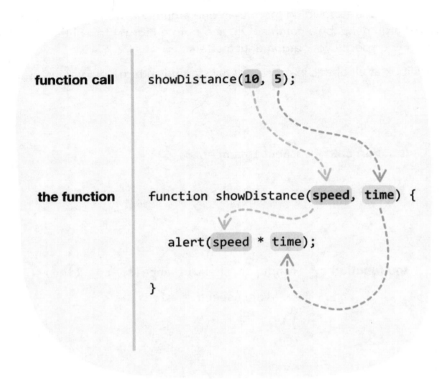

FIGURE 3.11

The argument names work like variables.

NOTE Mismatched Number of Arguments

If a function happens to take arguments and you don't provide any arguments as part of your function call, provide too few arguments, or provide too many arguments, things can still work. You can code your function defensively against these cases, and in the future, we will touch upon that a bit.

In general, to make the code you are writing clearer, you should provide the required number of arguments for the function you are calling.

Creating a Function that Returns Data

The last function variant we will look at is one that returns some data back to whatever called it. Here is what we want to do. We have our showDistance function, and we know that it looks as follows:

```
function showDistance(speed, time) {
  alert(speed * time);
}
```

Instead of having our showDistance function calculate the distance and display it as an alert, we want to store that value for some future use. We want to do something like this:

```
let myDistance = showDistance(10, 5);
```

The myDistance variable will store the results of the calculation the showDistance function does.

The Return Keyword

The way you return data from a function is by using the return keyword. Let's create a new function called getDistance that looks identical to showDistance with the only difference being what happens when the function runs to completion:

```
function getDistance(speed, time) {
  let distance = speed * time;
  return distance;
}
```

Notice that we are still calculating the distance by multiplying the speed and time. Instead of displaying an alert, we instead return the distance (as stored by the distance variable).

To call the getDistance function, we can just call it as part of initializing a variable:

```
let myDistance = getDistance(10, 5);
```

When the getDistance function gets called, it gets evaluated and returns a numerical value that then becomes assigned to the myDistance variable. That's all there is to it.

Exiting the Function Early

Once our function hits the `return` keyword, it stops everything it is doing at that point, returns whatever value you specified to the caller, and exits:

```
function getDistance(speed, time) {
    let distance = speed * time;
    return distance;

    if (speed < 0) {
      distance *= -1;
    }
}
```

Any code that exists after our `return` statement will not get reached. It will be as if that code never even existed.

In practice, we will use the `return` statement to terminate a function after it has done what we wanted it to do. That function could return a value to the caller like you saw in the previous examples, or that function could simply just exit:

```
function doSomething() {
    let foo = "Nothing interesting";
    return;
}
```

Using the `return` keyword to return a value is optional. The `return` keyword can be used standalone like we see here to just exit the function. If a function does not specify anything to return, a default value of `undefined` is returned instead.

THE ABSOLUTE MINIMUM

Functions are among a handful of things that you will use in almost every single JavaScript application. They provide the much sought-after capability to help make your code reusable. Whether you are creating your own functions or using the many functions that are built into the JavaScript language, you will simply not be able to live without them.

What you have seen so far are examples of how functions are commonly used. There are some advanced traits that functions possess that I did not cover here. Those uses will be covered in the future...a distant future. For now, everything you've learned will take you quite far when it comes to understanding how functions are used in the real world.

If you have any questions on the content here, don't fret! Post on the forums at **https://forum.kirupa.com** for quick help from both me as well as some of the web's smartest developers.

CONDITIONAL STATEMENTS: IF, ELSE, AND SWITCH

From the moment you wake up, whether you realize it or not, you start making decisions. Turn the alarm off. Turn the lights on. Look outside to see what the weather is like. Brush your teeth. Put on your robe and wizard hat. Check your calendar. Basically...you get the point. By the time you step outside your door, you consciously or subconsciously will have made hundreds of decisions with each decision having a certain effect on what you ended up doing.

For example, if the weather looks cold outside, you might decide to wear a hoodie or a jacket. You can model this decision as shown in Figure 4.1.

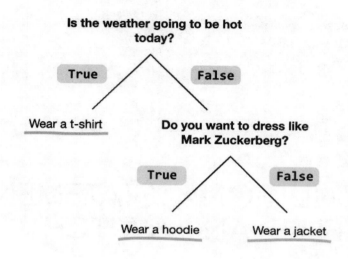

FIGURE 4.1

Modeling decisions.

At each stage of making a decision, you ask yourself a question that can be answered as **true** or **false**. The answer to that question determines your next step and ultimately whether you wear a t-shirt, hoodie, or jacket. Going broader, every decision you and I make can be modeled as a series of **true** and **false** statements. This may sound a bit chilly (ha!), but that's generally how we, others, and pretty much all living things go about making choices.

This generalization especially applies to everything our computer does. This may not be evident from the code we've written so far, but we are going to fix that. In this tutorial, we will cover what is known as **conditional statements**. These are the digital equivalents of the decisions we make where our code does something different depending on whether something is **true** or **false**.

Onward!

The If / Else Statement

The most common conditional statement we will use in our code is the **if / else statement** or just the **if statement**. The way this statement works is shown in Figure 4.2.

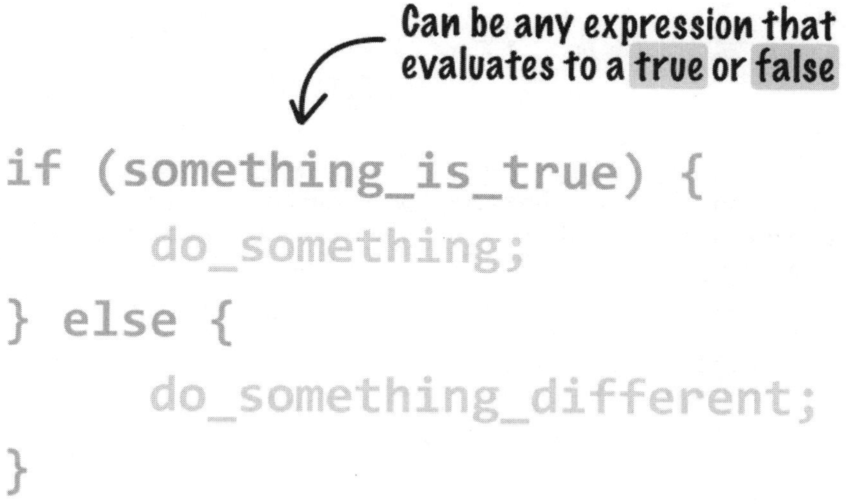

Can be any expression that evaluates to a `true` or `false`

```
if (something_is_true) {
    do_something;
} else {
    do_something_different;
}
```

FIGURE 4.2

How the if statement works.

To make sense of this, let's take a look at a simple example of an `if / else` statement in action. Create a new HTML document and add the following markup and code into it:

```
<!DOCTYPE html>
<html>

<head>
  <meta charset="utf-8">
  <title>If / Else Statements</title>
</head>

<body>
  <script>
    let safeToProceed = true;
```

```
   if (safeToProceed) {
     alert("You shall pass!");
   } else {
     alert("You shall not pass!");
   }
 </script>
</body>

</html>
```

Save this document with the name **if_else.htm** and preview it in your browser. If all worked as expected, you will see an alert with the text **You shall pass!** displayed (Figure 4.3).

FIGURE 4.3

You will see this alert.

The code responsible for making this work is the following lines from our example:

```
let safeToProceed = true;

if (safeToProceed) {
  alert("You shall pass!");
} else {
  alert("You shall not pass!");
}
```

Our **expression** (the thing following the keyword `if` that ultimately evaluates to **true** or **false**) is the variable `safeToProceed`. This variable is initialized to **true**, so the *true* part of our `if` statement kicked in.

Now, go ahead and change the value of the `safeToProceed` variable from a **true** to a **false**:

```
let safeToProceed = true;
```

```
if (safeToProceed) {

  alert("You shall pass!");

} else {

  alert("You shall not pass!");

}
```

This time when you run this code, you will see an alert with the text **You shall not pass!** because our expression now evaluates to **false** (Figure 4.4).

```
You shall not pass!
                                                    Close
```

FIGURE 4.4

The alert you get when the expression evaluates as false.

So far, all of this probably seems really boring. A large part of the reason for this is because we haven't turned up the complexity knob to focus on more realistic scenarios. We'll tackle that next by taking a deeper look at conditions.

Meet the Conditional Operators

In most cases, our expression will rarely be a simple variable that is set to **true** or **false** like it is in our earlier example. Our expression will involve what are known as **conditional operators** that help us to compare between two or more expressions to establish a **true** or **false** outcome.

The general format of such expressions is shown in Figure 4.5.

```
if (expression operator expression) {
    do_something;
} else {
    do_something_different;
}
```

FIGURE 4.5

General format of conditional operator expressions.

The **operator** (aka a **conditional operator**) defines a relationship between an expression. The end goal is to return a **true** or a **false** so that our `if` statement knows which block of code to execute. Key to making all this work are the conditional operators themselves. They are shown in Table 4.1.

TABLE 4.1   Operators

Operator	When it is true
==	If the first expression evaluates to something that is equal to the second expression.
>=	If the first expression evaluates to something that is greater or equal to the second expression.
>	If the first expression evaluates to something that is greater than the second expression.
<=	If the first expression evaluates to something that is lesser or equal to the second expression.
<	If the first expression evaluates to something that is less than the second expression.
!=	If the first expression evaluates to something that is not equal to the second expression.
&&	If the first expression and the second expression both evaluate to true.
||	If either the first expression or the second expression evaluate to true.

Let's take our general understanding of conditional operators and make it more specific by looking at another example...such as the following with our relevant `if`-related code highlighted:

```html
<!DOCTYPE html>
<html>

<head>
  <meta charset="utf-8">
  <title>Are you speeding?</title>
</head>

<body>
  <script>
    let speedLimit = 55;

    function amISpeeding(speed) {
      if (speed >= speedLimit) {
        alert("Yes. You are speeding.");
      } else {
        alert("No. You are not speeding. What's wrong with you?");
      }
    }

    amISpeeding(53);
    amISpeeding(72);
  </script>
</body>

</html>
```

Let's take a moment to understand what exactly is going on. We have a variable called `speedLimit` that is initialized to **55**. We then have a function called `amISpeeding` that takes an argument named `speed`. Inside this function, we have an `if` statement whose expression checks if the passed in `speed` value is greater than or equal (Hello >= conditional operator!) to the value stored by the `speedLimit` variable:

```
function amISpeeding(speed) {
  if (speed >= speedLimit) {
    alert("Yes. You are speeding.");
  } else {
    alert("No. You are not speeding. What's wrong with you?");
  }
}
```

The last thing our code does is actually call the `amISpeeding` function by passing in a few values for speed:

```
amISpeeding(53);
amISpeeding(72);
```

When we call this function with a speed of **53**, the `speed >= speedLimit` expression evaluates to **false**. The reason is that **53** is not greater than or equal to the stored value of `speedLimit` which is **55**. This will result in an alert showing that you aren't speeding.

The opposite happens when we call `amISpeeding` with a speed of **72**. In this case, we are speeding and the condition evaluates to a **true**. An alert telling us that we are speeding will also appear.

Creating More Complex Expressions

The thing you need to know about these expressions is that they can be as simple or as complex as you can make them. They can be made up of variables, function calls, or raw values. They can even be made up of combinations of variables, function calls, or raw values all separated using any of the operators you saw earlier. The only thing that you need to ensure is that your expression ultimately evaluates to a **true** or a **false**.

Here is a slightly more involved example:

```
let xPos = 300;
let yPos = 150;

function sendWarning(x, y) {
  if ((x < xPos) && (y < yPos)) {
    alert("Adjust the position");
```

```
  } else {
    alert("Things are fine!");
  }
}


sendWarning(500, 160);
sendWarning(100, 100);
sendWarning(201, 149);
```

Notice what our condition inside `sendWarning`'s `if` statement looks like:

```
function sendWarning(x, y) {
        if ((x < xPos) && (y < yPos)) {
                alert("Adjust the position");
        } else {
                alert("Things are fine!");
        }
}
```

There are three comparisons being made here. The first one is whether `x` is less than `xPos`. The second one is whether `y` is less than `yPos`. The third comparison is seeing if the **first statement and the second statement** both evaluate to **true** to allow the `&&` operator to return a **true** as well. We can chain together many series of conditional statements depending on what we are doing. The tricky thing, besides learning what all the operators do, is to ensure that each condition and sub-condition is properly insulated using parentheses.

All of what we are describing here and in the previous section falls under the umbrella of **Boolean Logic**. If you are not familiar with this topic, I recommend you glance through the **excellent quirksmode article** on this exact topic.

Variations on the If / Else Statement

We are almost done with the `if` statement. The last thing we are going to is look at are some of its relatives.

The if-only Statement

The first one is the solo `if` statement that doesn't have its `else` companion:

```
if (weight > 5000) {
  alert("No free shipping for you!");
}
```

In this case, if the expression evaluates to **true**, then great. If the expression evaluates to **false**, then your code just skips over the alert and just moves on to wherever it needs to go next. The `else` block is completely optional when working with `if` statements. To contrast the `if`-only statement, we have our next relative...

The Dreaded If / Else-If / Else Statement

Not everything can be neatly bucketed into a single `if` or `if` / `else` statement. For those kinds of situations, you can chain `if` statements together by using the `else if` keyword. Instead of explaining this further, let's just look at an example:

```
if (position < 100) {
  alert("Do something!");
} else if ((position >= 200) && (position < 300)) {
  alert("Do something else!");
} else {
  alert("Do something even more different!");
}
```

If the first `if` statement evaluates to **true**, then our code branches into the first alert. If the first `if` statement is **false**, then our code evaluates the `else if` statement to see if the expressions in it evaluate to a **true** or **false**. This repeats until our code reaches the end. In other words, our code simply navigates down through each `if` and `else if` statement until one of the expressions evaluates to **true**:

```
if (condition) {

  . . .

} else if (condition) {

  . . .

} else if (condition) {

  . . .

} else if (condition) {

  . . .

} else if (condition) {

  . . .

} else if (condition) {

  . . .

} else {

  . . .

}
```

If none of the statements have expressions that evaluate to **true**, the code inside the `else` block (if it exists) executes. If there is no `else` block, then the code will just go on to the next set of code that lives beyond all these `if` statements. Between the more complex expressions and `if / else if` statements, you can represent pretty much any decision that your code might need to evaluate.

Phew

And with this, you have learned all there is to know about the `if` statement. It's time to move on to a whole different species of conditional statement...

Switch Statements

In a world filled with beautiful `if`, `else`, and `else if` statements, the need for yet another way of dealing with conditionals may seem unnecessary. People who wrote code on room-sized machines and probably hiked uphill in snow (with wolves chasing them) disagreed, so we have what are known as `switch` statements. What are they? We are going to find out!

Using a Switch Statement

We are going to cut to the chase and look at the code first. The basic structure of a `switch` statement is as follows:

```
switch (expression) {
  case value1:
    statement;
    break;
  case value2:
    statement;
    break;
  case value3:
    statement;
    break;
  default:
    statement;
    break;
}
```

The thing to never forget is that a `switch` statement is nothing more than a conditional statement that tests whether *something* is true or false. That *something* is a variation of whether the **result of evaluating the expression equals a case value**. Let's make this explanation actually make sense by looking at a better example:

```
let color = "green";

switch (color) {
  case "yellow":
    alert("yellow color");
    break;
  case "red":
    alert("red color");
    break;
  case "blue":
    alert("blue color");
    break;
  case "green":
    alert("green color");
    break;
  case "black":
    alert("black color");
    break;
  default:
    alert("no known color specified");
    break;
}
```

In this simple example, we have a variable called `color` whose value is set to **green**:

```
let color = "green";
```

The `color` variable is also what we specify as our expression to the `switch` statement:

```
switch (color) {
  case "yellow":
    alert("yellow color");
    break;
```

```
  case "red":
    alert("red color");
    break;
  case "blue":
    alert("blue color");
    break;
  case "green":
    alert("green color");
    break;
  case "black":
    alert("black color");
    break;
  default:
    alert("no known color specified");
    break;
}
```

Our `switch` statement contains a collection of case blocks. Only one of these blocks will get hit with their code getting executed. The way this chosen one gets picked is by matching a block's case value with the result of evaluating the expression. In our case, because our expressions evaluate to a value of **green**, the code inside the case block whose case value is also **green** gets executed:

```
switch (color) {
  case "yellow":
    alert("yellow color");
    break;
  case "red":
    alert("red color");
    break;
  case "blue":
    alert("blue color");
    break;
  case "green":
    alert("green color");
    break;
  case "black":
    alert("black color");
    break;
```

```
    default:
        alert("no known color specified");
        break;
}
```

Note that **only** the code inside the **green** case block gets executed. That is thanks to the break keyword that ends that block. When your code hits the break, it exits the entire switch block and continues executing the code that lies below it. If you did not specify the break keyword, you will still execute the code inside the **green** case block. The difference is that you will then move to the next case block (the **black** one in our example) and execute any code that is there. Unless you hit another break keyword, your code will just move through every single case block until it reaches the end.

With all of this said, if you were to run this code, you would see an alert window that looks like Figure 4.6.

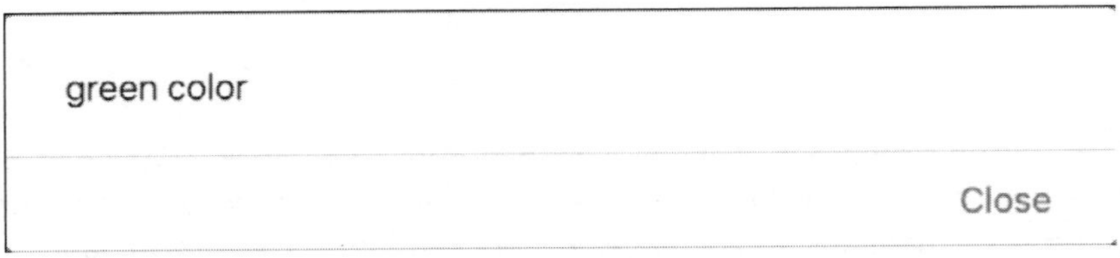

green color

Close

FIGURE 4.6

Alert window.

You can alter the value for the color variable to other valid values to see the other case blocks execute. Sometimes, no case block's value will match the result of evaluating an expression. In those cases, your switch statement will just do nothing. If you wish to specify a default behavior, add a default block:

```
switch (color) {
    case "yellow":
        alert("yellow color");
        break;
    case "red":
        alert("red color");
        break;
    case "blue":
        alert("blue color");
        break;
```

```
case "green":
  alert("green color");
  break;
case "black":
  alert("black color");
  break;
default:
  alert("no known color specified");
  break;
}
```

Note that the `default` block looks a bit different than your other case statements. It actually doesn't contain the word `case`.

Similarity to an If/Else Statement

At the beginning, we saw that a `switch` statement is used for evaluating conditions—just like the `if` / `else` statement that we spent a bulk of our time on here. Given that this is a major accusation, let's explore this in further detail by first looking at how an `if` statement would look if it were to be literally translated into a `switch` statement.

Let's say we have an `if` statement that looks as follows:

```
let number = 20;

if (number > 10) {
  alert("yes");
} else {
  alert("nope");
}
```

Because the value of our `number` variable is 20, our `if` statement will evaluate to a `true`. Seems pretty straightforward. Now, let's turn this into a `switch` statement:

```
switch (number > 10) {
  case true:
    alert("yes");
    break;
```

```
case false:
  alert("nope");
  break;
}
```

Notice that our expression is **number > 10**. The case value for the case blocks is set to true or false. Because **number > 10** evaluates to true, the code inside the true case block gets executed. While your expression in this case wasn't as simple as reading a color value stored in a variable like in the previous section, our view of how switch statements work still hasn't changed. Our expressions can be as complex as you would like. If they evaluate to something that can be matched inside a case value, then everything is golden...like a fleece!

Now, let's look at a slightly more involved example. This time, we will convert our earlier switch statement involving colors into equivalent if / else statements. The switch statement we used earlier looks as follows:

```
let color = "green";

switch (color) {
  case "yellow":
    alert("yellow color");
    break;
  case "red":
    alert("red color");
    break;
  case "blue":
    alert("blue color");
    break;
  case "green":
    alert("green color");
    break;
  case "black":
    alert("black color");
    break;
  default:
    alert("no color specified");
    break;
}
```

This `switch` statement converted into a series of if / else statements would look like this:

```
let color = "green";

if (color == "yellow") {
  alert("yellow color");
} else if (color == "red") {
  alert("red color");
} else if (color == "blue") {
  alert("blue color");
} else if (color == "green") {
  alert("green color");
} else if (color == "black") {
  alert("black color");
} else {
  alert("no color specified";
}
```

As we can see, if / else statements are very similar to `switch` statements and vice versa. The `default` case block becomes an `else` block. The relationship between the expression and the case value in a `switch` statement is combined into if / else conditions in an if / else statement.

Deciding Which to Use

In the previous section, we saw how interchangeable `switch` statements and if / else statements are. When we have two ways of doing something very similar, it is only natural to want to know when it is appropriate to use one over the other. In a nutshell, use whichever one you prefer. There are many arguments on the web about when to use `switch` vs an if / else, and the one thing is that they are all inconclusive.

My personal preference is to go with whatever is more readable. If you look at the comparisons earlier between `switch` and if / else statements, you'll notice that if you have a lot of conditions, your `switch` statement tends to look a bit cleaner. It is certainly less verbose and a bit more readable. What your cutoff mark is for deciding when to switch (ha!) between using a `switch` statement and an if / else statement is entirely up to you. I tend to draw the line at around four or five conditions.

Second, a `switch` statement works best when you are evaluating an expression and matching the result to a value. If you are doing something more complex involving weird conditions, value checking, etc., you probably want to use something different. That could involve something even more different than an `if` / `else` statement, by the way! We will touch upon those *different somethings* later.

To wrap this all up, the earlier guidance still stands: use whatever you like. If you are part of a team with coding guidelines, then follow them instead. Whatever you do, just be consistent. It makes your life as well as the life of anybody else who will be working in your code a little bit easier. For what it is worth, I've personally never been in a situation where I had to use a `switch` statement. Your mileage may vary.

THE ABSOLUTE MINIMUM

While creating true artificial intelligence goes beyond the scope of this book, you *can* write code to help your application make choices. This code will almost always take the form of an if/else statement where you provide the browser with a set of choices it needs to make:

```
let loginStatus = false;


if (name == "Admin") {
   loginStatus = true;
}
```

These choices are fed by conditions that need to evaluate to *true* or *false*.

In this chapter, we learned the mechanics of how to work with if/else statements and their (sort of) related cousins, the switch statements. In future chapters, you'll see us using these statements very casually, as if we've known them for years, so you'll be very familiar with how to write these statements by the time you reach the end of this book.

If you have any questions on the content here, don't worry! Be happy. Post on the forums at **https://forum.kirupa.com** for really quick help from both me as well as some of the web's nicest developers.

5

LOOPING WITH FOR, WHILE, AND DO...WHILE!

When you are coding something, there will be times when you want to repeat an action or run some code multiple times. For example, let's say we have a function called `saySomething` that we want to repeatedly call 10 times.

One way we could do this is by simply calling the function 10 times using copy and paste:

```
saySomething();
saySomething();
saySomething();
saySomething();
saySomething();
saySomething();
saySomething();
saySomething();
saySomething();
saySomething();
```

This works and accomplishes what we set out to do, but...we shouldn't do something like this. After all, duplicating code is never a good idea. If we had a nickel for every time you read that here, we'd have about four or five nickels. *#killing_it*

Now, even if we do decide to duplicate some code a few times manually, this approach doesn't really work in practice. The number of times we will need to duplicate our code will vary based on some external factors such as the number of items in a collection of data, some result from some web service, the number of letters in a word, and various other things that will keep changing. It won't always be a fixed number like **10**. Often, the number of times we want to repeat some code could be very VERY large. We don't want to copy and paste something a few hundred or thousand times in order to repeat something. That would be terrible.

What we need is a generic solution for repeating code with control over how many times the code repeats. In JavaScript, this solution is provided in the form of something known as a **loop**. There are three kinds of loops we can use to repeat some code:

- for loops
- while loops
- do...while loops

Each of these three loop variations allow us to specify the code we want to repeat (aka loop) and a way to stop the repetition when a condition is met. In the following sections, we'll learn all about them.

Onward!

NOTE Something beyond `alert`!

We've been using the `alert` function these past few chapters to get our code to display something on screen. In this chapter, we're going to look at one more way of displaying something on the screen that is a bit less intrusive. We're going to be using the `document.write` function:

```
document.write("Show this on screen!");
```

This function will print the text you provide to the page displayed in your browser without displaying a dialog that requires you to dismiss every time it appears. You'll see why we want something that is more lightweight when you learn more about loops and how we may want to print many things to the screen.

The `for` Loop

One of the most common ways to create a loop is by using the `for` statement to create a **for loop**. A for loop allows us to repeatedly run some code until an expression we specify returns **false**. To help clarify this definition, let's look at an example.

If we had to translate our earlier `saySomething` example using `for`, it would look as follows:

```
for (let i = 0; i < 10; i++) {
  saySomething();
}


function saySomething() {
  document.writeln("hello!");
}
```

If you want to follow along more actively and see this code for yourself, enter this code inside some `script` tags in an HTML document:

```html
<!DOCTYPE html>
<html>

<head>
  <meta charset="utf-8">
  <title>Loops!</title>

  <style>

  </style>
</head>

<body>
  <script>
    for (let i = 0; i < 10; i++) {
      saySomething();
    }

    function saySomething() {
      document.writeln("hello!");
    }
  </script>
</body>

</html>
```

Once your document is ready, save your document and preview it in your browser. After the page has loaded, what you would see is shown in Figure 5.1.

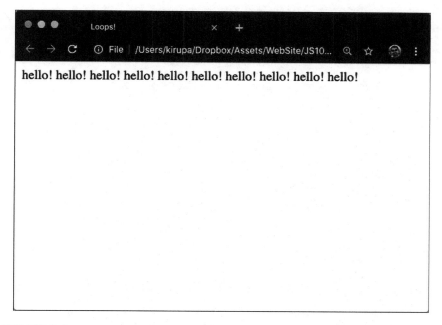

FIGURE 5.1

hello! repeats across the page.

The word **hello!** will be repeated ten times across your page. This is made possible thanks to the `for` loop, so we are going to thank it back by learning all about how it works. First, here is our star:

```
for (let i = 0; i < 10; i++) {
    saySomething();
}
```

This is a `for` loop. It probably looks very different from other statements we've seen so far, and that's because...well, it is very different. To understand the differences, let's generalize a `for` loop into the form shown in Figure 5.2.

```
for (start_point; condition; step) {

    // code to execute

}
```

FIGURE 5.2

General, high level for loop.

This high-level view corresponds to the actual values from our example (Figure 5.3).

```
for (let i = 0; i < 10; i++) {

    // code to execute

}
```

FIGURE 5.3

The actual values.

These three differently colored regions each play a very important role in how your loop functions. In order to use a `for` loop well, we must know what each region accomplishes, so we will spend the next few minutes diving deeper into each section.

The Starting Point

In the first region, we define the **starting point** for our loop. A common thing to put here is some code to declare and initialize a variable, similar to what we did in Figure 5.4.

```
for (let i = 0; i < 10; i++) {

    // code to execute

}
```

FIGURE 5.4

Declaring and initializing a variable i.

What we are telling JavaScript is to start our loop with the variable i initialized to **0**.

The Step

We are going to skip ahead to the **step** region next (Figure 5.5).

```
for (let i = 0; i < 10; i++) {

    // code to execute

}
```

FIGURE 5.5

The step.

In this stage, we specify how our starting point will evolve. For our example, what we are saying is that each time our loop runs, the value of i will be increased by 1. That is captured by the cryptic looking i++. We'll cover what the ++ means later when we look at how numbers and math in JavaScript work, but another way of representing this would be to say i = i + 1.

The Condition (aka How Long to Keep Looping)

Going back to the stage we skipped, we have the **condition** part of our loop that determines when the loop will stop running (Figure 5.6).

```
for (let i = 0; i < 10; i++) {

    // code to execute

}
```

FIGURE 5.6

The condition part of the loop.

In our example, the condition is that our i variable is less than the value of **10**:

- If our i variable is less than 10, this expression evaluates to **true** and our loop **continues to run**.

- If our i variable becomes equal to or greater than 10, the condition is **false**, and our loop **terminates**.

Putting It All Together

Ok, now that we have looked at each part of our for loop in greater detail, let's use our newly gained knowledge to run through it all at once to see what is going on. Our full example, repeated from earlier, is as follows:

```
for (let i = 0; i < 10; i++) {
    saySomething();
}
```

```
function saySomething() {
  document.writeln("hello!");
}
```

When our `for` loop is initially hit at the starting point, the `i` variable is created and initialized to **0**. Next, we go to the condition part of the loop that determines whether our loop should keep running or not. The condition checks if the value of `i` is less than 10. Is 0 less than 10? Yes it is, so this condition evaluates to **true** and the code contained inside the loop runs. Once this is done, the step part of our loop kicks in. In this stage, the `i` variable is incremented by 1 to have a value of 1. At this point, our loop has run through one cycle, commonly referred to as an *iteration*. Time to start the next iteration.

For the next iteration, the loop starts all over again except the variable `i` isn't re-initialized. Its value is **1** from the previous iteration, so that carries over. For the condition, we re-check whether the new value of 1 is less than 10...which it is. The code inside our loop (basically the `saySomething` function) and the step part of the loop where `i` increments by **1** happen. The value of `i` is then incremented by 1 to a value of **2**, and this iteration is done for the day...leaving the door open for the next iteration!

This process repeats iteration after iteration until the condition `i < 10` evaluates to **false**. Since we started the loop with `i` being **0**, the loop is set to terminate when the value of `i` is less than 10, and `i` increments by 1 in each iteration, this loop (and any code contained in it) will run 10 times before stopping. Phew!

Some for Loop Examples

In the previous section, we dissected a simple `for` loop and labeled all its inner workings. The thing about `for` loops and most everything in JavaScript is that a simple example doesn't always cover everything we might need. The best solution is to look at some more examples of `for` loops, and that's what we are going to be doing in the next few sections.

Breaking a Loop

Sometimes, we may want to end our loop before it reaches completion. The way we end a loop is by using the `break` keyword. Below is an example:

```
for (let i = 0; i < 100; i++) {
  document.writeln(i);

  if (i == 45) {
```

```
        break;
    }
}
```

When the value of i equals **45**, the break keyword stops the loop from continuing further. While this example was just a little bit contrived, when we do run into a real-world case for ending our loop, we now know what to do.

Skipping an Iteration

There will be moments when we want our loop to skip its current iteration and move on to the next one. That is cleverly handled by the continue keyword:

```
let floors = 28;

for (let i = 1; i <= floors; i++) {
  if (i == 13) {
    // no floor here
    continue;
  }

  document.writeln("At floor: " + i + "<br>");
}
```

Unlike break where our loop just stops and goes home, continue tells our loop to stop and move on to the next iteration. We will often find ourselves using continue when handling errors where we just want the loop to move on to the next item.

Going Backwards

There is no reason why our starting point **has** to have a variable initialized to 0 and then increment that variable upward:

```
for (let i = 25; i > 0; i--) {
  document.writeln("hello");
}
```

You can just as easily start high and then decrement until your loop condition returns a false.

You may have heard that doing something like this increases your loop's performance. The jury is **still out** on whether **decrementing** is actually faster than incrementing, but feel free to experiment and see if you notice any performance benefits.

You Don't Have to Use Numbers

When filling out your `for` loop, you don't have to only use numbers:

```
for (let i = "a"; i != "aaaaaaaa"; i += "a") {
  document.writeln("hmm...");
}
```

You can use anything you want as long as your loop will eventually hit a point where it can end. Notice that in this example we are using the letter a as our currency for running this loop. At each iteration, the value of `i` is incremented with the letter **a**, and the loop stops when `i` equals **aaaaaaaa**.

Oh, No He Didn't!

Oh yes! Yes, I did. I went there, took a picture, posted on Facebook, and came back:

```
let i = 0;
let yay = true;

for (; yay;) {
  if (i == 10) {
    yay = false;
  } else {
    i++;
    document.writeln("weird");
  }
}
```

You don't have to fill out the three sections of your `for` loop in order to make it work. As long as, in the end, you manage to satisfy the loop's terminating condition, you can do whatever you want...just like the example above shows.

The Other Loops

Living in the shadow of the beloved `for` loop are the `while` and `do...while` loop variants. In the interest of completeness, let's quickly look at both of them.

The `while` Loop

The `while` loop repeats some code until its condition (another expression) returns **false**. Take a look at the following example:

```
let count = 0;

while (count < 10) {
  document.writeln("looping away!");


  count++;
}
```

In this example, the condition is represented by the `count < 10` expression. With each iteration, our loop increments the `count` value by **1**:

```
let count = 0;

while (count < 10) {
  document.writeln("looping away!");


  count++;
}
```

Once the value of `count` becomes **10**, the loop stops because the `count < 10` expression will return **false**. If you look at everything the while loop does, it does look a great imitation of the `for` loop. While the `for` loop formally required you to define the starting, condition, and step stages, the `while` loop expects you to define those stages yourself in your own way.

The `do...while` Loop

Now, we get to the Meg Griffin of the loop variants. That would be the `do...while` loop whose purpose is even less defined than `while`. Where the `while` loop had its conditional expression first before the loop would execute, the `do...while` loop has its conditional expression at the end.

Here is an example:

```
let count = 0;

do {
    document.writeln("I don't know what I am doing here! <br>");

    count++;
} while (count < 10);
```

The main difference between a `while` loop and a `do...while` loop is that the contents of a `while` loop could never get executed if its conditional expression is `false` from the very beginning:

```
while (false) {
    document.writeln("Can't touch this!");
}
```

With a `do...while` loop, because the conditional expression is evaluated only after one iteration, your loop's contents are guaranteed to run at least once:

```
do {
    document.writeln("This code will run once!");
} while (false);
```

That can come in handy in some situations. Now, before we wrap things up, there is just one last bit of information I need to tell you before we move on. The `break` and `continue` statements that we saw earlier as part of the awesome `for` loop also work similarly when used inside the `while` and `do...while` loop variants.

THE ABSOLUTE MINIMUM

So, there you have it—a look at `for` loops and how we can use them along with very basic coverage of the `while` and `do...while` loops. Right now, we may not see ourselves using loops a whole lot. As we start getting into more involved situations involving collections of data, elements in your DOM, text manipulation, and other stuff, we'll be using loops a whole lot more. Basically...keep all the information we've seen here really close by!

If you have any questions on the content here, don't be stuck! Post on the forums at **https://forum.kirupa.com** for really quick help from both me as well as some of the web's smartest and friendliest developers.

COMMENTING YOUR CODE...FTW!

Everything we write in our code editor might **seem** like it is intended for our browser's eyes only:

```js
let xPos = -500;

function boringComputerStuff() {
  xPos += 5;

  if (xPos > 1000) {
    xPos = -500;
  }
}
boringComputerStuff();
```

As we will soon find out, that isn't the case. There is another audience for our code. That audience is made up of human beings.

Our code is often used or scrutinized by other people. This is especially true if you and I are working in a team with other JavaScript developers. We'll often be looking at their code, and they'll often be looking at our code. To make all this code look as efficient as possible, we need to ensure our code makes sense when someone other than us is looking at it. Even if you are working solo, this applies to you as well. That brilliant function that makes sense to you today might be gibberish when looked at next week.

There are many ways of solving this problem. One of the best ways is by using something known as **comments**. In this short article, we will learn what comments are, how to specify them in JavaScript, and learn some good practices on how to use them.

Onward!

What Are Comments?

Comments are the things we write as part of our code to communicate something to humans:

```
// This is for not inviting me to your birthday party!
let blah = true;


function sweetRevenge() {
  while (blah) {
    // Infinite dialog boxes! HAHAHA!!!!
    alert("Hahahaha!");
  }
}
sweetRevenge();
```

In this example, the comments are marked by the // character, and they provide some questionably useful information about the code being described.

The thing to keep in mind about comments is that they don't run and get executed like all the other code you write. **JavaScript ignores your comments**. It doesn't like you. It doesn't care what you have to say, so you don't have to worry about proper syntax, punctuation, spelling, and everything else you need to keep in mind when writing normal code. Comments exist only for us to help understand what a piece of code is doing.

There is one other purpose comments serve. We can use comments to mark lines of code that we don't want executed:

```
function insecureLogin(input) {
  if (input == "password") {
    // let key = Math.random() * 100000;
    // processLogin(key);
  }
  return false;
}
```

In this example, the following two lines can be seen in our code editor, but they won't run:

```
// let key = Math.random() * 100000;
// processLogin(key);
```

We'll often find ourselves using the code editor as a scratchpad, and comments are a great way to keep track of things we've tried in making our code work without affecting how your application ultimately runs.

Single Line Comments

There are several ways to specify comments in our code. One way is by specifying **single line comments** using the // mark followed by what we want to communicate. This is the comment variation we've seen several times already.

We can specify these comments in their own dedicated line:

```
// Return the larger of the two arguments
function max(a, b) {
  if (a > b) {
    return a;
  } else {
    return b;
  }
}
```

We can also specify these comments on the same line as a statement:

```
let zorb = "Alien"; // Annoy the planetary citizens
```

Where we specify comments is entirely up to you. Choose a location that seems appropriate for the comment you are writing.

Since I enjoy sounding like a broken record, to call out one more time, our comments don't run as part of our application. Only you, me, and possibly Dupree can see them. If that last line made no sense, what you are telling me is that you did not see one of the greatest comedies of our generation. I highly encourage you to put this book or tutorial down and take a few hours to rectify that.

Multi-Line Comments

The problem with single line comments is that you have to specify the `//` characters in front of every single line you want to comment. That can get really tiring—especially if you are writing a long comment or commenting out a large chunk of code.

For those situations, you have another way of specifying comments. You have the `/*` and `*/` characters to specify the beginning and ending of what are known as **multi-line comments**:

```
/*
let mouseX = 0;
let mouseY = 0;

canvas.addEventListener("mousemove", setMousePosition, false);

function setMousePosition(e) {
  mouseX = e.clientX;
  mouseY = e.clientY;
}
*/
```

Instead of adding `//` marks in front of each line like an animal, we can use the `/*` and `*/` characters to save us a lot of time and frustration.

In most applications, we'll use a combination of single line and multi-line comments depending on what we are trying to document. This means we need to be familiar with both of these commenting approaches.

TIP JSDoc Style Comments

When we are writing some code that you want used by others, you probably want an *easier way* to communicate what your code does beyond having people rummage through source code. That *easier way* exists, and it is made possible by a tool known as **JSDoc**! With JSDoc, you slightly modify how you write your comments:

```
/**
 * Shuffles the contents of your Array.
 *
 * @this {Array}
```

```
 * @returns {Array} The current array with the contents
fully shuffled.
 */
Array.prototype.shuffle = function () {
  let input = this;

  for (let i = input.length - 1; i >= 0; i--) {

    let randomIndex = Math.floor(Math.random() *
(i + 1));
    let itemAtIndex = input[randomIndex];

    input[randomIndex] = input[i];
    input[i] = itemAtIndex;
  }
  return input;
}
```

Once you have commented your files, you can use the JSDoc tool to export the relevant parts of your comments into an easily browseable set of HTML pages. This allows you to spend more time writing JavaScript while giving your users an easy way to understand what your code does and how to use various parts of it.

If you want to learn more on how to use JSDoc, check out their awesome **Getting Started page** for more details.

Commenting Best Practices

Now that we have a good idea of what comments are and the several ways we have to write them in JavaScript, let's talk a bit about how to properly use comments to help make our code easy to read:

- **Always comment your code as you are writing it.** Writing comments is dreadfully boring, but it is an important part of writing code. It is much more time efficient for you (and others) to understand what your code does from reading a comment as opposed to reading line after line of boring JavaScript.

- **Don't defer comment writing for later.** Deferring comment writing for a later time is the grown-up equivalent of procrastinating on a chore. If you don't comment your code as you are writing it, you'll probably just skip commenting entirely. That's not a good thing.

- **Use more English and less JavaScript.** Comments are one of the few places when writing JavaScript where you can freely use English (or whatever language you prefer communicating in). Don't complicate your comments unnecessarily with code. Be clear. Be concise. Use words.

- **Embrace whitespace.** When scanning large blocks of code, you want to ensure your comments stand out and are clear to follow. That involves being liberal with your Spacebar and Enter/Return key. Take a look at the following example:

```javascript
function selectInitialState(state) {
  let selectContent = document.querySelector("#stateList");
  let stateIndex = null;

  /*

      For the returned state, we would like to ensure that
      we select it in our UI. This means we iterate through
      every state in the drop-down until we find a match.
      When a match is found, we ensure it gets selected.

  */

  for (let i = 0; i < selectContent.length; i++) {

    let stateInSelect = selectContent.options[i].innerText;

    if (stateInSelect == state) {
      stateIndex = i;
    }
  }

  selectContent.selectedIndex = stateIndex;
}
```

Notice that our comment is appropriately spaced to distinguish it from the rest of the code. If your comments are strewn about in arbitrary locations where they are difficult to identify, that just unnecessarily slows you and whoever is reading your code down.

- **Don't comment obvious things.** If a line of code is self-explanatory, don't waste time explaining what it does unless there is some subtle behavior you need to call out as a warning. Instead, invest that time in commenting the less obvious parts of your code.

The best practices you see here will take you far in ensuring you write properly commented code. If you are working on a larger project with other people, I can assure you that your team already has some established guidelines on what proper commenting looks like. Take some time to understand those guidelines and follow them. You'll be happy. Your team will be happy.

THE ABSOLUTE MINIMUM

Comments are often viewed as a necessary evil. After all, would you rather take a few minutes documenting what *you* clearly already know, or would you rather implement the next cool piece of functionality? The way I like to describe comments is as follows: *It is a long-term investment.* The value and benefit of comments is often not immediately obvious. It becomes obvious when you start having other people looking over your code, and it becomes obvious when you have to revisit your own code after you've forgotten all about it and how it works. Don't sacrifice long-term time savings for a short-term kick. Invest in single line (//) and multi-line (/* and */) comments now before it is too late.

As always, if you have any questions on the content here, I and other friendly developers are here to help! Post on the forums at **https://forum.kirupa.com** to get unblocked quickly.

7

TIMERS

By default, our code runs synchronously. That is a fancy of way of saying that when a statement needs to execute, it executes immediately. There are no **ands**, **ifs**, or **buts** about it. The concept of delaying execution or deferring work to later isn't a part of JavaScript's default behavior. We kind of saw this when looking at loops earlier. The loop runs at lightning speed with no delay between each iteration. That is great for making quick calculations, but that isn't great if we want to make an update at a more measured (aka slower!) pace.

All of this doesn't mean the ability to stop work from running instantaneously doesn't exist! If we swerve just slightly off the main road, there are three functions that allow us to mostly do just that (and more)— setTimeout, setInterval, and requestAnimationFrame. In this article, we will look at what each of these functions do.

Onward!

Delaying with `setTimeout`

The `setTimeout` function allows us to delay executing some code. The way we use it is quite nice. This function allows us to specify what code to execute and how many milliseconds to wait before the code we specified executes. Putting that into JavaScript, it will look something like this:

```
let timeoutID = setTimeout(someFunction, delayInMilliseconds);
```

Going a bit more example-ish, if we wanted to call a function called `showAlert` after 5 seconds, the `setTimeout` declaration would look as follows:

```
function showAlert() {
  alert("moo!");
}
```

```
let timeoutID = setTimeout(showAlert, 5000);
```

Cool, right? Now, let's talk about something less interesting that we need to cover for completeness. That something has to do with the `timeID` variable that is initialized to our `setTimeout` function. It isn't there by accident. If we ever wanted to access this `setTimeout` timer again, we need a way to reference it. By associating a variable with our `setTimeout` declaration, we can easily accomplish that.

Now, you may be wondering why we would ever want to reference a timer once we've created it. There aren't too many reasons. The only reason I can think of would be to cancel the timer. For `setTimeout`, that is conveniently accomplished using the `clearTimeout` function and passing the timeout ID as the argument:

```
clearTimeout(timeoutID);
```

If you are never planning on canceling your timer, you can just use `setTimeout` directly without having it be part of the variable initialization.

Let's talk about when we would commonly use it in the real world. **UI development.** When we are doing UI development, deferring some action to a later time is unusually common. Here are some examples that I ran into just in the past month:

A menu slides in, and after a few seconds of the user no longer playing with the menu, the menu slides away.

You have a long running operation that is unable to complete, and a `setTimeout` function interrupts that operation to return control back to the user.

My favorite (and one that I wrote a tutorial about as well) is where you use the `setTimeout` function to **detect whether users are inactive or idle**!

If you do a search for `setTimeout` on this site or Google, you'll see many more real-world cases where `setTimeout` proves very useful.

Looping with `setInterval`

The next timer function we are going to look at is `setInterval`. The `setInterval` function is similar to `setTimeout` in that it also allows you to execute code after a specified amount of time. What makes it different is that it doesn't just execute the code once. It keeps on executing the code in a loop forever.

Here is how you would use the `setInterval` function:

```
let intervalID = setInterval(someFunction, delayInMilliseconds);
```

Except for the function name, the way you use `setInterval` is even identical to `setTimeout`. The first argument specifies the inline code or function you would like to execute. The second argument specifies how long to wait before your code loops again. You can also optionally initialize the `setInterval` function to a variable to store an interval ID—an ID that you can later use to do exciting things like cancel the looping. Yay!!!

OK! Now that we've seen all that, here is an example of this code at work for looping a function called `drawText` with a delay of 2 seconds between each loop:

```html
<!DOCTYPE html>
<html>

<head>
  <meta charset="utf-8">
  <title>Show me some text!</title>
</head>

<body>
  <script>
    let thingToPrint = "";

    function drawText() {
      thingToPrint += "#";
      document.writeln(thingToPrint);
    }

    setInterval(drawText, 2000);
  </script>
</body>

</html>
```

If we wish to cancel the looping, we can use the appropriately named `clearInterval` function:

```
clearInterval(intervalID);
```

Its usage is similar to its `clearTimeout` equivalent. We pass in the ID of the `setInterval` timer instance that we optionally retrieved while setting up our `setInterval` in the first place.

In real life, `setInterval` was the primary function you had for the longest time for creating animations in JavaScript. To get 30 or 60 frames a second, you would do something as follows by playing with the delay time value:

```
// 1000 divided by 60 is the millisecond value for 60fps
setInterval(moveCircles, 1000 / 60);
```

To see `setInterval` in action in some other realistic examples on this site itself, check out the bottom of the **Creating a Sweet Content Slider** (https://www. kirupa.com/html5/creating_a_sweet_content_slider.htm) article as well as the **Creating an Analog Clock** (https://www.kirupa.com/html5/create_an_analog_ clock_using_the_canvas.htm) article. They both feature `setInterval` quite prominently!

Animating Smoothly with `requestAnimationFrame`

Now, we get to one of my favorite functions ever: `requestAnimationFrame`. The `requestAnimationFrame` function is all about synchronizing your code with a browser repaint event. What this means is this: your browser is busy juggling a billion different things at any given time. These things include fiddling with layout, reacting to page scrolls, listening for mouse clicks, displaying the result of keyboard taps, executing JavaScript, loading resources, and more. At the same time your browser is doing all of this, it is also redrawing the screen at 60 frames per second...or at least trying its very best to.

When you have code that is intended to animate something to the screen, you want to ensure your animation code runs properly without getting lost in the shuffle of everything else your browser is doing. Using the `setInterval` technique mentioned earlier doesn't guarantee that frames won't get dropped when the browser is busy optimizing for other things. To avoid your animation code from being treated like any other generic JavaScript, you have the `requestAnimationFrame` function. This function gets special treatment by the browser. This special treatment allows it to time its execution perfectly to avoid dropped frames, avoid unnecessary work, and generally steer clear of other side effects that plague other looping solutions.

The way we use this function starts off a bit similar to `setTimeout` and `setInterval`:

```
let requestID = requestAnimationFrame(someFunction);
```

The only real difference is that we don't specify a duration value. The duration is automatically calculated based on the current frame rate, whether the current tab is active or not, whether your device is running on battery or not, and a whole host of other factors that go beyond what we can control or understand.

Anyway, this usage of the `requestAnimationFrame` function is merely the textbook version. In real life, you'll rarely make a single call to `requestAnimationFrame` like this. Key to all animations created in JavaScript is an animation loop, and it is this loop that we want to throw `requestAnimationFrame` at. The result of that throw looks something as follows:

```
function animationLoop() {
  // animation-related code

  requestAnimationFrame(animationLoop)
}


// start off our animation loop!
animationLoop();
```

Notice that our `requestAnimationFrame` specifies that the `animationLoop` function gets called the next time the browser decides to repaint. It looks like the `requestAnimationFrame` function calls `animationLoop` directly, which isn't the case. That isn't a bug in the code. While this kind of circular referencing would almost guarantee a frozen/hung browser, `requestAnimationFrame`'s implementation avoids that. Instead, it ensures the `animationLoop` function is called just the right amount of times needed to ensure things get drawn to the screen to create smooth and fluid animations. It does so without freezing the rest of your application functionality up.

To learn more about `requestAnimationFrame` and its primary use in creating awesome animations, you should check out all the content in the **Animations in JavaScript** section. In that section, I also dive deeper into **requestAnimationFrame** beyond the highlights we've looked at here.

THE ABSOLUTE MINIMUM

If you think that timers fall under a more niche category compared to some of the other more essential things like the if/else statements and loops we looked at earlier, you would probably be right in thinking that. You can build many awesome apps without ever having to rely on `setTimeout`, `setInterval`, or `requestAnimationFrame`. That doesn't mean it isn't essential to know about them, though. There will be a time when you'll need to delay when your code executes, loop your code continuously, or create a sweet animation using JavaScript. When that time arrives, you'll be prepared…or at least know what to Google for.

To see these timer functions used in the wild, check out these optional articles and examples that may help you out:

- **Creating Animations Using requestAnimationFrame** http://bit.ly/kirupaAnimationsJS
- **Creating a Sweet Content Slider** http://bit.ly/sliderTutorial
- **Creating an Analog Clock** http://bit.ly/kirupaAnalogClock
- **The Seizure Generator** http://bit.ly/kirupaSeizureGenerator (Seizure warning: The animation on this site strobes heavily.)

I've mentioned this a bunch of times so far, but JavaScript can be frustrating. Timers doubly so. If you ever run into any issues, I and other developers who have battled times for a long time are here to help! Post on the forums at **https://forum.kirupa.com** to get un-frustrated!

VARIABLE SCOPE

Let's revisit something relating to variables we saw a few chapters ago. Each variable we declare has a certain level of visibility that determines when we can actually use it. In human-understandable terms, just because we declare a variable doesn't mean that it can be accessed from anywhere in our code. There are some basic things we need to understand, and this whole area of understanding falls under a topic known as **variable scope**.

In this tutorial, I'm going to be explaining variable scope by looking at common cases that we've (mostly) already seen. This is a pretty deep topic, but we are just going to scratch the surface here. We'll see variable scope creep up in many subsequent tutorials where we will extend on what we learn here.

Onward!

Global Scope

We are going to start our exploration of scope at the very top with what is known as **global scope**. In real life, when we say that something can be heard globally, it means that we can be anywhere in the world and still be able to hear that... something

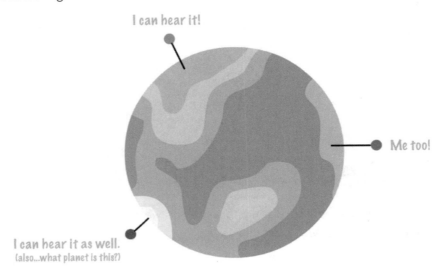

I can hear it!

Me too!

I can hear it as well.
(also...what planet is this?)

In JavaScript, much the same applies. If we say, for example, a variable is available globally, it means that any code on our page has access to read and modify this variable. The way we make something apply globally is by declaring it in our code completely outside of a function.

To illustrate this, let's take a look at the following example:

```
<!DOCTYPE html>
<html>

<head>
  <meta charset="utf-8">
  <title>Variable Scope</title>
</head>

<body>
  <script>
    let counter = 0;
```

```
    alert(counter);
  </script>
</body>


</html>
```

Here, we are simply declaring a variable called `counter` and initializing it to **0**. By virtue of this variable being declared directly inside the script tag without being placed inside a function, the `counter` variable is considered to be **global**. What this distinction means is that our `counter` variable can be accessed by any code that lives in our document.

The below code highlights this:

```
<!DOCTYPE html>
<html>


<head>
  <meta charset="utf-8">
  <title>Variable Scope</title>
</head>


<body>
  <script>
    let counter = 0;

    function returnCount() {
      return counter;
    }

    alert(returnCount());
  </script>
</body>


</html>
```

In this example, the `counter` variable is declared outside of the `returnCount` function. Despite that, the `returnCount` function has full access to the `counter` variable. When the code runs, the `alert` function calls the `returnCount` function that returns the value of the `counter` variable.

At this point, you are probably wondering why I am pointing this out. We've been using global variables all this time without really noticing it. All I am doing here is formally introducing you to a guest that has been hanging around your party for a while.

Local Scope

Now, things get a little interesting when we look at things that aren't globally declared. This is where understanding scope really starts paying dividends. As we saw earlier, a variable declared globally is accessible inside a function:

```
let counter = 0;

function returnCount() {
  return counter;
}
```

The opposite doesn't hold true. A variable declared inside a function will not work when accessed outside of a function:

```
function setState() {
  let state = "on";
}
setState();

alert(state) // undefined
```

In this example, the `state` variable is declared inside the `setState` function, and accessing the state variable outside of that function doesn't work. The reason is that the scope for our `state` variable is local to the `setState` function itself. A more generic way of describing this is by saying that your `state` variable is just **local**.

 NOTE Using Variables Without Declaring Them

If we initialize the `state` variable without formally declaring it, the scoping behavior is drastically different:

```
function setState() {
  state = "on";
}
setState();

alert(state) // "on"
```

In this case, even though our `state` variable makes its appearance inside the `setState` function first, not declaring it first with either `let` or `const` (or `var`, which is an older way of declaring variables) makes this variable live globally. In general, you don't want to declare a variable like this. Always prefix it with a `let` or `const`.

Miscellaneous Scoping Shenanigans

Since we are talking about JavaScript here, things would be too easy if we just left everything with variable scope as they stand now. In the following sections, I am going to highlight some quirks that you need to be familiar with.

Block Scoping

Our code is made-up of blocks...lots and lots of blocks. What exactly is a block? A block is a collection of JavaScript statements almost always wrapped by curly braces. For example, let us take a look at the following code:

```
let safeToProceed = false;

function isItSafe() {
  if (safeToProceed) {
    alert("You shall pass!");
  } else {
    alert("You shall not pass!");
  }
}

isItSafe();
```

Counting the pair of curly brackets, there are three blocks here. One block is the region contained by the `isItSafe` function itself:

```
let safeToProceed = false;

function isItSafe() {
  if (safeToProceed) {
    alert("You shall pass!");
  } else {
```

```
      alert("You shall not pass!");
   }
}
```

```
isItSafe();
```

The second block is the `if` statement region:

```
let safeToProceed = false;

function isItSafe() {
  if (safeToProceed) {
    alert("You shall pass!");
  } else {
    alert("You shall not pass!");
  }
}
```

The third block is the region covered by the `else` statement:

```
let safeToProceed = false;

function isItSafe() {
  if (safeToProceed) {
    alert("You shall pass!");
  } else {
    alert("You shall not pass!");
  }
}
```

Any variable declared inside a block using `let` or `const` is local to that block and any child blocks contained inside it. To better understand this, take a look at the following code that is a variation of the `isItSafe` function from earlier:

```
function isThePriceRight(cost) {
  let total = cost + 1;

  if (total > 3) {
    alert(total);
  } else {
```

```
      alert("Not enough!");
    }
  }


  isThePriceRight(4);
```

We declared the `total` variable as part of the function block. We are accessing this variable inside the `if` block. What do you think will happen? The `total` variable is totally (haha!) accessible here, because the `if` block is a child of the function block. To put it in the lingo of our times, the total variable is considered **in-scope** of the `alert` function.

What about the following situation?

```
function isThePriceRight(cost) {
  let total = cost + 1;

  if (total > 3) {
    let warning = true;
    alert(total);
  } else {
    alert("Not enough!");
  }

  alert(warning);
}


isThePriceRight(4);
```

We have a variable called `warning` declared inside our `if` block, and we have an `alert` function that tries to print the value of `warning`. In this case, because we are trying to access the `warning` variable in a block that is outside the one the variable was originally declared in, our `alert` function won't actually display the value of **true**. Given where our `alert` function is, the `warning` variable is considered to be **out-of-scope**.

 NOTE Declaring Variables with the `var` Keyword!

A few paragraphs ago, I casually mentioned that variables were once declared with the `var` keyword. The `let` (and `const`) keywords were new additions to help you declare variables, and wherever you may have used `var` in the past, you should use `let`

instead. We never discussed why `let` is preferable and said that we'll discuss it further when looking at variable scope. Well...here we are!

Variables declared with `var` scope to functions. They don't scope to blocks like our if/else ones. If we modify the example from earlier to have our `warning` variable be declared using `var` instead of `let`, our code will look as follows:

```
function isThePriceRight(cost) {
  let total = cost + 1;

  if (total > 3) {
    var warning = true;
    alert(total);
  } else {
    alert("Not enough!");
  }

  alert(warning);
}


isThePriceRight(4);
```

Earlier, the `alert` function for `warning` wouldn't display anything because the `warning` variable was out-of-scope when declared with `let`. With `var`, that isn't the case. You will see **true** displayed. The reason for this is because of the major difference between `let` and `var`. Variables declared with `var` are scoped at the function level, so as long as somewhere inside the function the variable is declared, that variable is considered to be in-scope. Variables declared with `let`, as we saw earlier, are scoped to the block level.

The level of leniency provided by `var` in the scoping department is a little too much, and this leniency makes it easy to make variable-related mistakes. For this reason, my preference is for all of us to use `let` when it comes to declaring variables.

How JavaScript Processes Variables

If you thought the earlier block scoping logic was weird, wait till you see this one. Take a look at the following code:

```
let foo = "Hello!";
alert(foo);
```

When this code runs, we can reasonably state that the value of **Hello!** will be displayed. We would reasonably be right. What if we made the following modification where we moved the variable declaration and initialization to the end?

```
alert(foo);
let foo = "Hello!";
```

In this situation, our code will error out. The foo variable is being accessed without being referenced. If we replaced the let with a var, here is what our code would look like:

```
alert(foo);
var foo = "Hello!";
```

When this code runs, the behavior is different than what we saw earlier. You will see **undefined** displayed. What exactly is going on here?

When JavaScript encounters a scope (global, function, etc.) , one of the first things it does is scan the full body of the code for any declared variables. When it encounters any variables, it initializes them by default with **undefined** for var. For let and const, it leaves the variables **completely uninitialized**. Lastly, it moves any variables it encounters to the top of the scope—the nearest block for let and const, the nearest function for var.

Let's dive in to see what this means. Our code initially looks like this:

```
alert(foo);
let foo = "Hello!";
```

When JavaScript makes a pass at this, what this code gets turned into is the following:

```
let foo;
alert(foo);
foo = "Hello!";
```

The foo variable, despite being declared at the bottom of our code, gets kicked up to the top. This is more formally known as **hoisting**. The thing about let (and const), is that when they get hoisted, they are left uninitialized. If you try to access an uninitialized variable, our code will throw an error and stop. If we modified our earlier example to use var, the way JavaScript would see things would look as follows:

```
var foo = undefined;
alert(foo);
foo = "Hello!";
```

The variable still gets hoisted, but it gets initialized to **undefined**. This ensures our code still runs.

The main takeaway from all of this is as follows: **please declare and initialize your variables before actually using them**. While JavaScript has some affordance for dealing with cases where we don't do that, those affordances are just awfully confusing.

Closures

No conversation about variable scope can be wrapped up without discussing closures. That is, until right now. I am not going to explain closures here, for it is a slightly more advanced topic that we will cover separately in Chapter 9.

Before you go to the next chapter, if you have any questions on the content here, post on the forums at **https://forum.kirupa.com** where I and other developers will be happy to help you out.

THE ABSOLUTE MINIMUM

Where your variables live has a major impact on where they can be used. Variables declared globally are accessible to your entire application. Variables declared locally will only be accessible to whatever scope they are found in. Within the range of global and local variables, JavaScript has a lot going on up its sleeve.

This chapter gave you an overview of how variable scope can affect your code, and you'll see some of these concepts presented front-and-center in the near future.

9

CLOSURES

By now, you probably know all about functions and all the fun functiony things that they do. An important part of working with functions, with JavaScript, and (possibly) life in general is understanding the topic known as **closures**. Closures touch upon a gray area where functions and variable scope intersect (Figure 9.1).

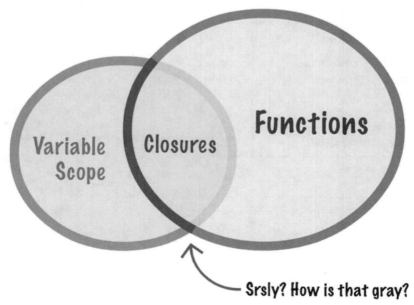

FIGURE 9.1

Closures.

Now, I am not going to say any more about closures, for this is something best explained by seeing code. Any words I add right now to define or describe what closures are will only serve to confuse things. In the following sections, we'll start off in familiar territory and then slowly venture into hostile areas where closures can be found.

Onward!

Functions within Functions

The first thing we are going to do is really drill in on what happens when you have functions within functions...and the inner function gets returned. As part of that, let's do a quick review of functions.

Take a look at the following code:

```
function calculateRectangleArea(length, width) {
  return length * width;
}


let roomArea = calculateRectangleArea(10, 10);
alert(roomArea);
```

The calculateRectangleArea function takes two arguments and returns the multiplied value of those arguments to whatever called it. In this example, the **whatever called it part** is played by the roomArea variable.

After this code has run, the roomArea variable contains the result of multiplying 10 and 10...which is simply 100 (Figure 9.2).

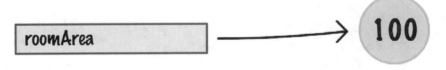

FIGURE 9.2

The result of roomArea.

As you know, what a function returns can pretty much be anything. In this case, we returned a number. You can very easily return some text (aka a **String**), the undefined value, a **custom object**, etc. As long as the code that is calling the function knows what to do with what the function returns, you can do pretty much whatever you want. You can even return another function. Let me rathole on this a bit.

Below is a very simple example of what I am talking about:

```
function youSayGoodBye() {

  alert("Good Bye!");

  function andISayHello() {
    alert("Hello!");
  }

  return andISayHello;
}
```

We can have functions that contain functions inside them. In this example, we have our youSayGoodBye function that contains an `alert` and another function called andISayHello (Figure 9.3).

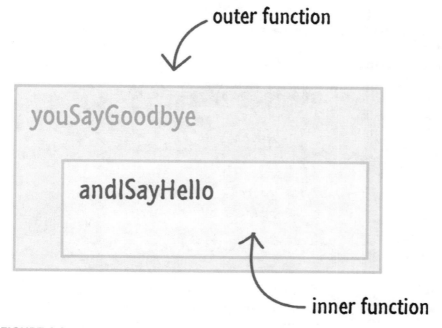

FIGURE 9.3

A function within a function.

The interesting part is what the youSayGoodBye function returns when it gets called. It returns the andISayHello function:

```
function youSayGoodBye() {

  alert("Good Bye!");

  function andISayHello() {
    alert("Hello!");
  }

  return andISayHello;
}
```

Let's go ahead and play this example out. To call this function, initialize a variable that points to youSayGoodBye:

```
let something = youSayGoodBye();
```

The moment this line of code runs, **all of the code** inside your youSayGoodBye function will get run as well. This means, you will see a dialog (thanks to the alert) that says **Good Bye!** (Figure 9.4).

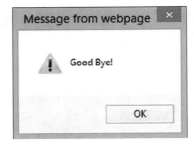

FIGURE 9.4

The Good Bye! dialog.

As part of running to completion, the andISayHello function will be created and then returned as well. At this point, our something variable only has eyes for one thing, and that thing is the andISayHello function (see Figure 9.5).

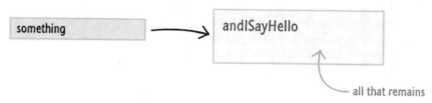

FIGURE 9.5

Something and the andISayHello function.

The `youSayGoodBye` outer function, from the `something` variable's point of view, simply goes away. Because the `something` variable now points to a function, you can invoke this function by just calling it using the open and close parentheses like you normally would:

```
let something = youSayGoodBye();
something();
```

When you do this, the returned inner function (aka `andISayHello`) will execute. Just like before, you will see a dialog appear, but this dialog will say **Hello!** (Figure 9.6) – which is what the `alert` inside this function specified.

FIGURE 9.6

Hello!

All of this should probably a review. The only thing that you may have found new is realizing once a function returns a value, it is no longer around. The only thing that remains is the returned value.

Ok, we are getting close to the promised hostile territory. In the next section, we will extend what we've just seen by taking a look at another example with a slight twist.

When the Inner Functions Aren't Self-Contained

In the previous example, our `andISayHello` inner function was self-contained and didn't rely on any variables or state from the outer function:

```
function youSayGoodBye() {

  alert("Good Bye!");

  function andISayHello() {
    alert("Hello!");
  }

  return andISayHello;
}
```

In many real scenarios, very rarely will we run into a case like this. We will often have variables and data that are shared between the outer function and the inner function. To highlight this, take a look at the following:

```
function stopWatch() {
  let startTime = Date.now();

  function getDelay() {
    let elapsedTime = Date.now() - startTime;
    alert(elapsedTime);
  }

  return getDelay;
}
```

This example shows a very simple way of measuring the time it takes to do something. Inside the `stopWatch` function, we have a `startTime` variable that is set to the value of `Date.now()`:

```
function stopWatch() {
  let startTime = Date.now();

  function getDelay() {
    let elapsedTime = Date.now() - startTime;
    alert(elapsedTime);
```

```
  }

  return getDelay;
}
```

We also have an inner function called `getDelay`:

```
function stopWatch() {
  let startTime = Date.now();

  function getDelay() {
    let elapsedTime = Date.now() - startTime;
    alert(elapsedTime);
  }

  return getDelay;
}
```

The `getDelay` function displays a dialog containing the difference in time between a new call to `Date.now()` and the `startTime` variable declared earlier.

Getting back to the outer `stopWatch` function, the last thing that happens is that it returns the `getDelay` function before exiting. As we can see, the code here is very similar to the earlier example. We have an outer function, we have an inner function, and we have the outer function returning the inner function.

Now, to see the `stopWatch` function at work, add the following lines of code:

```
let timer = stopWatch();

// do something that takes some time
for (let i = 0; i < 1000000; i++) {
  let foo = Math.random() * 10000;
}

// invoke the returned function
timer();
```

The full markup and code for this example looks as follows:

```
<!DOCTYPE html>
<html>
```

```html
<head>
  <meta charset="utf-8">
  <title>Closures</title>

  <style>

  </style>
</head>

<body>
  <script>
    function stopWatch() {
      var startTime = Date.now();

      function getDelay() {
        var elapsedTime = Date.now() - startTime;
        alert(elapsedTime);
      }

      return getDelay;
    }

    let timer = stopWatch();

    // do something that takes some time
    for (let i = 0; i < 1000000; i++) {
      let foo = Math.random() * 10000;
    }

    // invoke the returned function
    timer();
  </script>
</body>

</html>
```

If you run this example, we'll see a dialog displaying the number of milliseconds it took between your `timer` variable getting initialized, your `for` loop running to completion, and the `timer` variable getting invoked as a function (Figure 9.7).

FIGURE 9.7

The timer variable invoked as a function.

To explain in a different way, we have a stopwatch that we invoke, run some long-running operation, and invoke again to see how long the long-running operation took place.

Now that we can see our little stopwatch example working, let's go back to the `stopWatch` function and see what exactly is going on. Like I mentioned a few lines ago, a lot of what we see is similar to the `youSayGoodBye` / `andISayHello` example. There is a twist that makes this example different, and the important part to note is what happens when the `getDelay` function is returned to the `timer` variable.

Figure 9.8 is an incomplete visualization of what this looks like.

FIGURE 9.8

The stopWatch outer function is no longer active, and the timer variable is bound to the getDelay function.

The stopWatch outer function is no longer in play, and the timer variable is bound to the getDelay function. Now, here is the twist. The getDelay function relies on the startTime variable that lives in the context of the outer stopWatch function:

```
function stopWatch() {
    let startTime = Date.now();


    function getDelay() {
        let elapsedTime = Date.now() - startTime;
        alert(elapsedTime);
    }


    return getDelay;
}
```

When the outer stopWatch function goes away when getDelay is returned to the timer variable, what happens in the following line?

```
function getDelay() {
    let elapsedTime = Date.now() - startTime;
    alert(elapsedTime);
}
```

In this context, it would make sense if the startTime variable is actually undefined, right? But the example totally worked, so something else is going on here. That something else is the shy and mysterious closure. Here is a look at what happens to make our startTime variable actually store a value and not be undefined.

The JavaScript runtime that keeps track of all of your variables, memory usage, references, and so on is really clever. In this example, it detects that the inner function (getDelay) is relying on variables from the outer function (stopWatch). When that happens, the runtime ensures that any variables in the outer function that are needed are still available to the inner function **even if the outer function goes away**.

To visualize this properly, Figure 9.9 shows you what the timer variable looks like.

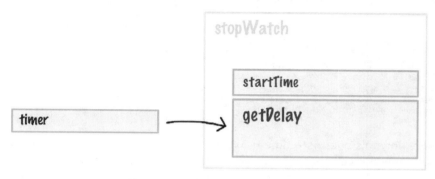

FIGURE 9.9

The timer variable.

It is still referring to the getDelay function, but the getDelay function also has access to the startTime variable that existed in the outer stopWatch function. This inner function, because it **enclosed** relevant variables from the outer function into its bubble (aka scope), is known as a **closure** (Figure 9.10).

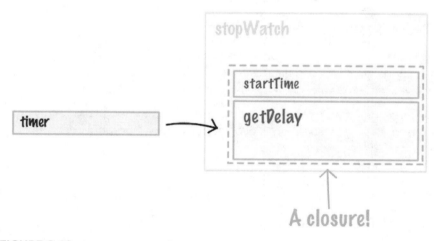

FIGURE 9.10

A closure defined diagramatically.

To define the closure more formally, it is a **newly created function that also contains its variable context** (Figure 9.11).

variables this **function** relies on

closure = function + outer context

usually created / returned by
another function

FIGURE 9.11

A more formal definition of closure.

To review this one more time using our existing example, the `startTime` variable gets the value of `Date.now` the moment the `timer` variable gets initialized and the `stopWatch` function runs. When the `stopWatch` function returns the inner `getDelay` function, the `stopWatch` function goes away. What doesn't go away are any shared variables inside `stopWatch` that the inner function relies on. Those shared variables are not destroyed. Instead, they are enclosed by the inner function aka the closure.

THE ABSOLUTE MINIMUM

By looking at closures through examples first, you really missed out on a lot of boring definitions, theories, and hand waving. In all seriousness, closures are very common in JavaScript. You will encounter them in many subtle and not-so-subtle ways:

If there is only thing you take out of all of this, remember the following: The *most important thing closures do is allow functions to keep on working even if their environment drastically changes or disappears.* Any variables that were in scope when the function was created are enclosed and protected to ensure the function still works. This behavior is essential for a very dynamic language like JavaScript where you often create, modify, and destroy things on the fly. Happy days!

We covered a lot of ground here. If you have any questions about what you've seen, please post on the forums at **https://forum.kirupa.com** to quickly get answers.

10

WHERE SHOULD YOUR CODE LIVE?

Let's take a break from our regularly scheduled...programming (ha!). So far, all of the code we have been writing has been contained fully inside an HTML document:

```html
<!DOCTYPE html>
<html>

<head>
  <meta charset="utf-8">
  <title>An Interesting Title Goes Here</title>

  <style>
    body {
      background-color: #EEE;
    }

    h1 {
      font-family: sans-serif;
      font-size: 36px;
    }

    p {
      font-family: sans-serif;
    }
  </style>
</head>

<body>
  <h1>Are you ready for this?</h1>
  <p>Are you ready for seeing (or already having seen!) the most
amazing dialog ever?</p>

  <script>
    alert("hello, world!");
  </script>
</body>

</html>
```

We are going to take a step back and revisit whether having this arrangement between HTML, CSS, and JS in the same document makes sense for all situations. To simplify how we talk about our document structure, let's replace the code view with a more...um, artistic view...involving some really nicely designed boxes (Figure 10.1).

FIGURE 10.1

Our representation of a web page.

In this world, the only thing that protects our HTML document from JavaScript is just a couple of `script` tags. Now, your JavaScript does not have to live inside our HTML document. We have another way, and this way involves a separate file where all of our JavaScript will instead live (Figure 10.2).

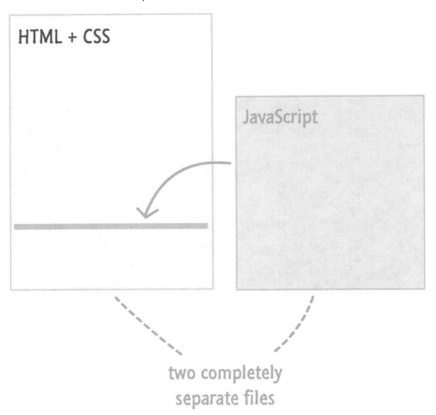

FIGURE 10.2

Our JS now lives in its own separate file!

In this approach, we don't have any real JavaScript that lives inside our HTML document. We still have our `script` tag, but this tag **simply points to the JavaScript file** instead of containing line after line of actual JavaScript code.

The thing to note is that none of these approaches are mutually exclusive. We can mix both approaches into an HTML document and have a hybrid approach where we have both an external JavaScript file as well as lines of JavaScript code fully contained inside the document (Figure 10.3).

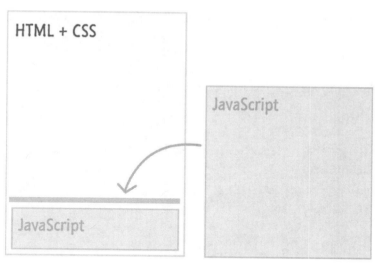

FIGURE 10.3

A mixed approach where our JS content lives in several different places.

To make things more interesting, we also have variations on the two approaches such as having multiple script sections in a HTML document, having multiple JS files, and so on. In the following sections, we'll look at both of these approaches in greater detail and discuss when you would choose to use one approach over the other.

By the end of all this, you will have a good understanding of the pros and cons of each approach so that you can do the right thing with the JavaScript in your web pages and applications.

Onward!

Approach #1: All the Code Lives in Your HTML Document

The first approach we will look at is one that we've been using all along so far. This is the approach where all of our JavaScript lives inside a `script` tag alongside the rest of your HTML document:

```
<!DOCTYPE html>

<html>

<body>
```

```
<h1>Example</h1>

<script>
  function showDistance(speed, time) {
    alert(speed * time);
  }

  showDistance(10, 5);
  showDistance(85, 1.5);
  showDistance(12, 9);
  showDistance(42, 21);
</script>
</body>

</html>
```

When our browser loads the page, it goes through and parses every line of HTML from top to bottom. When it hits the `script` tag, it will go ahead and execute all the lines of JavaScript as well. Once it has finished executing our code, it will continue to parse the rest of our document. This means the location the script tag lives in our page is important. We will discuss that later when looking at the Running Your Code at the Right Time chapter.

Approach #2: The Code Lives in a Separate File

The second approach is one where our main HTML document doesn't contain any JavaScript content. Instead, all of our JavaScript lives in a separate document. There are two parts to this approach. The first part deals with the JavaScript file. The second part deals with referencing this JavaScript file in the HTML. Let's look at both of these parts in greater detail.

The JavaScript File

Key to making this approach work is the separate file that contains our JavaScript code. It doesn't matter what you name this file, but its extension is typically **.js**. For example, my JavaScript file is called **example.js**.

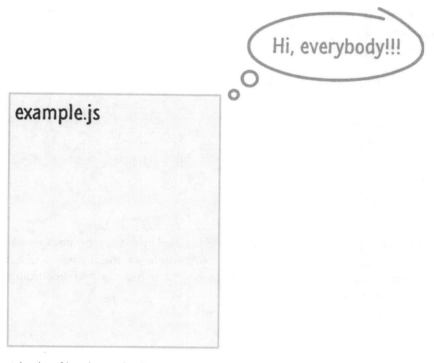

Inside this file, the only thing you will have is JavaScript:

```javascript
function showDistance(speed, time) {
    alert(speed * time);
}

showDistance(10, 5);
showDistance(85, 1.5);
showDistance(12, 9);
showDistance(42, 21);
```

Everything we would normally put inside a `script` tag in the HTML will go here. Nothing else will go into this file. Putting anything else like arbitrary pieces of HTML and CSS isn't allowed, and our browser will complain.

Referencing the JavaScript File

Once we have our JavaScript file created, the second (and final) step is to reference it in the HTML page. This is handled by our `script` tag. More specifically, it is handled by our `script` tag's `src` attribute that points to the location of our JavaScript file:

```
<!DOCTYPE html>

<html>

<body>
    <h1>Example</h1>

    <script src="example.js"></script>
</body>

</html>
```

In this example, if our JavaScript file is located in the same directory as our HTML, we can use a relative path and just reference the file name directly. If our JavaScript file lives in another folder, we would alter our path accordingly:

```
<!DOCTYPE html>

<html>

<body>
    <h1>Example</h1>

    <script src="some/other/folder/example.js"></script>
</body>

</html>
```

In this case, our script file is nested inside three folders with the name **some**, **other**, and **folder**. We can completely avoid relative paths and use an absolute path as well:

```
<!DOCTYPE html>

<html>

<body>
    <h1>Example</h1>

    <script src="https://www.kirupa.com/js/example.js"></script>
</body>

</html>
```

Either a relative path or absolute path will work just fine. For situations where the path between our HTML page and the script we are referencing will vary (such as inside a template, a server-side include, a 3rd party library, etc.), we'll be safer using an absolute path.

SCRIPTS, PARSING, AND LOCATION IN DOCUMENT

A few sections earlier, I briefly described how scripts get executed. Your browser parses your HTML page starting at the top and then moves down line by line. When a `script` tag gets hit, your browser starts executing the code that is contained inside the script tag. This execution is also done line-by-line starting at the top. Everything else that your page might be doing takes a backseat while the execution is going on. If the `script` tag references an external JavaScript file, your browser first downloads the external file before starting to execute its contents.

This behavior where your browser linearly parses your document has some interesting side effects that affect where in your document you want to place your `script` tags. Technically, your `script` tag can live anywhere in your HTML document. There is a preferred place you should specify your scripts, though. Because of how your browser parses the page and blocks everything while your scripts are executing, **you want to place your script tags toward the bottom of your HTML document after all of your HTML elements**.

If your `script` tag is towards the top of your document, your browser will block everything else while the script is running. This could result in users seeing a partially loaded and unresponsive HTML page if you are downloading a large script file or executing a script that is taking a long time to complete. Unless you really have a good need to force your JavaScript to run before your full document is parsed, ensure your `script` tags appear towards the end of your document as shown in almost all of the earlier examples. There is one other advantage to placing your scripts at the bottom of your page, but I will explain that much later when talking about the DOM and what happens during a page load.

So...Which Approach to Use?

We have two main approaches around where our code should live (Figure 10.4).

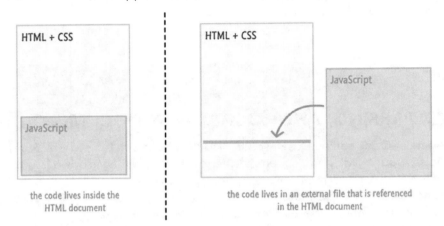

the code lives inside the HTML document

the code lives in an external file that is referenced in the HTML document

FIGURE 10.4

The two main approaches we have for dealing with our JS content.

The approach you end up choosing depends on your answer to the following question: **Is the identical code going to be used across multiple HTML documents?**

Yes, My Code Will Be Used on Multiple Documents!

If the answer is **yes**, then you probably want to put the code in an external file and then reference it across all of the HTML pages you want it executing in. The first reason you want to do this is to avoid having code repeated across multiple pages (Figure 10.5).

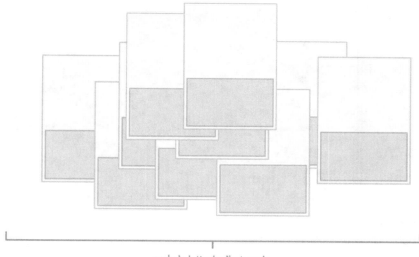

a whole lotta duplicate code

FIGURE 10.5

Having duplicated code is a problem!

Duplicate code makes maintenance a nightmare where a change to your script will require you updating every single HTML document with the exact change. If you are employing some sort of templating or SSI logic where there is only one HTML fragment containing your script, then the maintenance issue is less of a problem.

The second reason has to do with file size. When you have your script duplicated across many HTML pages, each time a user loads one of those HTML pages, they are downloading your script all over again. This is less of a problem for smaller scripts, but once you have more than a few hundred lines of code, the size starts adding up.

When you factor all our code into a single file, you don't have the issues I just outlined (Figure 10.6).

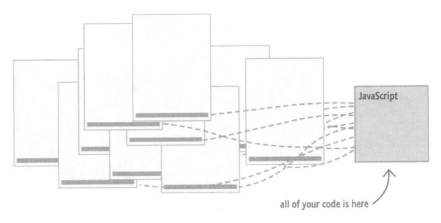

all of your code is here

FIGURE 10.6

A your code in one place.

Your code is easily maintainable because you update your code inside the one file only. Any HTML document that references this JavaScript file automatically gets the most recent version when it loads. By having all of your code in one file, your browser will download the code only once and **deliver the cached version of the file on subsequent accesses**.

No, My Code Is Used Only Once on a Single HTML Document!

If you answered **no** to the earlier question around whether your code is going to be used on multiple HTML documents, then you can do whatever you want. You can still choose to put your code into a separate file and reference it in your HTML document, but the benefits of doing that are less than what you saw earlier with the example involving many documents.

Placing your code entirely inside your HTML document is also fine for this situation. Most of the examples you will see in this site have all of the code within the HTML document itself. Our examples aren't really going to be used across multiple pages, and they aren't going to be so large where readability is improved by putting all of the code in a separate location.

THE ABSOLUTE MINIMUM

As you can see, even something as seemingly simple as determining where your code should live ends up taking many pages of explanation and discussion. Welcome to the world of HTML and JavaScript where nothing is really black and white. Anyway, getting back to the point of this article, a typical HTML document will contain many script files loaded from an external location. Some of those files will be your own; some, however, will be created by a third party and included into your document.

Also, do you remember the hybrid approach I showed at the very beginning where your HTML document contains both a reference to a separate JavaScript file as well as actual code within the document? Well, that approach is pretty common as well. Ultimately, the approach you end up using is entirely up to you. Hopefully, this chapter gave you a taste of the information needed to make the right choice. In Chapter 36, "Page Load Events and Other Stuff," we take a deeper look at what you saw here by looking at page loading-related events and certain special attributes that complicate things. Don't worry about them for now.

If you have any questions, feel free to post them on the forums at **https://forum.kirupa.com**. I and others will be thrilled to help you out!

IN THIS CHAPTER

- Learn how to go beyond alerts for displaying results
- Understand how the console works
- Learn the variety of logging solutions you have at your fingertips

CONSOLE LOGGING BASICS

When you are writing code, you will often find yourself in one of two situations. One situation is where you wonder if the code you just wrote is going to run at all. In the other situation, you know your code runs, but it isn't running correctly. There is something wrong...**somewhere**.

In both of these situations, what you need is some extra visibility into what your code is doing. A timeless approach for bringing this visibility involves the `alert` method:

```
let myButton = document.querySelector("#myButton");
myButton.addEventListener("click", doSomething, false);

function doSomething(e) {
  alert("Is this working?");
}
```

Using the `alert` method isn't bad. It works fine for simple situations, but as your code starts to do more, relying on them doesn't work as well. For starters, you'll probably go insane from dismissing the large number of dialogs that keep popping up while your code is running! You'll also want an easy way to persist the messages you are seeing. The fleeting nature of our `alert` dialogs makes any sort of long-term logging like that difficult.

In this tutorial, we're going to look at one of the greatest inventions of all time that makes it easy to help us figure out what our code is doing. We are going to be learning about something known as the **console**.

Onward!

Meet the Console

Even if you think you write the most perfect JavaScript, you'll be spending a fair amount of time in what is known as the **console**. If you've never used the console before, it is part of your browser's developer tools where all sorts of text and stuff gets printed for you to see and (occasionally) interact with.

It will look a little bit like what is shown in Figure 11.1

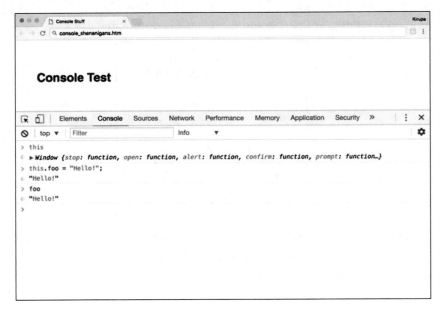

FIGURE 11.1

Meet the console.

At a very high level, your console helps with a bunch of things:

- You can read messages you have told your code to log and display

- You can modify your application state by setting (or overwriting) variables and values

- You can inspect the value of any DOM element, applied style, or code that is accessible and in scope

- You can use it as a virtual code editor and write/execute some code just for kicks

In this article, we won't focus on all the things your console is capable of doing. Instead, we're just going to take it easy and gradually get you comfortable with using the console to just display messages. We will cover all of the crazy console-related things eventually, so don't worry.

Displaying the Console

The first thing we are going to do is get your console up. The console is a part of your browser's developer tools. The way you bring up your browser developer tools is by fiddling with your browser's menus or by using the handy keyboard shortcuts. From inside your browser, press Ctrl + Shift + I on Windows or Cmd + Alt + I on Mac to bring up the developer tools.

Depending on your browser and platform, each of your developer tools will look a little different. The important thing is to find the Console tab and make sure the console gets displayed.

When you bring up the console in Chrome, you'll see something like what you see in Figure 11.2.

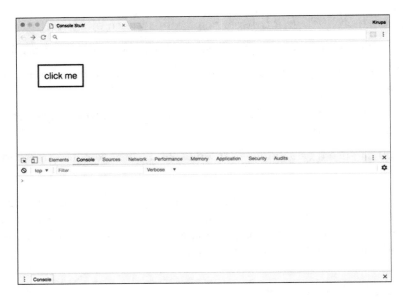

FIGURE 11.2

The Chrome console.

On Safari, the console will look a bit like Figure 11.3.

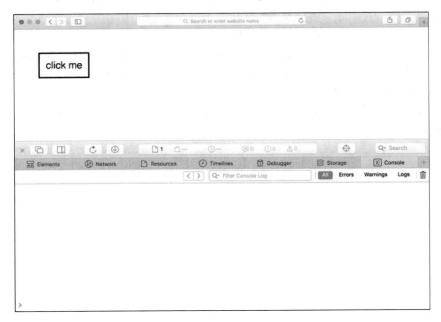

FIGURE 11.3

The Safari console.

Firefox's console looks like what is shown in Figure 11.4.

FIGURE 11.4

The Firefox console.

Bringing up the console in Microsoft Edge will look like Figure 11.5.

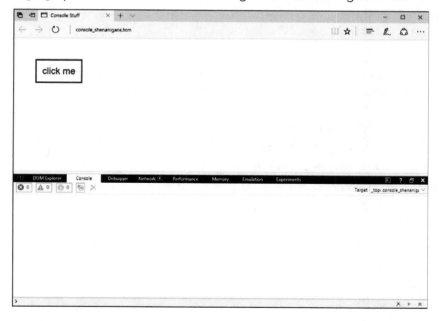

FIGURE 11.5

The Edge console.

The thing I want to highlight is that it doesn't matter which browser you use. The console looks and functions pretty much the same on all browsers. Just bring up the console in your favorite browser and get ready to start actually using the console in the following sections.

If You Want to Follow Along

Now, you can just read the following sections and learn a whole bunch of console-related things without lifting a finger. If that is what you would like to do, then skip all of this and jump to the next section.

On the other hand, if you want to get your hands a bit dirty and see some of the console shenanigans for yourself on your screen, create a new HTML document and add the following HTML, CSS, and JavaScript into it:

```html
<!DOCTYPE html>
<html>

<head>
  <title>Console Stuff</title>

  <style>
    #container {
      padding: 50px;
    }

    #myButton {
      font-family: sans-serif;
      font-size: 24px;
      font-weight: lighter;
      background-color: #FFF;
      border: 3px #333 solid;
      padding: 15px;
    }

    #myButton:hover {
      background-color: aliceblue;
    }
```

```
      </style>
  </head>

  <body>
    <div id="container">
      <button id="myButton">click me</button>
    </div>
    <script>

      let myButton = document.querySelector("#myButton");
      myButton.addEventListener("click", doSomething, false);

      function doSomething(e) {
        alert("Is this working?");
      }
    </script>
  </body>

</html>
```

What we have here is a really simple HTML page with a button that you can click. When you click on the button, an alert dialog (the same one we described earlier) will appear. In the following sections, we'll modify this example to help bring some of the console-related things to life!

Console Logging 101

The first thing we are going to do is tell our console to display things on screen. This is no different than what we did with the `alert` statement earlier, and it is almost just as easy. The key to all of this is the **Console API**. This API contains a bunch of properties and methods that allow you to display things to your console in a variety of ways. The first and probably most popular of these properties and methods is the `log` method.

Meet the Log Method

At its most basic level, the way you use the `log` method is as follows:

```
console.log("Look, ma! I'm logging stuff.")
```

You call it via the `console` object and pass in the text that you want to display. To see this in action, we can replace the `alert` from our example with the following:

```
function doSomething(e) {
  console.log("Is this working?");
}
```

When you run this code, take a look at your console after clicking on the **click me** button. If everything worked out properly, you will see the "Is this working?" text displayed inside it as shown in Figure 11.6.

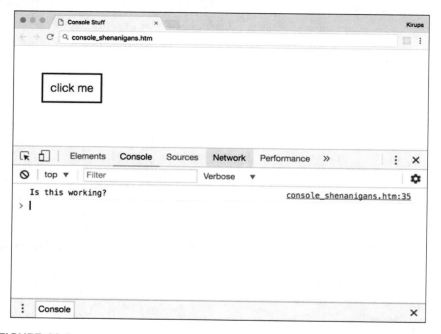

FIGURE 11.6

The **click me** *button displayed!*

If you keep clicking on the button, you'll see more instances of "Is this working?" getting logged as shown in Figure 11.7.

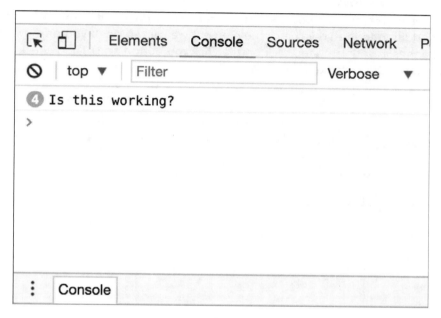

FIGURE 11.7

Each button click will end up getting represented in our Console.

How that looks will depend on the developer tools you are using. You will probably just see a counter to the left of your initial message getting incremented as shown in the screenshot. You may see the text "Is this working?" getting duplicated in each line as well. Don't be alarmed if what you see doesn't exactly match what you see in my screenshots. The important detail is that your call to console.log works and is logging messages for you to see in the console. Also, these messages aren't read only. You can select them. You can copy them. You can even print them and frame them on the wall behind you.

Going Beyond Predefined Text

Now that you've just seen the basics, let's go a bit deeper. When using the console, you aren't limited to only printing some predefined text. For example, a common thing you might do is print the value of something that exists only by evaluating an expression or accessing a value. To see what we mean by this, make the following change to your doSomething function:

```
function doSomething(e) {
    console.log("We clicked on: " + e.target.id);
}
```

What we are doing here is telling our console to display the text "We clicked on" in addition to the `id` value of the element we clicked on. If you preview these changes in your browser, click on the **click me** button again, and check out what is shown in the console, as in Figure 11.8.

FIGURE 11.8

The id of the button we clicked on is displayed!

The `id` value of the button you clicked on is displayed in addition to our pre-defined text. Now, getting the `id` value of an element is probably not the most exciting thing you might want to print, but you can print pretty much anything that would look good when represented as text. That's powerful!

Displaying Warnings and Errors

It is time to look beyond the `log` method! Our `console` object provides us with the `warn` and `error` methods that allow us to display messages formatted as warnings and errors, respectively, as shown in Figure 11.9.

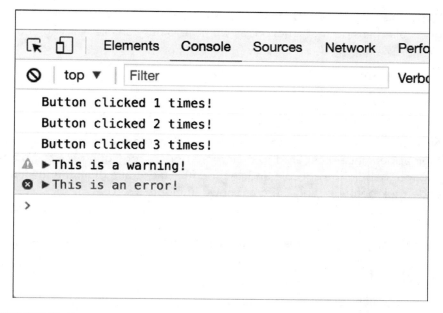

FIGURE 11.9

We can show errors and warnings...like a boss!

The way you use these two methods is no different from how you used the `log` method. Just pass in whatever you want to display. You can see an example of how to use these methods in the following snippet:

```
let counter = 0;

function doSomething(e) {
  counter++;

  console.log("Button clicked " + counter + " times!");

  if (counter == 3) {
    showMore();
  }
}

function showMore() {
  console.warn("This is a warning!");
  console.error("This is an error!");
}
```

When this code runs and our button is clicked three times, the showMore function gets called. Inside that function, all we have is our console warning and error:

```
function showMore() {
    console.warn("This is a warning!");
    console.error("This is an error!");
}
```

Now, there is something cool about warnings and errors that goes beyond just their appearance compared to their more boring log counterparts. You can expand them in the console and see the full stack trace of all the functions your code took before hitting them as shown in Figure 11.10.

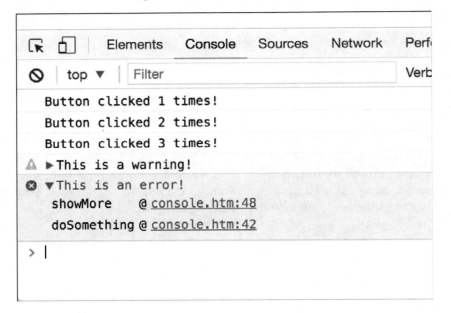

FIGURE 11.10

Seeing more details for our errors!

For large pieces of code with a lot of branching, this is really useful. The warn and error methods provide an excellent way for us to better understand the twisted paths our code took into getting into whatever state it ended up in!

THE ABSOLUTE MINIMUM

The console provides you with one of the best tools you have for understanding what your code is doing. Displaying messages is only one part of what the console allows you to do. Within our narrow focus on just displaying messages, there is a whole lot more that we can cover than what we've seen so far. We'll cover more things the console does later, but the few `console` techniques you've seen here will take you far in helping you find and squash bugs in your code.

If you have any questions, feel free to post them on the forums at **https://forum.kirupa.com**. I and others will be extremely totally happy to help you out!

THIS CHAPTER

- Understand what all this fuss about **Objects** is about
- Learn about the basic types you'll run into in JavaScript
- Find out that pizza has an educational value beyond just being deliciously awesome

OF PIZZA, TYPES, PRIMITIVES, AND OBJECTS

It's time to get serious. Srsly! In the past few chapters, we've been working with all kinds of values. We've worked with strings (text), numbers, booleans (aka **true** and **false**), functions, and various other built-in things that are part of the JavaScript language.

Following are some examples to jog our memory:

```
let someText = "hello, world!";
let count = 50;
let isActive = true;
```

Unlike other languages, JavaScript makes it really easy to specify and use these built-in things. We don't even have to think about or plan ahead to use any of them. Despite how simple using these different kinds of built-in things is, there is a lot of detail that is hidden from us. Knowing these details is important because it will not only help us make sense of our code more easily, it may even help us to more quickly pinpoint what is going wrong when things aren't working the way they should.

Now, as you can probably guess, *built-in-things* isn't the proper way to describe the variety of values that you can use in JavaScript. There is a more formal name for the variety of values you can use in your code, and that name is **types**. In this chapter, you are going to get a gentle introduction to what they are.

Onward!

Let's First Talk About Pizza

No, I haven't completely lost it. Since I am always eating something (or thinking about eating something), I am going to try to explain the mysterious world of types by first explaining the much simpler world of pizza.

In case you haven't had pizza in a while, this is what a typical pizza looks like:

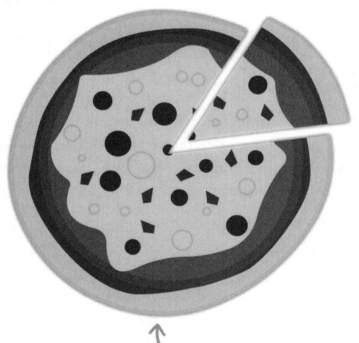

If your pizza doesn't look like this, take it back!™

A pizza doesn't just magically appear looking like this. It is made up of other ingredients – some simple and some not-so-simple:

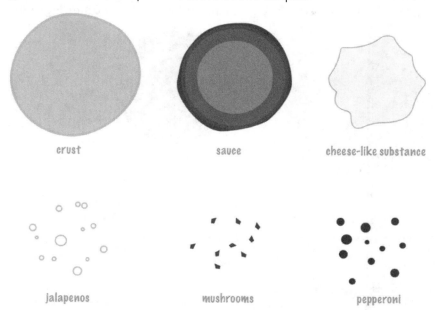

The simple ingredients are easy to spot. These would be your **mushrooms** and **jalapenos**. The reason these are simple is because you can't break these ingredients apart any further:

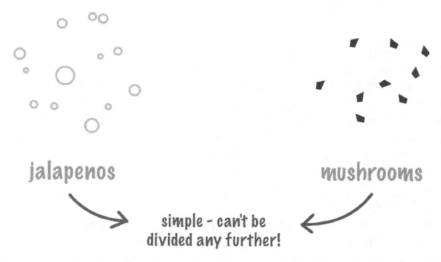

They aren't prepared. They aren't made up of other simple ingredients. Just like the dude, they abide.

The not-so-simple, complex ingredients would be your **cheese, sauce, crust,** and the **pepperoni**. These are more complex for all the reasons the simples one are... um...simple. These complex ingredients are made up of **other ingredients**:

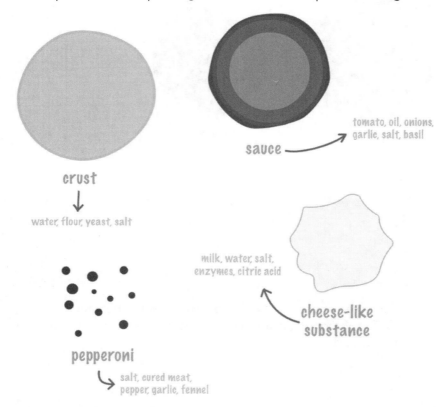

crust

water, flour, yeast, salt

sauce

tomato, oil, onions, garlic, salt, basil

milk, water, salt, enzymes, citric acid

cheese-like substance

pepperoni

salt, cured meat, pepper, garlic, fennel

Unfortunately for all of us, there is no one simple ingredient called cheese or pepperoni out there. We need to combine and prepare and add some more ingredients to make up some of the complex ingredients we see here. There is a subtle wrinkle to call out about complex ingredients. Their composition isn't limited to just simple ingredients. Complex ingredients can themselves be made up of other complex ingredients. How scandalous?!!

From Pizza to JavaScript!

While this may be hard to believe, everything we learned about pizzas in the previous section was there for a purpose. The description of the simple and complex ingredients very neatly applies to types in JavaScript. Each individual ingredient could be considered a counterpart to a type that you can use (Figure 12.1).

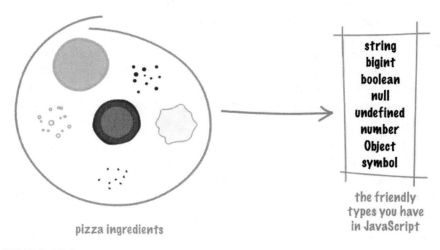

pizza ingredients

string
bigint
boolean
null
undefined
number
Object
symbol

the friendly
types you have
in JavaScript

FIGURE 12.1

A list of the simple types we have in JavaScript.

Just like the cheese, sauce, pepperoni, mushrooms, and bacon in our version of a pizza, the types in JavaScript are `string`, `number`, `boolean`, `null`, `undefined`, `bigint`, `symbol`, and `Object`. Some of these types may be very familiar to you already, and some of them may not be. While we will look at all of these types in much greater detail in future chapters, the Table 12.1 provides a very brief summary of what they do.

TABLE 12.1 Types

Type	What it does
string	The basic structure for working with text
number	As you can guess, it allows you to work with numbers
boolean	Comes alive when you are using **true** and **false**
null	Represents the digital equivalent of nothing...or **moo** :P
undefined	While sort of similar to `null`, this is returned when a value should exist but doesn't...like when you declare a variable but don't assign anything to it
bigint	Allows you to work with really large or really small numbers that go beyond what a typical "number" might support
symbol	Something unique and immutable (can't be changed) that you can optionally use as an identifier for Object properties
Object	Acts a shell for other types including other objects

Now, while each of the types is pretty unique in what it does. There is a simple grouping they fall under. Just like with our pizza's simple and complex ingredients, our types can be simple or complex as well. Except, in JavaScript terminology involving types, simple and complex are more formally known as **primitive** and **object** respectively. Another way of saying this is that our types in JavaScript are either known as **primitive types** (or just **primitives**) and **object types** (or just **objects**).

Our primitive types are `string`, `number`, `boolean`, `null`, `bigint`, `symbol`, and `undefined` types. Any values that fall under their umbrella can't be divided any further. They are the jalapenos and mushrooms of the JavaScript world. Primitives are pretty easy to define and bucket into something understandable. There is no depth to them, and we pretty much get what we see when we encounter one.

Our object types, represented by `Object` in our table, are a bit more mysterious, so the last thing we want to cover before unleashing you with details about all of these types is what objects in JavaScript actually are.

What Are Objects?

The concept of objects in a programming language like JavaScript maps nicely to its real-world equivalents. In the real world, you are literally surrounded by objects. Your computer is an object. A book on a shelf is an object. A potato is (arguably) an object. Your alarm clock is an object. A poster you got on eBay is also an object. I could go on forever, but (for everyone's sake) I'm going to stop here.

Some objects like a paperweight don't do much:

paperweight!
(it is not a rock!)

They just sit there. Other objects, like a television, go above and beyond the call of mere existence and do a lot of things:

A typical television takes input, allows you to turn it on or off, change the channel, adjust the volume, and do all sorts of television-y things.

The thing to realize is that objects come in different shapes, sizes, and usefulness. Despite the variations, objects are all the same at a high-level. They are an **abstraction**. They provide an easy way for you to use them without having to worry about what goes on under the covers. Even the simplest objects hide a certain level of complexity that you simply don't have to worry about.

For example, it doesn't matter what goes on inside your TV, how the wires are connected, or what type of glue is used to hold everything together. Those are unnecessary details. All that you care about is that the TV does what it is told. When you want it to change the channel, the channel should change. When you adjust the volume, the volume should adjust. Everything else is just noise.

Basically, think of an object as a black box. There are some predefined/documented things it does. How it does them is something you can't easily see. How it does its magic is also something you don't really care about as long as it works. We'll change that notion later when we learn to actually create the insides of an object, but let's relish this simple and happy world for now.

The Predefined Objects Roaming Around in JavaScript

Besides the built-in types you saw earlier, you also have a handful of predefined objects in JavaScript that you can use out-of-the-box. These objects allow you to work with everything from collections of data to dates to even text and numbers. Table 12.2 lists these objects along with, just like before, a short blurb on what they do:

TABLE 12.2 Objects

Type	What it does
Array	Helps store, retrieve, and manipulate a collection of data
Boolean	Acts as a wrapper around the `boolean` primitive; still very much in love with **true** and **false**
Date	Allows you to more easily represent and work with dates
Function	Allows you to invoke some code among other esoteric things
Math	The nerdy one in the group that helps you better work with numbers
Number	Acts as a wrapper around the `number` primitive
RegExp	Provides a lot of functionality for matching patterns in text
String	Acts as a wrapper around the `string` primitive

The way you use these built-in objects is a little bit different than how you use primitives. Each object has its own quirk on how you can use them as well. Explaining each object and how it is meant to be used is something that I will defer to for later, but here is a very short snippet of commented code to show you what is possible:

```javascript
// an array
let names = ["Jerry", "Elaine", "George", "Kramer"];
let alsoNames = new Array("Dennis", "Frank", "Dee", "Mac");


// a round number
let roundNumber = Math.round("3.14");


// today's date
let today = new Date();
```

```
// a boolean object
let booleanObject = new Boolean(true);

// infinity
let unquantifiablyBigNumber = Number.POSITIVE_INFINITY;

// a string object
let hello = new String("Hello!");
```

One thing that you may find puzzling is the existence of the Object-form of the string, boolean, symbol, bigint, and number primitives. On the surface, the Object-form and primitive-form of these types look very similar. Here is an example:

```
let movie = "Pulp Fiction";
let movieObj = new String("Pulp Fiction");

console.log(movie);
console.log(movieObj);
```

What you will see printed will be identical. Below the surface, though, both movie and movieObj are very different. One is literally a primitive of type string, and the other is of type Object. This leads to some interesting (and possibly incomprehensible) behavior that I will gradually touch upon as we explore the handful of built-in types that we've seen so far.

THE ABSOLUTE MINIMUM

If this feels like a movie that abruptly ended just as things were getting interesting, I don't blame you for thinking that way. The main takeaway is that your primitives make up the most basic types that you can use in your code. Your objects are a bit more complex and are made up of other primitives or objects. We'll see more of that in a little bit when we dive deeper. Beyond that, we learned the names for the common built-in types and some basic background material about all of them.

What you are going to see in subsequent chapters is a deeper look at all of these types and the nuances of working with them. Think of this chapter as the gentle on-ramp that suddenly drops you onto the rails of a crazy rollercoaster.

13

ARRAYS

Let's imagine you are jotting down a list on a piece of paper. Let's call the piece of paper **groceries**. Now, in the paper, you write a numbered list starting with zero with all the items that belong there, as shown in Figure 13.1.

| 0. Milk |
| 1. Eggs |
| 2. Frosted Flakes |
| 3. Salami |
| 4. Juice |

That's some neat handwriting!

FIGURE 13.1

A list of items that resembles a grocery list.

By simply creating a list of things, what you have right now is a real-world example of an array! The piece of paper called *groceries* would be your array. The items that you need to purchase are known as the array values.

In this tutorial, you will learn all about what I like to go grocery shopping for. You may indirectly get an introduction to the very common built-in type, the array.

Onward!

Creating an Array

The popular way all the cool kids create arrays these days is to use an open and close bracket. Below is our `groceries` variable that is initialized to an empty array:

```
let groceries = [];
```

You have your variable name on the left, and you have a pair of brackets on the right that initializes this variable as an empty array. This bracket-y approach for creating an array is better known as the **array literal notation**.

Now, you will commonly want to create an array with some items inside it from the very beginning. To create these non-empty arrays, place the items you want inside the brackets and separate them by commas:

```
let groceries = ["Milk", "Eggs", "Frosted Flakes", "Salami",
"Juice"];
```

Notice that my groceries array now contains **Milk**, **Eggs**, **Frosted Flakes**, **Salami**, and **Juice**. I just have to reiterate how important the commas are. Without the commas, you'll just have one giant item instead. All right, now that you've learned how to declare an array, let's look at how you can actually use it to store and work with data.

Accessing Array Values

One of the nice things about arrays is that you not only have easy access to the array, but you also have easy access to the array values...similar to highlighting an item in your grocery list (Figure 13.2).

FIGURE 13.2

Arrays enable you to access individual items selectively.

The only thing you need to know is what the procedure is for accessing an individual item.

Inside an array, each item is assigned a number starting with zero. In Figure 3.2, **Milk** is given the value 0, **Eggs** the value 1, **Frosted Flakes** the value 2, and so on. The formal term for these numbers is called the index value.

Let's say that our groceries array is declared as follows:

```
let groceries = ["Milk", "Eggs", "Frosted Flakes", "Salami",
"Juice"];
```

If I wanted to access an item from the array, all I need to do is pass in the index value of the item I am interested in:

```
groceries[1]
```

The index value is passed in to your array using square brackets. In this example, you are referring to the **Eggs** value because the index position 1 refers to it. If you passed in a 2, you would return **Frosted Flakes**. You can keep passing in an index value until you have no more values left.

The range of numbers you can use as your index values is one less than your array's length. The reason is that, as shown in the diagram earlier, your index values start with a value of 0. If your array only has 5 items, trying to display `grocery[6]` or `grocery[5]` will result in a message of **undefined**.

Let's go one step further. In most real-world scenarios, you will want to programmatically go through your array as opposed to accessing each item individually.

You can take what I explained in the previous paragraph and use a `for` loop to accomplish this:

```
for (let i = 0; i < groceries.length; i++) {
   let item = groceries[i];
}
```

Notice the range of your loop starts at 0 and ends just one before your array's full length (as returned by the `length` property). This works because, like I mentioned earlier, your array index values go from 0 to one short of the value returned for the array's length. And yes, the `length` property returns a count of all the items in your array!

Adding Items to Your Array

Rarely will you leave your array in the state you initialized it in originally. You will want to add items to it. To add items to your array, you will use the `push` method:

```
groceries.push("Cookies");
```

The `push` method is called directly on your array, and you pass in the data you want to add to it. By using the `push` method, your newly added data will always find itself at the end of the array.

For example, after running the code on our initial array, you will see Cookies added to the end of your groceries array (Figure 13.3).

FIGURE 13.3

Our array is now larger with the addition of Cookies at the end.

If you want to add data to the beginning of your array, you use the `unshift` method:

```
groceries.unshift("Bananas");
```

When data is added to the beginning of your array, the index value for all of the existing items increases to account for the newly inserted data (Figure 13.4).

0. Bananas

1. Milk

2. Eggs

3. Frosted Flakes

4. Salami

5. Juice

6. Cookies

FIGURE 13.4

Our newly added item is inserted at the beginning.

The reason is that the first item in your array will always have an index value of 0. This means that the space originally occupied by the 0th item needs to push itself and everything below it out to make room for the new data.

Both the push and unshift methods, besides adding the elements to the array when you use them, return the new length of the array as well:

```
console.log(groceries.push("Cookies")); // returns 6
```

Not sure why that is useful, but keep it under your hat in case you do need it.

Removing Items from the Array

To remove an item from the array, you can use the `pop` or `shift` methods. The pop method removes the last item from the array and returns it:

```
let lastItem = groceries.pop();
```

The `shift` method does the same thing on the opposite end of the array. Instead of the last item being removed and returned, the `shift` method removes and returns the first item from the array:

```
let firstItem = groceries.shift();
```

When an item is removed from the beginning of the array, the index positions of all remaining elements are decremented by 1 to fill in the gap (Figure 13.5).

FIGURE 13.5

What happens when an item is removed from our array.

Note that when you are adding items to your array using `unshift` or `push`, the returned value from that method call is the new length of your array. That is not what happens when you call the `pop` and `shift` methods, though! When you are removing items using `shift` and `pop`, the value returned by the method call is the removed item itself!

Finding Items in the Array

To find items inside your array, you have a handful of built-in methods: `indexOf`, `lastIndexOf`, `includes`, `find`, `findIndex`, and `filter`. For the sake of simplicity, we will focus on `indexOf` and `lastIndexOf` for now. These two methods work by scanning your array and returning the index position of the matching element.

The `indexOf` method returns the first occurrence of the item you are searching for:

```
let groceries =["Milk", "Eggs", "Frosted Flakes", "Salami",
"Juice"];
let resultIndex = groceries.indexOf("Eggs",0);


console.log(resultIndex); // 1
```

Notice that the `resultIndex` variable stores the result of calling `indexOf` on our groceries array. To use `indexOf`, I pass in the element I am looking for along with the index position to start from:

```
groceries.indexOf("Eggs", 0);
```

The value returned by `indexOf` in this case will be 1.

The `lastIndexOf` method is similar to `indexOf` in how you use it, but it differs a bit on what it returns when an element is found. Where `indexOf` finds the first occurrence of the element you are searching for, `lastIndexOf` finds the last occurrence of the element you are searching for and returns that element's index position.

When you search for an element that does not exist in your array, both `indexOf` and `lastIndexOf` return a value of -1.

Merging Arrays

The last thing we are going to do is look at how to create a new array that is made up of two separate arrays. Let's say you have two arrays called good and bad:

```
let good = ["Mario", "Luigi", "Kirby", "Yoshi"];
let bad = ["Bowser", "Koopa Troopa", "Goomba"];
```

To combine both of these arrays into one array, use the `concat` method on the array you want to make bigger and pass the array you want to merge into it as the argument. What will get returned is a new array whose contents are both good and bad:

```
let goodAndBad = good.concat(bad);
console.log(goodAndBad);
```

In this example, because the `concat` method returns a new array, the `goodAndBad` variable ends up becoming an array that stores the results of our concatenation operation. The order of the elements inside `goodAndBad` is good first and bad second.

Mapping, Filtering, and Reducing Arrays

So far, we looked at several ways to add items, remove items, and other basic bookkeeping tasks. One of the other things arrays bring to the table is really simple ways for you to manipulate the data that is contained inside them. These simple ways are brought to you via the **map**, **reduce**, and **filter** methods.

The Old School Way

Before we talk about `map`, `reduce`, and `filter` and how they make accessing and manipulating data inside an array a breeze, let us look at the non-breezy approach first. This is an approach that typically involves a `for` loop, keeping track of where in the array you are, and shedding a certain amount of tears.

To see this in action, let's say we have an array of names:

```
let names = ["marge", "homer", "bart", "lisa", "maggie"];
```

This aptly named `names` array contains a list of names that are currently lowercased. What we want to do is capitalize the first letter in each word to make these names look proper. Using the `for` loop approach, this can be accomplished as follows:

```
let names = ["marge", "homer", "bart", "lisa", "maggie"];

let newNames = [];

for (let i = 0; i < names.length; i++) {
  let name = names[i];
  let firstLetter = name.charAt(0).toUpperCase();
```

```
    newNames.push(firstLetter + name.slice(1));

}


console.log(newNames);
```

Notice that we go through each item, capitalize the first letter, and add the properly capitalized name to a new array called newNames. There is nothing magical or complicated going on here, but you'll often find yourself taking the items in your array, manipulating (or accessing) the items for some purpose, and returning a new array with the manipulated data. It's a common enough task with a lot of boilerplate code that you will keep replicating unnecessarily. In large codebases, making sense of what is going on in a loop adds unnecessary overhead. That's why map, filter, and reduce were introduced. You get all the flexibility of using a for loop without the unwanted side effects and extra code. Who wouldn't want this?!

Modifying Each Array Item with Map

The first of the array methods we will look at for manipulating our array data is map. We will use the map method to take all the items in our array and modify them into something else that is an entirely new array (Figure 13.6).

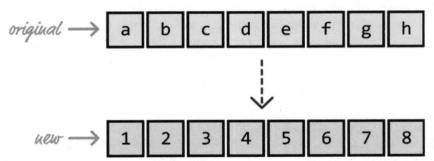

FIGURE 13.6

Our original array and new array!

The way you use it looks as follows:

```
let newArray = originalArray.map(someFunction);
```

This single line looks nice and friendly, but it hides a lot of complexity. Let's de-mystify it a bit. The way map works is as follows: You call it on the array that you wish to affect (originalArray), and it takes a function (someFunction) as the argument. This function will run on each item in the array—allowing you to write code to modify each item as you wish. The end result is a new array whose contents are the result of `someFunction` having run and potentially modified each item in the original array. Sounds simple enough, right?

Using `map`, let's revisit our earlier problem of taking the lowercased names from the array and capitalizing them properly. We'll look at the full code first and then focus on the interesting details next. The full code is as follows:

```
let names = ["marge", "homer", "bart", "lisa", "maggie"];


function capitalizeItUp(item) {
  let firstLetter = item.charAt(0).toUpperCase();
  return firstLetter + item.slice(1);
}


let newNames = names.map(capitalizeItUp);
console.log(newNames);
```

Take a moment to see how this code works. The interesting part is the `capitalizeItUp` function that is passed in as the argument to the `map` method. This function runs on each item, and notice that the array item you are currently on is passed in to this function as an argument. You can reference the current item argument via whatever name you prefer. We are referencing this argument using the boring name of `item`:

```
function capitalizeItUp(item) {
  let firstLetter = item.charAt(0).toUpperCase();
  return firstLetter + item.slice(1);
}
```

Inside this function, we can write whatever code we want to manipulate the current array item. The only thing we need to do is return the new array item value:

```
function capitalizeItUp(item) {
  let firstLetter = item.charAt(0).toUpperCase();
  return firstLetter + item.slice(1);
}
```

That's all there is to it. After all of this code runs, `map` returns a new array with all of the capitalized items in their correct locations. The original array is never modified, so keep that in mind.

TIP Meet Callback Functions

Our `capitalizeItUp` function is also known more generically by another name. That name is **callback function**. A callback function is a function that does two things:

- It is passed in as an argument to another function
- It is called from inside the other function

You will see callback functions referenced all the time...such as when we look at `filter` and `reduce` in a few moments. If this is the first time you are hearing about them, you now have a better idea of what they are. If you've heard of them before, well...good for you!

Filtering Items

With arrays, you'll often find yourself filtering (aka removing) items based on a given criterion (Figure 13.7).

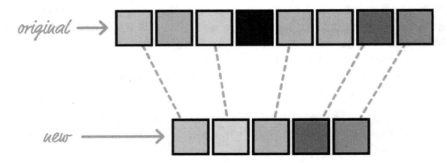

FIGURE 13.7

We start with many items but end up with fewer items.

For example, let's say we have an array of numbers:

```
let numbers = [1, 2, 3, 4, 5, 6, 7, 8, 9, 10, 11, 12];
```

Right now, our numbers array has both even numbers as well as odd numbers. Let's say we want to ignore all of the odd numbers and only look at the even ones. The way we can do that is by using our array's `filter` method and filtering out all of the odd numbers so only the even numbers remain.

The way we use the `filter` method is similar to what we did with `map`. It takes one argument, a callback function, and this function will determine whether each array item will be filtered out or not. This will make more sense when we look at some code. Take a look at the following:

```
let numbers = [1, 2, 3, 4, 5, 6, 7, 8, 9, 10, 11, 12];

let evenNumbers = numbers.filter(function (item) {
  return (item % 2 == 0);
});


console.log(evenNumbers);
```

We create a new array called `evenNumbers` that will store the result of `filter` running on our `numbers` array. The contents of this array will be the even numbers only thanks to our callback function checking each item to see whether the result of `item % 2` (aka checking if the remainder when you divide by 2) is 0. If the callback function returns a **true**, the item is carried over to the filtered array. If the callback function returns **false**, the item is ignored.

One thing to note here is that our callback function isn't an explicitly named function like our `capitalizeItUp` function we saw earlier. It is simply an anonymous one, but it still gets the job done. You'll see this anonymous form commonly where a callback function needs to be specified, so become familiar with this style of defining a function.

Getting One Value from an Array of Items

The last array method we will look at is `reduce`. This is a bizarre one. With both `map` and `filter`, we went from one array with a starting set of values to another array with a different set of values. With the `reduce` method, we will still start with an array. What we will end up with will be a single value (Figure 13.8).

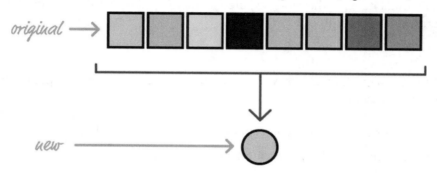

FIGURE 13.8

From many to...one!

This is definitely one of those cases where we need an example to explain what is going on.

Let's reuse our numbers array from earlier:

```
let numbers = [1, 2, 3, 4, 5, 6, 7, 8, 9, 10, 11, 12];
```

What we want to do is add up all the values here. This is the kind of thing the `reduce` method was built for where we reduce all the values in our array into a single item. Take a look at the following code:

```
let total = numbers.reduce(function(total, current) {
  return total + current;
}, 0);


console.log(total);
```

We call reduce on our numbers array, and we pass in two arguments to it:

- The callback function

- Initial value

We start our summing at an initial value of 0, and our callback function is responsible for adding up each item in the array. Unlike earlier where our callback function took only the current array item as its argument, the callback function for reduce is slightly more involved. You need to deal with **two** arguments here as well:

- The first argument contains the total value of all the actions you've done so far

- The second argument is the familiar current array item

By using these two arguments, you can easily construct all sorts of scenarios involving keeping track of something. In our example, since all we want is the sum of all items in the array, we are summing up the `total` with the value of `current`. The end result will be **31**.

More on the Callback Function Arguments

For our callback functions, we've only specified one argument representing the current array item for `map` and `filter`. We specified two arguments representing the total value as well as the current item for `reduce`. Our callback functions have two optional arguments you can specify:

- The current index position of your current array item

- The array you are calling `map`, `filter`, or `reduce` on

For map and `filter`, these would be the second and third arguments you specify. For `reduce`, it would be the third and fourth arguments. You may go your entire life without ever having to specify these optional arguments, but if you ever run into a situation where you need them, you now know where to find them.

We are almost done here. Let's look at an example that shows the output of `reduce` to be something besides a number. Take a look at the following:

```
let words = ["Where", "do", "you", "want", "to", "go", "today?"];


let phrase = words.reduce(function (total, current, index) {
  if (index == 0) {
    return current;
  } else {
    return total + " " + current;
  }
}, "");


console.log(phrase);
```

In this example, we are combining the text-based content of our `words` array to create a single value that ends up showing **Where do you want to go today?** Notice what is going on in our callback function. Besides doing the work to combine each item into a single word, we are specifying the optional third argument that represents our current item's index position. We use this index value to special case the first word to deal with whether we insert or not insert a space character at the beginning.

A Short Foray into Functional Programming

As the last few sections have highlighted, the map, `filter`, and `reduce` methods greatly simplify how we work with arrays. There is another HUGE thing that these three methods scratch the surface of. That thing is something known as **functional programming**. Functional programming is a way of writing your code where you use functions that:

- Can work inside other functions

- Avoid sharing or changing state

- Return the same output for the same input

There are more nitpicky details that we can list here, but this is a good start. Anyway, you can see how functional programming principles apply to the various callback functions we've used so far. Our callback functions match these three criteria perfectly, for they are functions that can be dropped into or out of any situation as long as the arguments still work. They definitely don't modify any state, and they work fully inside the map, `filter`, or `reduce` methods. Functional programming is a fun topic that needs a lot more coverage than what we've looked at in the last few sentences, so we'll leave things be for now and cover it in greater detail in the future.

THE ABSOLUTE MINIMUM

That is almost all there is to know about arrays...well, at least the things you will use them for most frequently. At the very least, you will have learned how to use them to create a grocery list!

Some additional resources and examples:

- **Shuffling an Array**: http://bit.ly/kirupaArrayShuffle
- **Picking a Random Item from an Array**: http://bit.ly/kirupaRandomItemArray
- **Removing Duplicates from an Array**: http://bit.ly/kirupaRemoveDuplicates
- **Hashtables versus Arrays**: http://bit.ly/kirupaHvA

IN THIS CHAPTER

- Understand how text is treated in JavaScript
- Learn how to perform common string operations
- Look at the various string properties

14

STRINGS

I have a hunch that you are a human being. As a human, you probably relate really well with words. You speak it. You write it. You also tend to use a lot of it in the things you program. As it turns out, JavaScript likes words a whole lot as well. The letters and funny looking symbols that make up your (and my) language has a formal name. They are known as **strings**. Strings in JavaScript are nothing more than a series of characters. Despite how boring that sounds, accessing and manipulating these characters is a skill that we must be familiar with. That's where this tutorial comes in.

Onward!

The Basics

The way we can work with strings is by just using them in our code. We just need to make sure to enclose them in single or double quotes. Below are some examples:

```
let text = "this is some text";
let moreText = 'I am in single quotes!';

console.log("this is some more text");
```

Besides just listing strings, we'll often combine a couple of strings together. We easily do that by just using the + operator:

```
let initial = "hello";
console.log(initial + " world!");

console.log("I can also " + "do this!");
```

In all of these examples, we are able to see the string. The only reason I point out something this obvious is that, when we can see the contents of your string as literally as we do, these strings are more appropriately known as **string literals**. That doesn't change the fact that the resulting structure is still a built-in primitive type called a **string** (you know...a simple pizza ingredient from the previous chapter).

If we had to visualize what the text and moreText strings look like, they would look like Figure 14.1.

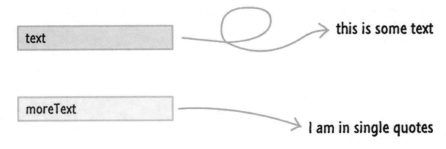

FIGURE 14.1

A visualization of strings.

We just have our two variables pointing to some literal chunks of text. There isn't anything else that is going on. If you are wondering why I wasted this space in visualizing something so obvious, the visualizations will get more complex once we move into Object territory. You'll see hints of that in this chapter itself.

Anyway, all of this isn't particularly important…yet. The only important thing to keep in mind is that you need to wrap your string literals in either quotation marks (") or apostrophes (') to designate them as a region of text. If you don't do that, bad things happen, and your code probably won't run.

That's all there is to the basics. The fun stuff comes from using all of the functionality JavaScript provides for working with strings. We'll look at that and more in the following sections.

String Properties and Methods

When we are working with strings, the underlying String object implementation contains a lot of properties that make working with text (usually) easier. In the following sections, instead of going over every property and boring both of us to death, I'll just focus on the important ones in the context of tasks you will be doing.

Accessing Individual Characters

While a string looks like one cohesive unit, it is actually made up of a series of characters. We can access each character in several ways. The most common way is by using array/bracket notation and passing in a number that corresponds to the index position of the character:

```
let vowels = "aeiou";
console.log(vowels[2]);
```

In this example, we will see the **i** character because it is the item at the second index position. To better visualize what just happened, the diagram in Figure 14.2 will help.

FIGURE 14.2

Our vowels mapped with index positions.

Here is something we should keep in mind when the word **index** is thrown around. Index positions in JavaScript start at 0 and move up from there. That is why our index position is 2, but the count of the element at that position is actually 3. This gets less weird the more you work with JavaScript and other languages that don't contain the words **Visual** and **Basic** where indexes start from 1.

To go one step further, we can access all characters in our string by just looping through the index positions. The start of the loop will be 0, and the end of your loop will be determined by the length of your string. The length of your string (aka a count of the number of characters) is returned by the `length` property.

Here is an example of the preceding paragraph in action:

```
let vowels = "aeiou";


for (let i = 0; i < vowels.length; i++) {
  console.log(vowels[i]);
}
```

While we may not be looping through a string all the time, it is very common to use the length property to get a count of the number of characters in your string.

If we don't get along with the array/bracket notation, we also have the `charAt` method that returns a character at a specified index position:

```
let vowels = "aeiou";
console.log(vowels.charAt(2));
```

The end result is identical to what we see using the array notation. I wouldn't use this method unless you care about really old browsers like Internet Explorer 7. Yep, I didn't think you did either.

WAIT...WHAT?

If you are wondering where in the world string primitives have the ability to access properties only available to `String` objects, suspend your curiosity for a few moments until the next chapter where we'll look at this in much greater detail.

Combining (aka Concatenating) Strings

To combine two strings together, we can just use the + or += operators and just add them like you would a series of numbers:

```
let stringA = "I am a simple string.";
let stringB = "I am a simple string, too!";


console.log(stringA + " " + stringB);
```

Notice that, in the third line, we add both `stringA` and `stringB` together. Between them, we specify an empty space character (" ") to ensure there is a space between each of the individual strings. You can mix and match string literals with string primitives and string objects and still get your text all combined together.

For example, this is all valid:

```
let textA = "Please";
let textB = new String("stop!");
let combined = textA + " make it " + textB;


console.log(combined);
```

Despite all of the mixing going on, the type of the `combined` variable is simply a **string** primitive.

For combining strings, we also have the `concat` method. We can call this method from any string and specify a sequence of string primitives, literals, and objects that we want to combine into one...megastring:

```
let foo = "I really";
let blah = "why anybody would";
let blarg = "do this";


let result = foo.concat(" don't know", " ", blah, " ", blarg);


console.log(result);
```

For the most part, just use the + and += approach for combining strings. It is faster than the `concat` approach. With everything else being equal, who wouldn't want some extra speed in their code?

Getting Substrings out of Strings

Sometimes, what we are interested in is a sequence of characters somewhere in the middle of your string. The two properties that help satisfy this interest are `slice` and `substr`. Let's say we have the following string:

```
let theBigString = "Pulp Fiction is an awesome movie!";
```

Let's mess with this string for a bit.

The `slice` Method!

The `slice` method allows us to specify the start and end positions of the part of the string that you want to extract:

```
let theBigString = "Pulp Fiction is an awesome movie!";
console.log(theBigString.slice(5, 12));
```

In this example, we extract the characters between index positions 5 and 12. The end result is that the word **Fiction** is what will get returned.

The start and end position values do not have to be positive. If you specify a negative value for the end position, the end position for your string is what is left when you count backwards from the end:

```
let theBigString = "Pulp Fiction is an awesome movie!";
console.log(theBigString.slice(0, -6));
```

If we specify a negative start position, your start position is the count of whatever you specify starting from the end of the string:

```
let theBigString = "Pulp Fiction is an awesome movie!";
console.log(theBigString.slice(-14, -7));
```

We just saw three variations of how the `slice` method can be used. I've never used anything but the first version with a positive start and end position, and you'll probably fall in a similar boat.

The `substr` Method!

The next approach we will look at for splitting up your string is the `substr` method. This method takes two arguments as well:

```
let newString = substr(start, length);
```

The first argument is a number that specifies your starting position, and the second argument is a number that specifies the length of your substring. This makes more sense when we look at some examples:

```
let theBigString = "Pulp Fiction is an awesome movie!";
console.log(theBigString.substr(0, 4)); // Pulp
```

We start the substring at the zeroth position and count four characters up. That is why **Pulp** is returned. If we want to just extract the word **Fiction**, this is what our code would look like:

```
let theBigString = "Pulp Fiction is an awesome movie!";
console.log(theBigString.substr(5, 7)); // Fiction
```

If we don't specify the length, the substring that gets returned is the string that goes from the start position to the end:

```
let theBigString = "Pulp Fiction is an awesome movie!";
console.log(theBigString.substr(5)); // Fiction is an awesome
movie!
```

There are a few more variations of values we can pass in for `substr`, but these are the big ones.

Splitting a String/`split`

That which you can concatenate, you can also split apart. I am pretty sure a wise person once said that. Another way we can split apart a string is by using the `split` method. Calling this method on a string returns an array of substrings. These substrings are separated by a character or Regular Expression (aka RegEx) that we use to determine where to split apart our string.

Let's look at a simple example where this makes more sense:

```
let inspirationalQuote = "That which you can concatenate, you can
also split apart.";
let splitWords = inspirationalQuote.split(" ");

console.log(splitWords.length); // 10
```

In this example, we are splitting the `inspirationalQuote` text on the space character. Every time a space character is encountered, what is left of the string before it is removed and made an item in the array that gets returned by this method.

Here is another example:

```
let days = "Monday,Tuesday,Wednesday,Thursday,Friday,
Saturday,Sunday";
let splitWords = days.split(",");


console.log(splitWords[6]); // Sunday
```

We have the `days` variable, which stores a string of days separated only by a comma. If we wanted to separate out each day, we could use the `split` method with the separator character being the comma. The end result is an array of seven items where each item is the day of the week from the original string.

You'll be surprised at how often you will find yourself using the `split` method to break apart a sequence of characters that can be as simple as a sentence or something more complex like data returned from a web service.

Finding Something Inside a String

If we ever need to find a character or characters inside a string, we can use the `indexOf`, `lastIndexOf`, and `match` methods. Let's look at the `indexOf` method first.

What the `indexOf` method does is take the character(s) we are looking for as its argument. If what we are looking for is found, it returns the index position in the string where the first occurrence...occurs. If no matches are found, this method gifts you with a `-1`. Let's look at an example:

```
let question = "I wonder what the pigs did to make these birds so
angry?";
console.log(question.indexOf("pigs")); // 18
```

We are trying to see if pigs exist in our string. Because what we are looking for does exist, the `indexOf` method lets us know that the first occurrence of this word occurs at the 18th index position. If we look for something that doesn't exist, like the letter **z** in this example, a -1 gets returned for:

```
let question = "I wonder what the pigs did to make these birds so
angry?";

console.log(question.indexOf("z")); // -1
```

The `lastIndexOf` method is very similar to `indexOf`. As you can sorta maybe guess by the name, `lastIndexOf` returns the last occurrence of what you are looking for:

```
let question = "How much wood could a woodchuck chuck if a
woodchuck could chuck wood?";

console.log(question.lastIndexOf("wood")); // 65
```

There is one more argument you can specify to both `indexOf` and `lastIndexOf`. In addition to providing the characters to search for, you can also specify an index position on your string to start your search from:

```
let question = "How much wood could a woodchuck chuck if a
woodchuck could chuck wood?";

console.log(question.indexOf("wood", 30)); // 43
```

The last thing to mention about the `indexOf` and `lastIndexOf` methods is that you can match any instance of these characters appearing in your string. These functions do not differentiate between whole words or what you are looking for being a substring of a larger set of characters. Be sure to take that into account.

Before we wrap this up, let's look at the `match` method. With the `match` method, you have a little more control. This method takes a Regex as its argument:

```
let phrase = "There are 3 little pigs.";
let regexp = /[0-9]/;

let numbers = phrase.match(regexp);

console.log(numbers[0]); // 3
```

What gets returned is also an array of matching substrings, so you can use your Array ninja skills to make working with the results a breeze. Learning how to work with regular expressions is something that we'll look at much later.

Upper and Lower Casing Strings

Finally, let's end this coverage on Strings with something easy that doesn't require anything complicated. To uppercase or lowercase a string, we can use the appropriately named `toUpperCase` and `toLowerCase` methods. Let's look at this example:

```
let phrase = "My name is Bond. James Bond.";


console.log(phrase.toUpperCase()); // MY NAME IS BOND. JAMES BOND.
console.log(phrase.toLowerCase()); // my name is bond. james bond.
```

See, told you this was easy!

THE ABSOLUTE MINIMUM

Strings are one of the handful of basic data types you have available in JavaScript, and you just saw a good overview of the many things you can do using them. One issue that I skirted around is where your string primitives seem to mysteriously have all of these properties that are common only to Objects. We'll look at that one in the next chapter!

Some additional resources and examples:

- **The Devowelizer:** http://bit.ly/kirupaDeVowelize
- **Capitalize the First Letter of a String:** http://bit.ly/kirupaCapLetter
- **10 Ways to Reverse a String:** http://bit.ly/kirupaWaysToReverseString

If you have any String-related questions...or just questions about life and JavaScript in general, head on over to **https://forum.kirupa.com** to get an answer.

15

WHEN PRIMITIVES BEHAVE LIKE OBJECTS

In the earlier **Strings** chapter and less so in the **Of Pizza, Types, Primitives, and Objects** chapter, we got a sneak peek at something that is probably pretty confusing. I've stated many times that primitives are very plain and simple. Unlike Objects, they don't contain properties that allow you to fiddle with their values in interesting (or boring) ways. Yet, as clearly demonstrated by all the stuff we can do with strings, our primitives seem to have a mysterious dark side to them:

```
let greeting = "Hi, everybody!!!";
let shout = greeting.toUpperCase(); // where did
toUpperCase come from?
```

As we can see from this brief snippet, our `greeting` variable, which stores a primitive value in the form of text, seems to have access to the `toUpperCase` method. How is this even possible? Where did that method come from? Why are we here? Answers to confusing existential questions like this will make up the bulk of what you will see in this page. Also, I apologize for writing that previous sentence in passive voice. Happen again it won't.

Onward!

Strings Aren't the Only Problem

Because of how fun and playful they are (kind of like a Golden Retriever!), it's easy to pick on strings as the main perpetrator of this primitive/Object confusion. As it turns out, many of the built-in primitive types are involved in this racket as well. Table 15.1 displays some popular built-in `Object` types with **most** of the guilty parties (`Symbol` and `BigInt` will be sitting this one out) that **also** exist as primitives highlighted:

TABLE 15.1 Object types with those that are primitive highlighted

Type	What it does
Array	helps store, retrieve, and manipulate a collection of data
Boolean	acts as a wrapper around the `boolean` primitive; still very much in love with **true** and **false**
Date	allows you to more easily represent and work with dates
Function	allows you to invoke some code among other esoteric things
Math	the nerdy one in the group that helps you better work with numbers
Number	acts as a wrapper around the `number` primitive
RegExp	provides a lot of functionality for matching patterns in text
String	acts as a wrapper around the `string` primitive

Whenever we are working with boolean, number, or string primitives, we have access to properties their Object equivalent exposes. In the following sections, you'll see what exactly is going on.

Let's Pick on Strings Anyway

Just as you were taught by your parents growing up, we typically use a string in the literal form:

```
let primitiveText = "Homer Simpson";
```

As we saw in the table earlier, strings also have the ability to be used as objects. There are several ways to create a new object, but the most common way to create an object for a built-in type like our string is to use the new keyword followed by the word String:

```
let name = new String("Batman");
```

The String in this case isn't just any normal word. It represents what is known as a **constructor function** whose sole purpose is to be used for creating objects. Just like there are several ways to create objects, there are several ways to create String objects as well. The way I see it, knowing about one way that you really *shouldn't* be creating them with is enough.

Anyway, the main difference between the primitive and object forms of a string is the sheer amount of additional baggage the object form carries with it. If we had to visualize our String object called name, Figure 15.1 shows what that would look like.

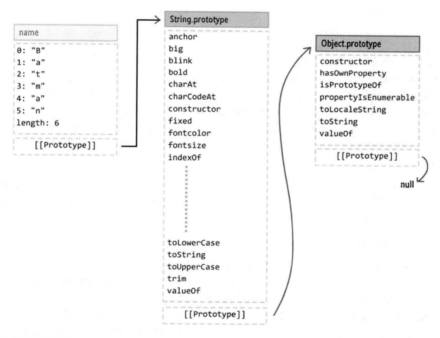

FIGURE 15.1

A deeper look at what our String object looks like.

We have your name variable containing a pointer to the text, **Homer Simpson**. You also have all of the various properties and methods that go with the String object—things you may have used like indexOf, toUpperCase, and so on.

You'll get a massive overview of what exactly this diagram represents when we look at Objects in greater detail, so don't worry too much about what you see here. Just know that the object form of any of the primitives carries with it a lot of functionality.

Why This Matters

Let's return to our earlier point of confusion. Our string is a primitive. How can a primitive type allow you to access properties on it? The answer has to do with JavaScript being really weird. Let's say we have the following string:

```
let game = "Dragon Age: Origins";
```

The game variable is very clearly a string primitive that is assigned to some literal text. If I want to access the length of this text, we would do something as follows:

```
let game = "Dragon Age: Origins";
console.log(game.length);
```

As part of evaluating game.length, JavaScript will convert your primitive string into an object. For a brief moment, your lowly primitive will become a beautiful object in order to figure out what the length actually is. The thing to keep in mind is that all of this is temporary. Because this temporary object isn't grounded or tied to anything after it serves its purpose, it goes away and you are left with the result of the length evaluation (a number) and the game variable still being a string primitive.

This transformation only happens for primitives. If we ever explicitly create a String object, then what we create is permanently kept as an object. Let's say we have the following:

```
let gameObject = new String("Dragon Age:Origins");
```

In this case, our gameObject variable very clearly points to something whose type is Object. This variable will continue to point to an Object type unless you modify the string or do something else that causes the reference to be changed. The primitive morphing into an object and then morphing back into a primitive is something unique to primitives. Your objects don't partake in such tomfoolery.

You can easily verify everything I've said by examining the type of your data. That is done by using the typeof keyword. Here is an example of me using it to confirm everything I've just told you about:

```
let game = "Dragon Age: Origins";
console.log("Length is: " + game.length);
```

```
let gameObject = new String("Dragon Age:Origins");

console.log(typeof game); // string
console.log(typeof game.length); // number
console.log(typeof gameObject); // object
```

Now, aren't you glad you learned all this?

THE ABSOLUTE MINIMUM

Hopefully this brief explanation helps you to reconcile why our primitives behave like objects when they need to. At this point, you might have a different question around why anybody would have designed a language that does something this bizarre. After all, if a primitive turns into an object when it needs to do something useful, why not just stay an object always? The answer has to do with memory consumption.

As we saw from our discussion on how much more baggage the object form of a primitive carries when compared to just a primitive, all of those pointers to additional functionality cost resources. The solution in JavaScript is a compromise. All literal values like text, numbers, and booleans are kept as primitives if they are declared and/or used as such. Only when they need to, are they converted to their respective Object forms. To ensure our app continues to keep a low memory footprint, these converted objects are quickly discarded (aka **garbage collected**) once they've served their purpose.

Got a question? Head on over to **https://forum.kirupa.com** to ask and get an answer from a bunch of cool and friendly developer peers.

NUMBERS

A large part of your time in JavaScript will be spent dealing with numbers. Even if you aren't working with numbers directly, you'll indirectly encounter them when doing even the most basic of tasks such as keeping count of something, working with arrays, etc.

In this chapter, I will introduce numbers in JavaScript by looking at how you can use them to accomplish many common tasks. Along the way, we will dive a little bit beyond the basics to broadly explore some interesting number-related things you might find useful.

Onward!

Using a Number

In order to use a number, all you have to do is…well, use it. Below is a simple example of me declaring a variable called `stooges` that is initialized to the number 3:

```
let stooges = 3;
```

That is it. There are no hoops to jump through. If you wanted to use more complex numbers, just use them as if nothing is different:

```
let pi = 3.14159;
let color = 0xFF;
let massOfEarth = 5.9742e+24;
```

In the above example, I am using a decimal value, a hexadecimal value, and a really large value using exponents. In the end, your browser will automatically do the right thing. Note that the "right thing" doesn't just exist in the positive space. You can use negative numbers easily as well. To use negative numbers, just place a minus (-) character before the number you want to turn into a negative value:

```
let temperature = -42;
```

What you've seen in this section makes up the bulk of how you will actually use numbers. In the next couple of sections, let's go a little bit deeper and look at some of the other interesting things you can do with numbers.

TIP   Trivia: Numbers in JavaScript

If you are curious why working with numbers is so easy, the reason is because JavaScript isn't big on numerical types. You don't have to declare a number as being of type `int`, `double`, `byte`, `float`, etc. like you may have had to do in other languages. The only exception is if you need a really large or really small number, and that is when `BigInt` comes in. We will talk about `BigInt` later… someday.

Oh, also…in JavaScript, all numbers are converted into 64-bit floating point numbers.

Operators

No introduction to numbers would be complete (…or started) without showing you how you can use mathematical operators in code to implement things you learned in first-grade Math class.

Let's look at the common operators in this section.

Doing Simple Math

In JavaScript, you can create simple mathematical expressions using the +, -, *, /, and % operators to add, subtract, multiply, divide, and find the remainder (modulus) of numbers respectively. If you can use a calculator, you can do simple math in JavaScript.

Here are some examples that put these operators to use:

```
let total = 4 + 26;
let average = total / 2;
let doublePi = 2*3.14159;
let subtractItem = 50 - 25;
let remainder = total % 7;
let more = (1 + average * 10) / 5;
```

In the last line in the above example, notice that I am defining a particular order of operations by using parenthesis around the expression I want to evaluate as a group. Again, all of this is just calculator stuff.

JavaScript evaluates expressions in the following order:

1. Parentheses

2. Exponents

3. Multiply

4. Divide

5. Add

6. Subtract

There are various mnemonic devices out there to help you remember this. The one I grew up with since elementary school is "**P**lease **E**xcuse **M**y **D**ear **A**unt **S**ally."

Incrementing and Decrementing

A common thing you will do with numbers will involve incrementing or decrementing a variable by a certain amount. Below is an example of me incrementing the variable i by 1:

```
let i = 4;
i = i + 1;
```

You don't have to increment or decrement by just 1. You can use any arbitrary number:

```
let i = 100;
i = i - 2;
```

All of this doesn't just have to just be addition or subtraction. You can perform other operations as well:

```
let i = 100;
i = i / 2;
```

You should start to see a pattern here. Regardless of what operator you are using, you'll notice that you are cumulatively modifying your i variable. Because of how frequently you will use this pattern, you have some operators that simplify this a bit (Table 16.1).

TABLE 16.1   Operators for simplifying incrementing and decrementing

Expression	What it does
i++	Increments i by 1 (i = i + 1)
i--	Decrements i by 1 (i = i - 1)
i += n	Increments i by n (i = i + n)
i -= n	Decrements i by n (i = i - n)
i *= n	Multiplies by n (i = i * n)
i /= n	Divides i by n (i = i / n)
i %= n	Finds the remainder of i when divided by n (i = i % n)
i **= n	Exponential operator where i is raised to the power of n

If I use these operators on the three examples you saw earlier, the code will look as follows:

```
i++;
i -= 2;
i /= 2;
```

Before we wrap this up, there is one quirk you should be aware of. It has to do with the -- and ++ operators for incrementing or decrementing a value by 1. Whether the ++ and -- operators appear before or after the variable they are incrementing matters.

Let's look at this example:

```
let i = 4;
let j = i++;
```

After executing these two lines, the value of i will be 5...just like you would expect. The value of j will be 4. Notice that in this example, the operator appears after the variable.

If we place the operator in front of the variable, the results are a bit different:

```
let i = 4;
let j = ++i;
```

The value of i will still be 5. Here is the kicker...the value of j will be 5 also.

What changed between these two examples is the position of the operator. The position of the operator determines **whether the incremented value will be returned or the pre-incremented value will be returned**. Now, aren't you glad you learned that?

Hexadecimal and Octal Values

Beyond using normal decimal values, you can use hexadecimal (base 16) and octal (base 8) values as well. When working with octal values, make sure to start your number with a 0:

```
let leet = 0o2471;
```

For hexadecimal values, you need start your number with 0x:

```
let leet = 0x539;
```

In many situations, you'll find yourself dealing with octal and hexadecimal values in the form of strings. If they are strings, you cannot manipulate them as you would normal numbers. You need to convert the string to a number first.

The way you do that is by using the parseInt function:

```
let hexValue = parseInt('FFFFFF', 16);
let octalValue = parseInt('011', 8);
```

The parseInt function takes your hexadecimal or octal value followed by the base you are converting from.

Special Values—Infinity and NaN

The last thing we will look at are two global properties that you will encounter that aren't numerical values. These values are `Infinity` and `NaN`.

Infinity

You can use the `Infinity` and `-Infinity` values to define infinitely large or small numbers:

```
let myLoveForYou = Infinity * 2;
```

The chances of you having to use `Infinity` are often very slim. Instead, you will probably see it returned as part of something else your code does. For example, you will see `Infinity` returned if you divide by 0.

NaN

The `NaN` keyword stands for "Not a Number", and it gets returned when you do some numerical operation that is invalid. For example, `NaN` gets returned in the following case:

```
let nope = 1920 / "blah";
```

The reason is that you cannot divide a number and a string. There are non-contrived cases where you will see this value returned, and we'll look at some later.

Going from a String to a Number

Sometimes, you will have numbers that are buried inside strings. To get all the scoop on that, read the **Going from a String to a Number** tutorial.

The Math Object

Numbers are used in a variety of mathematical expressions, and they often go beyond simple additions, subtractions, multiplications, and divisions. Your math classes back in the day would have been a whole lot easier if that's all there was to it. To help you more easily do complicated numerical things, you have the `Math` object. This object provides you with a lot of functions and constants that will come in handy, and we are going to very briefly look at some of the things this object does.

This is Boring!

I am not going to lie to you. Looking at all the stuff the `Math` object provides is pretty boring. Unless you really want to know about all of this now, I would prefer you just very quickly skim through the following sections and refer back as needed. The `Math` object isn't going anywhere (it has no friends), so it will be waiting for you at a later time.

The Constants

To avoid you having to explicitly define mathematical constants like pi, Euler's constant, natural log, and so on, the `Math` object defines many common constants for you (Table 16.2).

TABLE 16.2 Constants

Usage	What it stands for
`Math.E`	Euler's constant
`Math.LN2`	Natural logarithm of 2
`Math.LN10`	Natural logarithm of 10
`Math.LOG2E`	Base 2 logarithm of E
`Math.LOG10E`	Base 10 logarithm of E
`Math.PI`	3.14159 (that's all I remember, and I'm too lazy to look up the rest!)
`Math.SQRT1_2`	Square root of 1/2
`Math.SQRT2`	Square root of 2

Of all of these constants, the one I've used the most is `Math.PI`:

I just wanted an excuse
to post this picture

You will use this in everything from drawing circles on your screen to specifying trigonometric expressions. In fact, I can't ever remember having used any of these other constants outside of `Math.PI`. Here is an example of a function that returns the circumference given the radius:

```javascript
function getCircumference(radius) {
  return 2 * Math.PI * radius;
}


console.log(getCircumference(2));
```

You would use `Math.PI` or any other constant just as you would any named variable.

Rounding Numbers

Your numbers will often end up containing a ridiculous amount of precision:

```javascript
let position = getPositionFromCursor(); // 159.3634493939
```

To help you round these numbers up to a reasonable integer value, you have the `Math.round()`, `Math.ceil()`, and `Math.floor()` functions that take a number as an argument (Table 16.3).

TABLE 16.3 Rounding functions

Function	What it does
Math.round()	Returns a number that is rounded to the nearest integer. You round up if your argument is greater than or equal to .5. You stay at your current integer, if your argument is less than .5.
Math.ceil()	Returns a number that is greater than or equal to your argument
Math.floor()	Returns a number that is less than or equal to your argument

The easiest way to make sense of the above table is to just see these three functions in action:

```
Math.floor(.5); // 0
Math.ceil(.5); // 1
Math.round(.5); // 1

Math.floor(3.14); // 3
Math.round(3.14); // 3
Math.ceil(3.14); // 4

Math.floor(5.9); // 5
Math.round(5.9); // 6
Math.ceil(5.9); // 6
```

These three functions always round you to an integer. If you want to round to a precise set of digits, check out the last half of my **Rounding Numbers in JavaScript** tutorial.

Trigonometric Functions

My favorite of the functions, the Math object gives you handy access to almost all of the trigonometric functions you will need as shown in Table 16.4.

TABLE 16.4 Trigonometric functions

Function	What it does
Math.cos()	Gives you the cosine for a given argument
Math.sin()	Gives you the sine for a given argument
Math.tan()	Gives you the tan for a given argument
Math.acos()	Gives you the arccosine (isn't that such a cool name?) for a given argument
Math.asin()	Gives you the arcsine for a given argument
Math.atan()	Gives you the arctan for a given argument

To use any of these, just pass in a number as the argument:

```
Math.cos(0); // 1
Math.sin(0); // 0
Math.tan(Math.PI / 4); // 1
Math.cos(Math.PI); // 1
Math.cos(4 * Math.PI); // 1
```

These trigonometric functions take arguments in the form of radian values. If your numbers are in the form of degrees, be sure to convert them to radians first.

Powers and Square Roots

Continuing down the path of defining the Math object functions, you have Math.pow(), Math.exp(), and Math.sqrt() as explained in Table 16.5.

TABLE 16.5 Functions for powers and square roots

Function	What it does
Math.pow()	Raises a number to a specified power
Math.exp()	Raises the Euler's constant to a specified number
Math.sqrt()	Returns the square root of a given argument

Let's look at some examples:

```
Math.pow(2, 4); //equivalent of 2^4 (or 2 * 2 * 2 * 2)
Math.exp(3); //equivalent of Math.E^3
Math.sqrt(16); //4
```

Note that `Math.pow()` takes two arguments. This might be the first built-in function we've looked at that takes two arguments. This little detail is somehow mildly exciting.

Getting the Absolute Value

If you want the absolute value of a number, simply use the `Math.abs()` function:

```
Math.abs(37); //37
Math.abs(-6); //6
```

That's all I got for this.

Random Numbers

To generate a somewhat random number between 0 and a smidgen less than 1, you have the `Math.random()` function. This function doesn't take any arguments, but you can simply use it as part of a mathematical expression:

```
let randomNumber = Math.random() * 100;
```

Each time your `Math.random` function is called, you will see a different number returned for `Math.random()`. To learn all about how to work with this function to generate random numbers, read the **Random Numbers in JS** tutorial.

THE ABSOLUTE MINIMUM

That's all there is to it for this introductory chapter on numbers and the `Math` object in JavaScript. As you can see, it doesn't get much easier than this. JavaScript provides a very no-frills approach to working with them, and this chapter gave you a slight peek at the edges in case you need to go there.

Some additional resources and examples that will help you to better understand how numbers in JavaScript can be used:

- **Going from a String to a Number:** http://bit.ly/kirupaStrToNum
- **Random Numbers in JS:** http://bit.ly/kirupaRandom
- **Advanced Random Numbers in JS:** http://bit.ly/AdvRandom
- **Why Don't My Numbers Add Up:** http://bit.ly/kirupaFPG
- **Random Colors in JS:** http://bit.ly/kirupaRandomColors

Numbers in JavaScript is a fun topic that can be confusing at times. If you find yourself stuck or confused, get clarity by posting on **https://forum.kirupa.com**.

IN THIS CHAPTER

- Learn the difference between data properties and accessor properties
- Learn about getters and setters
- Identify when to use an accessor property vs. a data property

GETTERS AND SETTERS

The properties we have been working with so far are known as **data properties**. These are the properties where we give them a name and assign a value to them:

```
let foo = {
  a: "Hello",
  b: "Monday";
}
```

To read back the value, all we do is just access it directly:

```
console.log(foo.a);
```

Writing a value to this property is sorta what we would expect as well:

```
foo.a = "Manic";
```

Outside of setting and reading a value, there really isn't much more we can do. That is the sad tale of a data property. Now, as part of reading and writing properties, what if we had the ability to:

- Maintain our existing syntax for reading and writing property values
- Gain the ability to run some custom code behind the scenes

That would be pretty cool, right? As it turns out, we have the ability to do all of this. It is brought to you by another friendly and hardworking property variant known as an **accessor property**! In the following sections we'll learn all about them and run into the real stars of this show, the mysterious getters and setters.

Onward!

A Tale of Two Properties

On the surface, accessor properties and data properties look very similar. With a data property, you can read and write to a property:

```
theObj.storedValue = "Unique snowflake!"; // setting
console.log(theObj.storedValue); // reading
```

With an accessor property, you can pretty much do the exact same thing:

```
myObj.storedValue = "Also a unique snowflake!"; // setting
console.log(myObj.storedValue); // reading
```

We can't tell by looking at how a property is used to see if it is a data property or an accessor property. To tell the difference, we have to go where the property is actually defined. Take a look at the following code where we have a few properties defined inside our zorb object:

```
let zorb = {
  message: "Blah",

  get greeting() {
    return this.message;
  },

  set greeting(value) {
    this.message = value;
  }
};
```

First up is message, a regular old data property:

```
let zorb = {
  message: "Blah",

  get greeting() {
```

```
    return this.message;
  },

  set greeting(value) {
    this.message = value;
  }
};
```

We know this is a data property because it is just a property name and a value. There isn't anything else going on here. Now, here is where things get a little exciting. The next property we have is greeting, and it doesn't look like any property we've seen in the past:

```
let zorb = {
  message: "Blah",

  get greeting() {
    return this.message;
  },

  set greeting(value) {
    this.message = value;
  }
};
```

Instead of a simple name and value arrangement like we saw with message, the greeting property is broken up into two **functions** preceded by either a get or set keyword:

```
let zorb = {
  message: "Blah",

  get greeting() {
    return this.message;
  },

  set greeting(value) {
    this.message = value;
  }
};
```

These keyword and function pairs are commonly known as **getters** and **setters** respectively. What makes them special is that we don't access `greeting` as a function. We access it just like we would any old property:

```
zorb.greeting = "Hola!";
console.log(zorb.greeting);
```

The real interesting stuff happens at the getter and setter level, so we will dive deeper into them next.

Meet Getters and Setters

Based on what we know so far, *getter* and *setter* are just fancy names for functions that behave like properties. When we try to read an accessor property (`zorb.greeting`), the getter function gets called:

```
let zorb = {
  message: "Blah",

  get greeting() {
    return this.message;
  },

  set greeting(value) {
    this.message = value;
  }
};
```

Similarly, when we set a new value to our accessor property (`zorb.greeting = "Hola!"`), the setter function gets called:

```
let zorb = {
  message: "Blah",

  get greeting() {
    return this.message;
  },

  set greeting(value) {
    this.message = value;
  }
};
```

The full power of a getter and setter lies in the code we can execute when reading or writing a property. **Because we are dealing with functions under the covers, we can run any code we want**. In our zorb example, we used our greeting getter and setter to closely mimic what a data property would do. We can set a value, and we can read back the value that we just set. Pretty boring right? It doesn't have to be that way, and the following examples kick the interestingness of our getters and setters up a bunch of notches.

Shout Generator

Here is an example where whatever message we specify gets turned into all caps:

```
var shout = {
  _message: "HELLO!",

  get message() {
    return this._message;
  },

  set message(value) {
    this._message = value.toUpperCase();
  }
};

shout.message = "This is sparta!";
console.log(shout.message);
```

Notice that, as part of setting the value for the message property, we store the entered value in all caps thanks to the toUpperCase method all String objects carry around. All this ensures that, when we try to read back the message we had stored, we see the fully capitalized version of whatever we entered.

Logging Activity

In our next example, we have our superSecureTerminal object that logs all usernames:

```
var superSecureTerminal = {
  allUserNames: [],
  _username: "",
```

```
    showHistory() {
      console.log(this.allUserNames);
    },

    get username() {
      return this._username;
    },

    set username(name) {
      this._username = name;
      this.allUserNames.push(name);
    }
  }
```

This logging is handled inside the username setter where each username we provide gets stored in the allUserNames array and the showHistory function displays the stored usernames to the screen. Before we move on, let's actually put this code to the test. We are going to access superSecureTerminal differently from what we have done in the past. We are going to take some of our **Object creation knowledge** and do the following:

```
var myTerminal = Object.create(superSecureTerminal);
myTerminal.username = "Michael Gary Scott";
myTerminal.username = "Dwight K. Schrute";
myTerminal.username = "Creed Bratton";
myTerminal.username = "Pam Beasley";

myTerminal.showHistory();
```

We are creating a new object called myTerminal that is based on the superSecureTerminal object. From here, we can do everything with the myTerminal object and call it business as usual.

Property Value Validation

The last example we will look at is one where our setters do some validation on the values sent to them:

```
let person = {
  _name: "",
  _age: "",
```

```
    get name() {
      return this._name;
    },

    set name(value) {
      if (value.length > 2) {
        this._name = value;
      } else {
        console.log("Name is too short!");
      }
    },

    get age() {
      return this._age;
    },

    set age(value) {
      if (value < 5) {
        console.log("Too young!");
      } else {
        this._age = value;
      }
    },

    get details() {
      return "Name: " + this.name + ", Age: " + this.age;
    }
  }
```

Notice that we check for an acceptable input in both our name and age properties. If the name we provide is fewer than 2 characters, we show an alert. If the age is less than 5, we show an alert as well. Being able to check if a value we assign to a property is good or not is probably one of the best features that getters and setters bring to the table.

THE ABSOLUTE MINIMUM

Should we all stop creating regular data properties and going with the fancier accessor properties? Not really. It depends on your current needs and potential future needs. If a property you know will never really need the extra flexibility that getters and setters provide, you can just keep them as data properties. If you ever need to revisit that, going from a data property to an accessor property is something that happens entirely behind the scenes. You and I have the ability to change that without altering how the property itself will be used. Cool, right?

If you find yourself stuck or confused with any part of this, get clarity by posting on **https://forum.kirupa.com**.

IN THIS CHAPTER

- Understand at a deeper level how Objects work
- Learn to create custom objects
- Demystify the prototype property
- Do some inheriting

A DEEPER LOOK AT OBJECTS

In the *Introduction to Objects schtuff* in Chapter 11, "Of Pizzas, Types, Primitives, and Objects," we received a very high-level overview of what objects in JavaScript are and how to think about them. That was good enough to cover the basics and some of the built-in types, but we need to go a little deeper. In this chapter, we will make that earlier chapter seem like the tip of a ginormous iceberg:

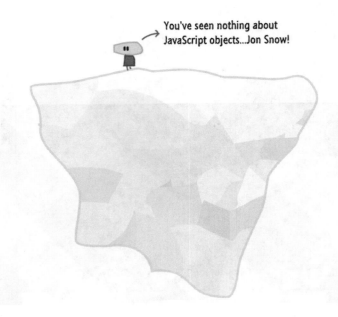

What we are going to do here is have a re-look at objects in greater detail and touch on the more advanced topics such as using the `Object` object, creating our own custom objects, inheritance, prototypes, and the `this` keyword. If all that I've listed so far makes no sense, it will after we've reached the end of this chapter...I guarantee it.

Onward!

Meet the Object

At the very bottom of the food chain, we have the `Object` type that lays the groundwork for both custom objects as well as built-in types like `Function`, `Array`, and `RegExp`. Pretty much everything except `null` and `undefined` is directly related to an `Object` or can become one as needed.

As we saw from the introduction to objects forever ago, the functionality that `Object` brings to the table is pretty minimal. It allows us to specify a bunch of named key and value pairs that we lovingly call **properties**. This isn't all that different from what we see in other languages with data structures like hashtables, associative arrays, and dictionaries.

Anyway, all of this is pretty boring. What we are going to do is learn more about objects by getting our hands dirty by working with them directly.

Creating Objects

The first thing we will look at is how to create an object. There are several ways to go about this, but all the cool kids are creating objects these days by using the funny-looking (yet compact) **object literal syntax**:

```
let funnyGuy = {};
```

That's right. Instead of typing in `new Object()` like our great-grandparents did, we can just initialize our object by saying `{}`. At the end of this line getting executed, we will have created an object called `funnyGuy` whose type is `Object`:

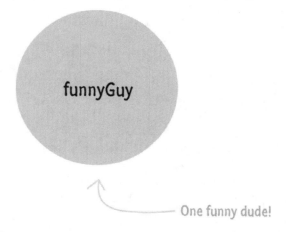

One funny dude!

There is a little more to creating objects than what we've just seen with the object literal syntax, but we'll cover all of that in due time. DUE. TIME.

Adding Properties

Once we have an object, there are several paths we can take to add properties on it. The path we will take is a simple and performant one that uses the array-like bracket notation with our new property name acting as the index.

Let's continue with where we left off with our `funnyGuy` object:

```
let funnyGuy = {};
```

Let's say we want to add a new property called `firstName` and give it a value of **Conan**. The way we would add this property is by using a dot notation syntax as follows:

```
funnyGuy.firstName = "Conan";
```

That's all there is to it. Once we have added this property, we can access it using the same syntax:

```
let funnyFirstName = funnyGuy.firstName;
```

Now, before we move on, since we are already here (and probably paid for a few more hours of parking), let's add another property called `lastName` and give it the value of **O'Brien**:

```
funnyGuy.lastName = "O'Brien";
```

THERE IS ALSO A BRACKET NOTATION

For both settings as well as reading properties, we used what is known as the **dot notation approach**. There is an alternate approach for setting and reading properties that uses brackets instead of the dot:

```
let funnyGuy = {};

funnyGuy["firstName"] = "Conan";
funnyGuy["lastName"] = "O'Brien";
```

Whether you prefer dots or brackets is up to you (or your team if you are working with a bunch of people), but there is one area that brackets are uniquely qualified for. That area is when we are dealing with properties whose names we need to dynamically generate. In the case of `firstName` and `lastName`, we had these property names hardcoded. Take a look at the following snippet:

```
let myObject = {};

for (let i = 0; i < 5; i++) {
  let propertyName = "data" + i;

  myObject[propertyName] = Math.random() * 100;
}
```

We have an object called `myObject`—notice how we are setting properties on it. We don't have a hardcoded list of property names, Instead, we create the property name by relying on the index values from our array. Once we have figured out the property name, we then use that data to create a property on `myObject`. The property names we will generate will be **data0**, **data1**, **data2**, **data3**, and **data4**. This ability to dynamically specify a property name as part of setting or reading from an object is something the bracket syntax makes easily possible.

At this point, we are in good shape. Our complete `funnyGuy` code will look as follows:

```
let funnyGuy = {};

funnyGuy.firstName = "Conan";
funnyGuy.lastName = "O'Brien";
```

When this code runs, we will have created our `funnyGuy` object and set two properties called `firstName` and `lastName` on it.

What we have just seen is how to create an object and set properties on it in **separate** steps. If we know what properties we want to set from the beginning, we can combine some steps together:

```
let funnyGuy = {
  firstName: "Conan",
  lastName: "O'Brien"
};
```

The end result of this code is identical to what we saw earlier where we created our `funnyGuy` object first and set the properties afterwards.

There is yet another detail about adding properties that we should look at. By now, we have looked at a variety of different objects that have properties whose values are made of up numbers, strings, and so on. Did you know that a property value can be another object itself? That's right! Take a look at the following `colors` object whose `content` property stores an object:

```
let colors = {
  header: "blue",
  footer: "gray",
  content: {
    title: "black",
    body: "darkgray",
    signature: "light blue"
  }
};
```

The way you specify an object inside an object is as direct as specifying a property and using the bracket syntax for setting the property value to an object. If we want to add a property to a nested object, we can combine everything we've seen so far to do this.

Let's say we want to add a property called **frame** to the nested `content` object we saw a few seconds earlier. The way we can do that is by doing something that looks like this:

```
colors.content.frame = "yellow";
```

We start with our `colors` object, move to our `content` object, and then specify the property and value that we want. If you prefer to use the bracket notation for accessing the `content` property, you can do this instead:

```
colors["content"]["frame"] = "yellow";
```

If you want to mix things up between the dot and bracket notations, this also works:

```
colors.content["frame"] = "yellow";
```

Before we wrap this up, I mentioned at the beginning that you have several paths that you can take to add properties to an object. We looked at one such path. A more complex path that you can take could involve the `Object.defineProperty` and `Object.defineProperties` methods. These methods allow you to set a property and its value, but they allow you to do much more...like specify whether a property can be enumerated, specify whether a property can be customized, and more. It's definitely overkill for what we will want to do 99% of the time in the beginning, but know this: if overkill is what you want, then these two methods deliver. **The MDN documentation** does a good job providing examples of how you can use them to add one or many properties to an object.

Removing Properties

If you thought adding properties to an object was fun, removing properties from an object is a bit boring. It is also simpler. Let's continue to work with our colors object:

```
let colors = {
  header: "blue",
  footer: "gray",
  content: {
    title: "black",
    body: "darkgray",
    signature: "light blue"
  }
};
```

What we want to do is remove the `footer` property. We have two ways of doing this depending on whether we want to access the footer property using the bracket notation or whether we want to access it using the dot notation:

```
delete colors.footer;
```

```
// or
```

```
delete colors["footer"];
```

The key to making this all work is the `delete` keyword. Simply use the `delete` keyword and follow it up with the property you'd like to remove. That's all there is to it.

Now, this wouldn't be JavaScript if I didn't mention a caveat. This one has to do with performance. If you will be deleting a lot of properties on a frequent basis across a large number of objects, `delete` is much slower than just setting the value of the property to something like **undefined**:

```
colors.footer = undefined;
```

```
// or
```

```
colors["footer"] = undefined;
```

The flipside is that setting a property to **undefined** means the property still exists in memory. You'll need to calculate the tradeoffs (speed vs. memory) in your situation and optimize for the one that makes the most sense for you.

What Is Going on Behind the Scenes?

We saw how to create objects and make some typical modifications on them. Because objects really are the core of what makes JavaScript do all of its JavaScriptey things, it is important for us to have a deeper understanding of what is happening. This isn't just for the sake of trivial knowledge, though it will be fun to impress your friends and family over dinner with what you have learned. A large part of working with JavaScript is building objects based on other objects and doing other traditional object-oriented things. All of those things will make more sense when we have a better idea of what really goes on when we are working with objects.

Let's start with our `funnyGuy` object again:

```
let funnyGuy = {};
```

Now, what can we do with an empty object? We have no properties defined on it. Is our `funnyGuy` object truly alone and isolated with nothing at all going for it? As it turns out, the answer is a resounding **nope**. The reason has to do with how objects we create in JavaScript are automatically interlinked with the bigger `Object` and all the functionality it brings to the table. The best way to make sense of this interlinking, is to visualize it. Take a really REALLY deep breath and look at Figure 18.1.

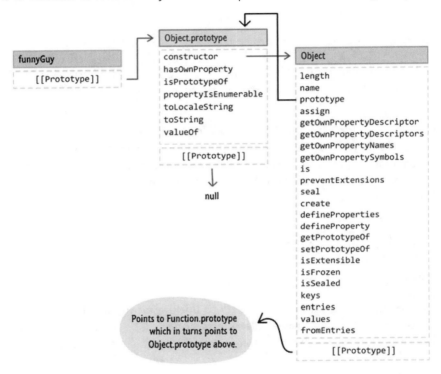

FIGURE 18.1

What our seemingly simple `funnyGuy` object actually has going on!

In this diagram, we have mapped out what really happens behind the scenes when we create our empty `funnyGuy` object.

In this view, we still start off with our `funnyGuy` object. That part is still the same. What is different is everything else. See, our `funnyGuy` is simply an empty object. It has no properties that we defined on it. It does have properties that come defined out of the box, and these properties link our `funnyGuy` object to the underlying `Object` type without us having to do any work. This link allows us to call traditional `Object` properties on `funnyGuy` like the following:

```
let funnyGuy = {};
funnyGuy.toString();  // [object Object]
```

To hammer the point home, this link is what allows `toString` to work when called on our seemingly empty `funnyGuy` object. Now, calling this link a **link** isn't accurate. Our link is actually known as a prototype (and often represented as `[[Prototype]]`) that ends up pointing to another object. A*nother* object can have its own `[[Prototype]]` that points to yet another object and so on. All of this linking is known as the **prototype chain**. Traveling across the prototype chain is a big part of what JavaScript does when trying to find a property you are calling. For us calling `toString` on our `funnyGuy` object, Figure 18.2 shows us what is actually happening.

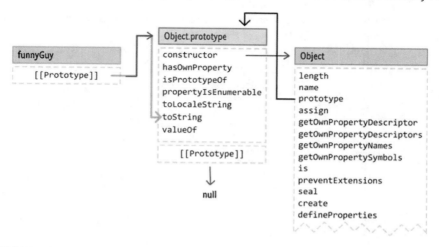

FIGURE 18.2

Walking the prototype chain to find the property we are looking for.

With the prototype chain, even if our object doesn't have a particular property that we are looking for defined, JavaScript will walk through the chain and see if every stop along the way has that property defined instead. Now, our `funnyGuy` object's prototype chain is just itself and `Object.prototype`. It isn't a complex chain at all. As we work with more complex objects, the prototype chain will get very long and more complex. We'll dip our toes into this complexity shortly.

NOTE Object Isn't a Part of the Prototype Chain

In our previous visualizations, we see our Object having a dedicated entry with lines going between properties on it and the `Object.prototype`. The thing to note is that Object is not a part of the prototype chain. It plays a role in how objects implement the relationship between their `constructor` and a poorly named `prototype` property (not related to our `[[Prototype]]`), and we'll touch upon the Object's role later on. For completeness, I will continue to show Object's role in future visualizations of our objects, but do keep a note that it doesn't play a role in our prototype chain traversal.

Next, as we can see, our `funnyGuy` object right now is very basic. Let's add the `firstName` and `lastName` properties from earlier to make things a bit more interesting:

```
let funnyGuy = {
    firstName: "Conan",
    lastName: "O'Brien"
};
```

With these two properties thrown into the mix, our earlier visualization will now look as shown in Figure 18.3.

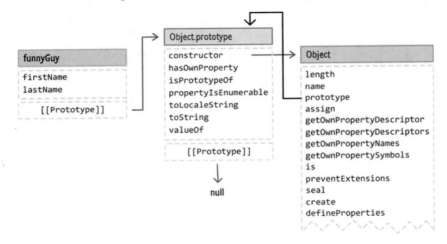

FIGURE 18.3

*Say **hello** to the `firstName` and `lastName` properties.*

The `firstName` and `lastName` properties are a part of the `funnyGuy` object and visualized as such as well. With this initial coverage of the object out of the way, it's time for us to go a bit more detailed.

Creating Custom Objects

Working with the generic `Object` and putting properties on it serves a useful purpose, but its awesomeness fades away really quickly when we are creating many objects that are basically the same thing. Take a look at the following snippet:

```
let funnyGuy = {
  firstName: "Conan",
  lastName: "O'Brien",

  getName: function () {
    return "Name is: " + this.firstName + " " + this.lastName;
  }
};


let theDude = {
  firstName: "Jeffrey",
  lastName: "Lebowski",

  getName: function () {
    return "Name is: " + this.firstName + " " + this.lastName;
  }
};


let detective = {
  firstName: "Adrian",
  lastName: "Monk",

  getName: function () {
    return "Name is: " + this.firstName + " " + this.lastName;
  }
};
```

This snippet builds on our `funnyGuy` object and introduces two new objects that are very similar to it, `theDude` and `detective`. Our visualization of all of this will now look as shown in Figure 18.4.

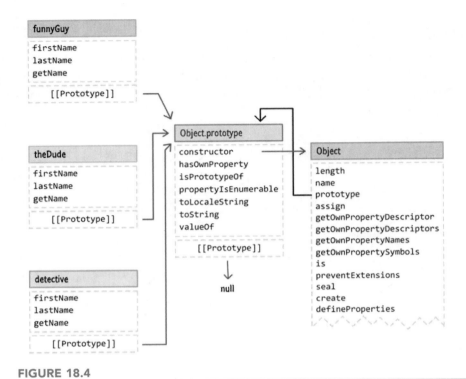

FIGURE 18.4

Each new object we created extends from `Object.prototype`.

At first glance, there seems to be quite a bit of duplication going on. Each of our new objects carries with it its own copy of the `firstName`, `lastName`, and `get-Name` properties. Now, not all duplication is bad. Yes, that does go against what I had stated earlier, but hear me out. In the case of objects, we need to figure out what properties make sense to be duplicated and which ones don't. From our example, the `firstName` and `lastName` properties will typically have a unique value per object. Keeping these duplicated on each object makes sense. The `getName` property, though, acts as a helper and doesn't contain anything one particular object will want to uniquely customize:

```
getName: function () {
  return "Name is: " + this.firstName + " " + this.lastName;
}
```

Duplicating this one doesn't make sense, so we should look at making `getName` more generally available without the duplication. How can we go about doing this?

Well...it turns out there is a clean way to do this by creating an intermediate **parent** object that contains the generic properties. Our **child** objects can inherit from this parent object instead of inheriting from `Object` directly. To get more specific, we are going to create a new `person` object that contains `getName`. Our `funnyGuy`, `theDude`, and `detective` objects will inherit from `person`. This arrangement will ensure that the properties we need duplicated get duplicated and the properties we need shared get shared. To help all of this cryptic text make sense, Figure 18.5 highlights what we are trying to do.

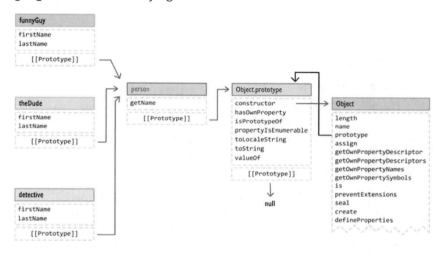

FIGURE 18.5

Adding an intermediate `person` object with our (now shared) `getName` property.

Notice that `person` is now a part of the prototype chain, happily nestled between `Object.prototype` and our child objects. How do we go about doing this? One approach that we've seen earlier is by relying on `Object.create`. When using `Object.create`, we can specify an object to create our object from, for example:

```
let myObject = Object.create(fooObject);
```

When we do this, what happens behind the scenes is the following: our `myObject` object's **prototype** will be `fooObject`. It becomes a part of the prototype chain. Now that we have taken a detour and expanded our understanding of `Object.create` with what we've seen in this chapter, let's go back to our original problem of how we get `funnyGuy`, `theDude`, and `detective` to inherit from our `person` object.

The code for doing all of this would be as follows:

```
let person = {
  getName: function () {
    return "The name is " + this.firstName + " " + this.lastName;
  }
};
```

```
let funnyGuy = Object.create(person);
funnyGuy.firstName = "Conan";
funnyGuy.lastName = "O'Brien";

let theDude = Object.create(person);
theDude.firstName = "Jeffrey";
theDude.lastName = "Lebowski";

let detective = Object.create(person);
detective.firstName = "Adrian";
detective.lastName = "Monk";
```

Because of how the prototype chain works, we can call `getName` on any of our funnyGuy, theDude, or `detective` objects, and the right things would happen:

```
detective.getName(); // The name is Adrian Monk
```

If we decide to enhance our `person` object, we can do so just once and have any objects that inherit from it benefit from our enhancement without any repetition. Let's say that we add a `getInitials` method that returns the first letter of the first and last name:

```
let person = {
  getName: function () {
    return "The name is " + this.firstName + " " + this.lastName;
  },
  getInitials: function () {
    if (this.firstName && this.lastName) {
      return this.firstName[0] + this.lastName[0];
    }
  }
};
```

We add this `getInitials` method on our person object. To use this method, we can call it on any object that extends `person`, like our `funnyGuy`:

```
funnyGuy.getInitials(); // CO
```

This ability to create intermediate objects to help divide up the functionality in our code is a powerful thing. It allows us to be more efficient in how we create objects and what functionality we provide on each one. Neat, right?

The `this` Keyword

One thing you may have noticed in our previous snippets is the use of the `this` keyword, especially when we used it in our `person` object to refer to properties created on its children instead. Let's go back to our `person` object and, more specifically, the `getName` property:

```
let person = {
  getName: function () {
    return "The name is " + this.firstName + " " + this.lastName;
  },
  getInitials: function () {
    if (this.firstName && this.lastName) {
      return this.firstName[0] + this.lastName[0];
    }
  }
};
```

When we call `getName`, depending on which object we called it from, we'll see the appropriate name returned. For example, let's say we do the following:

```
let spaceGuy = Object.create(person);
spaceGuy.firstName = "Buzz";
spaceGuy.lastName = "Lightyear";


console.log(spaceGuy.getName()); // Buzz Lightyear
```

When we run this, we'll see **Buzz Lightyear** printed to our console. If we look at the `getName` property again, there is absolutely no existence of the `firstName` or `lastName` properties on the `person` object. When a property doesn't exist, we saw earlier that we walk down the prototype chain from parent to parent as shown in Figure 18.6.

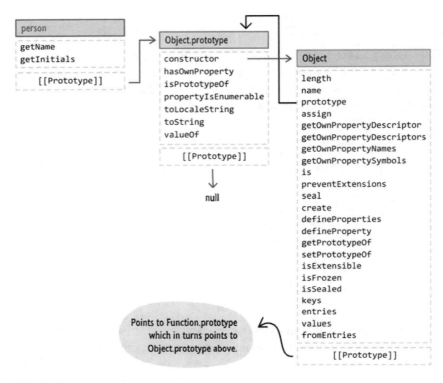

FIGURE 18.6

The prototype chain for our person object.

In our case, the only stop on the chain would be `Object.prototype`. There is no existence of the `firstName` or `lastName` properties on `Object.prototype` either. How is it that this `getName` method happens to work and return the right values?

The answer has to do with the `this` keyword that precedes `firstName` and `lastName` as part of the `return` statement in getName:

```
let person = {
  getName: function () {
    return "The name is " + this.firstName + " " + this.lastName;
  },
  getInitials: function () {
```

```
    if (this.firstName && this.lastName) {
      return this.firstName[0] + this.lastName[0];
    }
  }
};
```

The `this` keyword refers to the object that our `getName` method is bound to. That object is, in this case, `spaceGuy` because that is the object that we are using as the entry point to all of this prototype navigation goodness as highlighted in Figure 18.7.

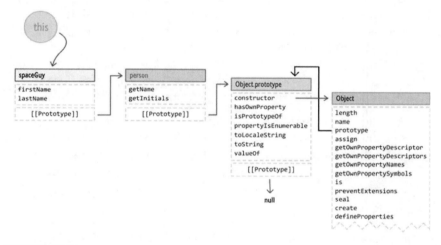

FIGURE 18.7

The `this` keyword refers to `spaceGuy`!

At the point where the `getName` method is evaluated and the `firstName` and `lastName` properties have to be resolved, the lookup starts at whatever the `this` keyword is pointing to. This means our lookup starts with the `spaceGuy` object—an object that turns out actually contains the `firstName` and `lastName` properties! That is why we get the correct result when the code for `getName` (and `getInitials` as well) is called.

Knowing what the `this` keyword refers to is something barrels of ink have been spilled on, and covering it fully goes a bit beyond what we want to talk about. The good thing is that what you've seen now will you get you pretty far.

THE ABSOLUTE MINIMUM

Because so much fuss is made about JavaScript's object orientedness, it is only natural that a topic that covers it would be as wide and deep as what you've seen here. A bulk of what you saw here dealt with inheritance directly or indirectly where objects are derived and based on other objects. Unlike other, more class-ical languages that use classes as templates for objects, JavaScript has no such concept of a class in a strict sense. JavaScript uses what is known as a **prototypical inheritance model**. You don't instantiate objects from a template. Instead, you create objects either from scratch or, more commonly, by copying/cloning another object. JavaScript fits in this gray area where it doesn't fit the mold of a class-ical language, but it does have many class-like constructs (some of which you will see in a later chapter) which doesn't make it a wild animal at a table where other class-ical languages may congregate. I wouldn't get too caught up in labels here.

In the bazillion pages here, I tried to reinforce JavaScript's new functionality for working with objects and extending them for your own needs. There is still more to cover, so take a break and we'll touch upon some more interesting topics in the near future that extend what you've seen in more powerful, expressive, and awesome ways.

Some additional resources and examples:

- **Understanding "Prototypes" in JS:** http://bit.ly/kirupaJSPrototypes
- **A Plain English Guide to JS Prototypes:** http://bit.ly/kirupaPrototypesGuide
- **How Does JavaScript ".prototype" Work?:** http://bit.ly/kirupaPrototypeWork

This is a big and strange topic, so please do post on **https://forum.kirupa.com** if you run into any problems.

IN THIS CHAPTER
- Extend your objects' functionality
- Learn more about the prototype chain

19

EXTENDING BUILT-IN OBJECTS

As we know very well by now, JavaScript comes from the factory with a good supply of built-in objects. These objects provide some of the core functionality for working with text, numbers, collections of data, dates, and a whole lot more. As you become more familiar with JavaScript and start doing interesting-er and cleverer things, you'll often find that you want to do more and go farther than what the built-in objects allow.

Let's take a look at an example of when something like this might occur. Below is an example of how we can shuffle the contents of an array:

```javascript
function shuffle(input) {
  for (let i = input.length - 1; i >= 0; i--) {

    let randomIndex = Math.floor(Math.random() * (i + 1));
    let itemAtIndex = input[randomIndex];

    input[randomIndex] = input[i];
    input[i] = itemAtIndex;
  }
  return input;
}
```

The way we use this `shuffle` function is by simply calling it and passing in the array whose contents we want shuffled:

```
let shuffleArray = [1, 2, 3, 4, 5, 6, 7, 8, 9, 10];
shuffle(shuffleArray);

// and the result is...
console.log(shuffleArray);
```

After this code has run, the end result is that the contents of our array are now rearranged. Now, this functionality is pretty useful. I would say this is sooo useful, the shuffling ability should be a part of the `Array` object and be as easily accessible as `push`, `pop`, `slice`, and other doo-dads the `Array` object has.

If the `shuffle` function were a part of the `Array` object, we could simply use it as follows:

```
let shuffleArray = [1, 2, 3, 4, 5, 6, 7, 8, 9, 10];
shuffleArray.shuffle();
```

This is an example of us extending a built-in object (the `Array`) with some functionality that we defined (the `shuffle`). In the next few sections, we are going to look at how exactly to accomplish this, why it all works, and why extending built-in objects is pretty controversial.

Onward!

Say Hello to `prototype`...again—Sort of!

Extending a built-in object with new functionality sounds complicated, but it is really simple once you understand what needs to be done. To help with this, we are going to look at a combination of sample code and diagrams all involving the very friendly `Array` object:

```
let tempArray = [1, 2, 3, 4, 5, 6, 7, 8, 9, 10];
```

If we were to diagram the full hierarchy of the `tempArray` object, it would look as shown in Figure 19.1.

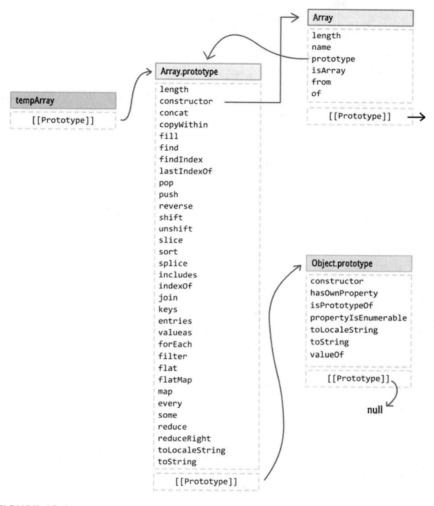

FIGURE 19.1

The tangled web of objects (and possibly lies!) that live just beneath the surface.

On the left, we have our tempArray object that is an instance of Array.proto-type…which is, in turn, an instance of the basic Object.prototype. Now, what we want to do is extend what our array is capable of with our shuffle function. What this means is that we need to figure out a way to get our shuffle function inserted into our Array.prototype as shown in Figure 19.2.

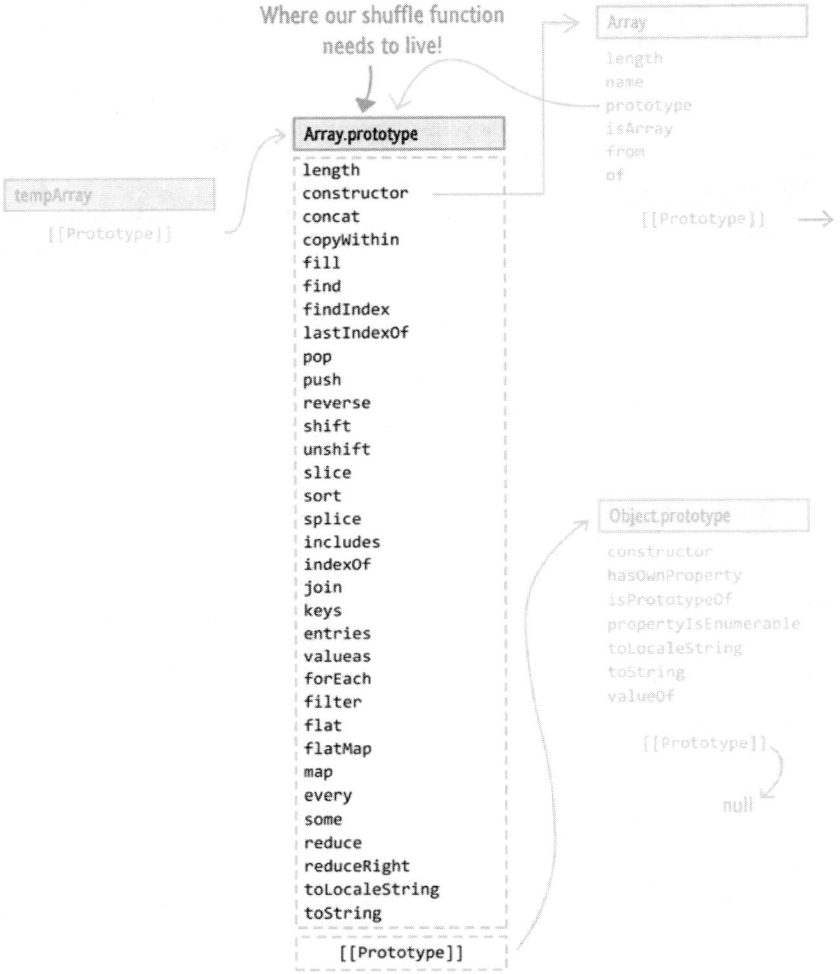

FIGURE 19.2

Where we want our shuffle function to live!

Here is the part where the quirkiness of JavaScript shines through. We don't have access to the code that makes up all of the array functionality. We can't find the function or object that makes up the `Array` and insert our shuffle function into it like we might for a custom object that we defined. Our built-in objects, such as the `Array`, are defined deep inside our browser's volcanic underbelly where no human being can go. We need to take another approach.

That **another approach** involves casually sneaking in and attaching our functionality to the `Array` object's `prototype` property. That would look something like this:

```
Array.prototype.shuffle = function () {
  let input = this;

  for (let i = input.length - 1; i >= 0; i--) {

    let randomIndex = Math.floor(Math.random() * (i + 1));
    let itemAtIndex = input[randomIndex];

    input[randomIndex] = input[i];
    input[i] = itemAtIndex;
  }
  return input;
}
```

Notice that our `shuffle` function is declared on `Array.prototype`! As part of this attachment, we made a minor change to how the function works. The function no longer takes an argument for referencing the array you need shuffled:

```
function shuffle(input) {
  .
  .
  .
  .
  .
}
```

Instead, because this function is now a part of the `Array`, the `this` keyword inside the function body points to the array that needs shuffling:

```
Array.prototype.shuffle = function () {
  let input = this;
  .
  .
  .
  .
}
```

Taking a step back, once we run this code, our `shuffle` function will find itself shoulder-to-shoulder with all of the other built-in methods the `Array` object exposes through `Array.prototype` as highlighted in Figure 19.3.

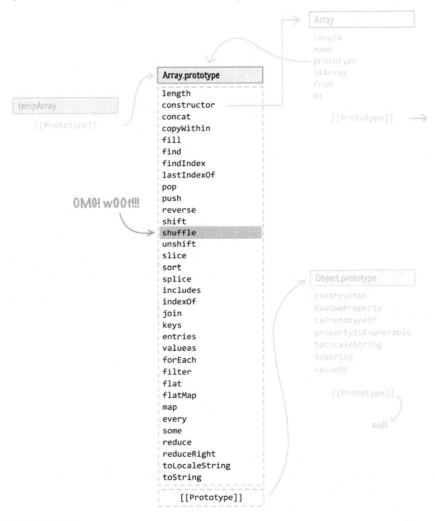

FIGURE 19.3

Great success! The shuffle function is now where it belongs.

If we wanted to access the `shuffle` capabilities, we can now do so using the approach we had initially desired:

```
let numbers = [1, 2, 3, 4, 5, 6, 7, 8, 9, 10];
numbers.shuffle();
```

Best of all, any new arrays we create will also have access to the shuffle functionality by default thanks to how prototype inheritance works.

Extending Built-in Objects is Controversial

Given how easy it is to extend a built-in object's functionality by declaring methods and properties using the `prototype` property, it's easy to think that everybody loves the ability to do all of this. As it turns out, extending built-in objects is a bit controversial. The reasons for this controversy revolve around...

You Don't Control the Built-in Object's Future

There is nothing preventing a future implementation of JavaScript from including its own version of shuffle that applies to `Array` objects. At this point, you have a collision where your version of `shuffle` and the browser's version of `shuffle` are in conflict with each other—especially if their behavior or performance characteristics wildly differ. Ruh-roh!

Some Functionality Should Not Be Extended or Overridden

Nothing prevents you from using what you've learned here to modify the behavior of existing methods and properties. For example, this is me changing how the `slice` behavior works:

```
Array.prototype.slice = function () {
  let input = this;
  input[0] = "This is an awesome example!";

. return input;
}

let tempArray = [1, 2, 3, 4, 5, 6, 7, 8, 9, 10]
tempArray.slice();

// and the result is...
console.log(tempArray);
```

While this is a terrible example, this does show how easy it was for me to break existing functionality.

FURTHER READING

To see a more comprehensive discussion and further reading around this controversy, check out this StackOverflow thread: **http://stackoverflow.com/questions/8859828/**.

THE ABSOLUTE MINIMUM: WHAT SHOULD YOU DO?

My answer to what you need to do is simple: **Use your best judgment!** The two cases I outlined are only a few of the numerous issues that people raise when extending built-in objects is discussed. For the most part, all of the objections are valid. The question you need to ask is, "Are these objections valid for my particular scenario?" My guess is that they probably won't be.

From personal experience, I have never had any issues extending built-in objects with my own functionality. I wrote this shuffle function years ago, and no browser as of now has even hinted at implementing their own version of it. I am certainly not complaining! Second, for any functionality I do add, I test to make sure that it works well across the browsers I am currently targeting. As long as your testing is somewhat comprehensive (probably the latest one or two versions of the major browsers), you should be good to go.

If you are worried about future-proofing your app, name any properties or methods in such a way that only your app would use them. For example, the chances of `Array.prototype.kirupaShuffle` being introduced by any future browser release is pretty close to zero. :P

Anyway, now that we've sufficiently covered some detailed topics around objects in this and the previous chapters, let's go back to looking at some of the other types you will run into before we move on to some really exciting stuff in a little bit.

If you have any questions about extending objects or anything about life in general, post on the forums at **https://forum.kirupa.com**.

USING CLASSES

When it comes to working with objects, we have covered a lot of ground so far. We saw how to create them, we learned about prototypical inheritance, and we even looked at the dark art of extending objects as well. In doing all of this, we worked at a very low level and were exposed to how the object-flavored sausage is made. That's great for really understanding what is going on. That's not so great when making sense of complex object happenings in your app. To simplify all of this, with the ES6 version of JavaScript, you have support for this thing called **classes**.

Those of you with a background in other object-oriented programming languages are probably familiar with that term. Don't worry if you are not. In the world of JavaScript, classes are nothing special. They are nothing more than just a handful of new keywords and conventions that *simplify what we have to type* when working with objects. In the following sections, we'll get a taste of what all that means.

Onward!

The Class Syntax and Object Creation

We are going to learn about the class syntax the same way our grandparents did—by writing code. Because there is a lot of ground to cover, we won't try to bite off everything at once. We'll start by focusing on how to use the class syntax when creating objects. As you'll see, there is a lot going on there that will keep us plenty busy!

Creating an Object

You can think of a class as a template—a template objects refer to when they are being created. Let's say that we want to create a new class called **Planet**. The most basic version of that class will look as follows:

```
class Planet {


}
```

We use a keyword called `class` followed by the name we want to give our class. The body of our class will live inside curly brackets, { and }. As you can see, our class is currently empty. That's not very exciting, but it is OK for now. We want to start off simple.

To create an object based on this class, all you need to do is the following:

```
let myPlanet = new Planet();
```

We declare the name of our object and use the `new` keyword to create (aka instantiate) our object based on the `Planet` class. If we had to visualize what is happening under the hood, Figure 20.1 shows what you would see:

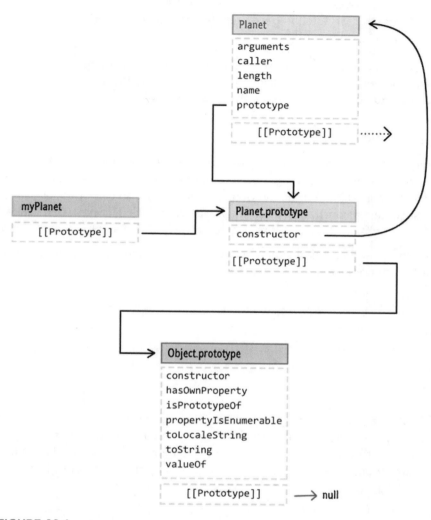

FIGURE 20.1

What myPlanet is made up of behind the scenes.

This looks a bit different from what we saw when creating objects using Object. create(). The difference has to do with us creating our myPlanet object by using the new keyword. When we create objects with the new keyword, the following things happen:

1. Our new object is simply of type **Planet**.

2. Our new object's [[Prototype]] is our *new* function or class's prototype property.

3. A constructor function gets executed that deals with initializing our newly created object

I won't bore you too much with additional details, but there is one important thing that we are going to dive into further. That thing deals with the so-called **constructor** that we mentioned in the 3rd item above.

Meet the Constructor

The constructor is a function (or method) that lives inside your class's body. It is responsible for initializing the newly created object, and it does that by running any code contained inside it during object creation. This isn't an optional detail. All classes must contain a constructor function. If your class doesn't contain one (kinda like our `Planet` right now), JavaScript will automatically create an empty constructor for you.

Let's go ahead and define a constructor for our `Planet` class. Take a look at the following modification:

```
class Planet {
  constructor(name, radius) {
    this.name = name;
    this.radius = radius;
  }
}
```

To define a constructor, we use a special `constructor` keyword to create what is basically a function. Just like a function, you can also specify any arguments you would like to use. In our case, we specify a **name** and **radius** value as arguments and use them to set the name and radius properties on our object:

```
class Planet {
  constructor(name, radius) {
    this.name = name;
    this.radius = radius;
  }
}
```

You can definitely do a lot more (or a lot less!) interesting things from inside your constructor, but the main thing to keep in mind is that this code will run every single time we are creating a new object using our `Planet` class. Speaking of which, here is how you call our `Planet` class to create an object:

```
let myPlanet = new Planet("Earth", 6378);
console.log(myPlanet.name); // Earth
```

Notice that the two arguments we need to set on our constructor are actually set directly on the `Planet` class itself. When our `myPlanet` object gets created, the constructor is run and the **name** and **radius** values we passed in get set on our object. Figure 20.2 shows what this looks like.

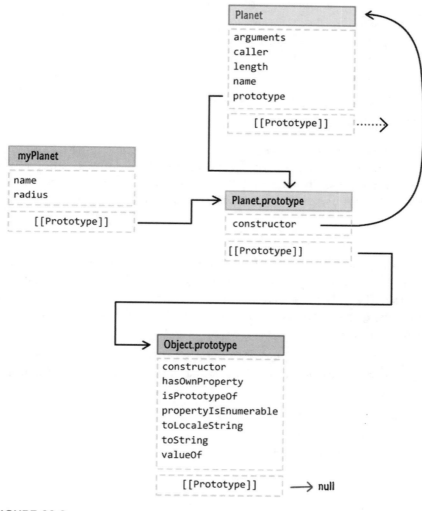

FIGURE 20.2

We can see our `myPlanet` object containing the `name` and `radius` properties.

While we are learning about the `class` syntax and the details surrounding it, never forget that all of this is just frosting—delicious syntactic sugar designed to make your life easy. If we didn't use the `class` syntax, we could also have done something like this:

```
function Planet(name, radius) {
  this.name = name;
  this.radius = radius;
};


let myPlanet = new Planet("Earth", 6378);
console.log(myPlanet.name); // Earth
```

The end result is almost identical to what we gained with the `class` syntax. How we got there is the only thing that is different. Don't let this comparison give you the wrong impression, though. Other useful uses of the `class` syntax won't be as easy to convert using the more traditional approaches as we've seen here.

What Goes Inside the Class

Our class objects look a lot like functions, but they have some quirks. We saw that one of the things that goes into the body of your class is this special constructor function. The only other things that can go inside your class are other **functions/ methods**, **getters**, and **setters**. That's it. No variable declarations and initializations are welcome.

To see all of this at work, let's add a `getSurfaceArea` function that prints the surface area of our planet to the console. Go ahead and make the following change:

```
class Planet {
  constructor(name, radius) {
    this.name = name;
    this.radius = radius;
  }

  getSurfaceArea() {
    let surfaceArea = 4 * Math.PI * Math.pow(this.radius, 2);
    console.log(surfaceArea + " square km!");
    return surfaceArea;
  }
}
```

You call getSurfaceArea off our created object to see it in action:

```
let earth = new Planet("Earth", 6378);
earth.getSurfaceArea();
```

When this code runs, you'll see something like 511 million square kilometers printed out. That's good. Since we mentioned the other things that can go inside our class body are getters and setters, let's throw those in as well. We'll use them to help us represent our planet's gravity:

```
class Planet {
  constructor(name, radius) {
    this.name = name;
    this.radius = radius;
  }

  getSurfaceArea() {
    let surfaceArea = 4 * Math.PI * Math.pow(this.radius, 2);
    console.log(surfaceArea + " square km!");
    return surfaceArea;
  }

  set gravity(value) {
    console.log("Setting value!");
    this._gravity = value;
  }

  get gravity() {
    console.log("Getting value!");
    return this._gravity;
  }
}

let earth = new Planet("Earth", 6378);
earth.gravity = 9.81;
earth.getSurfaceArea();

console.log(earth.gravity) // 9.81
```

That's all there is to it. One cool thing about adding these things to our class body is that they all **will not live on the created object**. They will live on the prototype (Planet.prototype) instead, as shown by Figure 20.3.

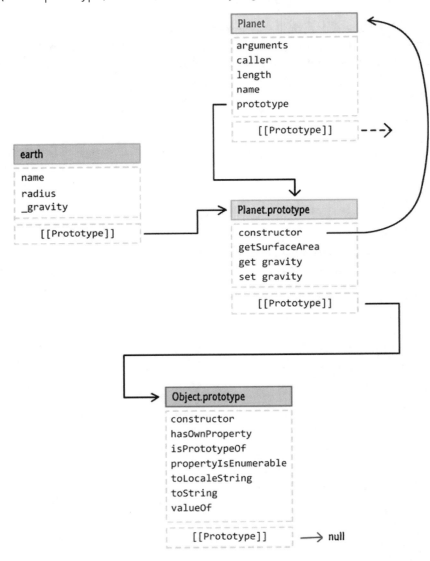

FIGURE 20.3

We don't have to do anything special to target the prototype object.

That is a good thing, for we don't want every object to unnecessarily carry around a copy of the class's internals when a shared instance would work just fine! Given that, you can see that represented in the above diagram. Our `gravity` getter and setter along with our `getSurfaceArea` function live entirely on our prototype!

WHY DO THE FUNCTIONS INSIDE MY CLASS LOOK WEIRD?

One thing you may have noticed is that the appearance of our functions inside the class body looks a bit odd. They are missing the `function` keyword, for example. That weirdness (for once) is actually not related to classes. When defining functions inside an object, you have a shorthand syntax you can use.

Instead of writing something like this:

```
let blah = {
  zorb: function() {
    // something interesting
  }
};
```

You can abbreviate the `zorb` function definition as follows:

```
let blah = {
  zorb() {
    // something interesting
  }
};
```

It is this abbreviated form that you will see and use when specifying functions inside your class body.

Extending Objects

The last thing we will look at has to do with extending objects in this class-based world. To help with this, we are going to be working with a whole new type of planet known as the **Potato Planet**.

The Potato Planet

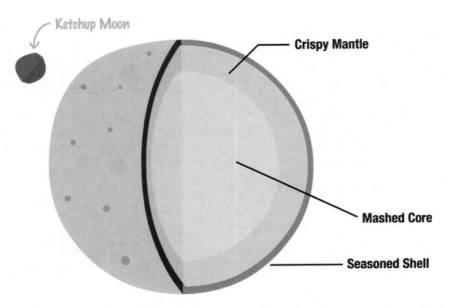

Ketchup Moon

Crispy Mantle

Mashed Core

Seasoned Shell

A potato planet contains everything a regular planet brings to the table, but a potato planet is made up entirely of potatoes...as opposed to the silly molten rocks and gas that the other planets are made up of. What we are going to do is define our potato planet as a class. Its functionality will largely mirror that of the `Planet` class, but we will have some additional doodads like a `potatoType` argument in the constructor and the `getPotatoType` method that prints to the console the value of `potatoType`.

A not-so-good approach would be to define our potato planet class as follows:

```
class PotatoPlanet {
  constructor(name, radius, potatoType) {
    this.name = name;
    this.radius = radius;
    this.potatoType = potatoType;
  }

  getSurfaceArea() {
    let surfaceArea = 4 * Math.PI * Math.pow(this.radius, 2);
    console.log(surfaceArea + " square km!");
```

```
      return surfaceArea;
  }


  getPotatoType() {
    var thePotato = this.potatoType.toUpperCase() + "!!1!!!";
    console.log(thePotato);
    return thePotato;
  }


  set gravity(value) {
    console.log("Setting value!");
    this._gravity = value;
  }


  get gravity() {
    return this._gravity;
  }
}
```

We have our `PotatoPlanet` class, and it contains not just the new potato-related things but it also all of the functionality our `Planet` class had as well. This approach isn't great because we are duplicating code. Now, instead of duplicating our code, what if we had a way of extending the functionality our `Planet` class provides with the few additional pieces of functionality that our `PotatoPlanet` would need? Wouldn't that be a better approach? Well...as luck would have it, we do have such a way via the `extends` keyword. By having our `PotatoPlanet` class extend our `Planet` class, we can do something like the following:

```
class Planet {
  constructor(name, radius) {
    this.name = name;
    this.radius = radius;
  }


  getSurfaceArea() {
    let surfaceArea = 4 * Math.PI * Math.pow(this.radius, 2);
    console.log(surfaceArea + " square km!");
    return surfaceArea;
  }
```

```
  set gravity(value) {
    console.log("Setting value!");
    this._gravity = value;
  }

  get gravity() {
    return this._gravity;
  }
}
```

```
class PotatoPlanet extends Planet {
  constructor(name, width, potatoType) {
    super(name, width);

    this.potatoType = potatoType;
  }

  getPotatoType() {
    let thePotato = this.potatoType.toUpperCase() + "!!1!!!";
    console.log(thePotato);
    return thePotato;
  }
}
```

Notice how we are declaring our `PotatoPlanet` class. We are using the
extends keyword and specifying the class we will be extending from, which is
`Planet`:

```
class PotatoPlanet extends Planet {
  .
  .
  .

}
```

From there, the other thing to keep in mind has to do with the `constructor`. If we are going to be extending a class without needing to modify the constructor, we can totally skip specifying the constructor inside our class:

```
class PotatoPlanet extends Planet {
  sayHello() {
    console.log("Hello!");
  }
}
```

In our case, since we are modifying what the constructor does by adding a property for the type of potato, we define our constructor again with one important addition:

```
class PotatoPlanet extends Planet {
  constructor(name, width) {
    super(name, width);

    this.potatoType = potatoType;
  }

  getPotatoType() {
    var thePotato = this.potatoType.toUpperCase() + "!!1!!!";
    console.log(thePotato);
    return thePotato;
  }
}
```

We make an explicit call to the parent (`Planet`) constructor by using the `super` keyword and passing in the relevant arguments needed. This `super` call ensures that whatever the `Planet` part of our object needs as part of its functioning is triggered.

To use our `PotatoPlanet`, we would create our object and populate its properties or call methods on it just like we would for any plain, non-extended object. Here is an example of us creating an object of type `PotatoPlanet` appropriately called spudnik:

```
let spudnik = new PotatoPlanet("Spudnik", 12411, "Russet");
spudnik.gravity = 42.1;
spudnik.getPotatoType();
```

The cool thing is that spudnik has access to not only functionality we defined as part of our `PotatoPlanet` class, but all of the functionality provided by the

`Planet` class we are extending is also available as well. We can see why that is the case by revisiting a more complex version of our prototype/object relationship diagram as seen in Figure 20.4.

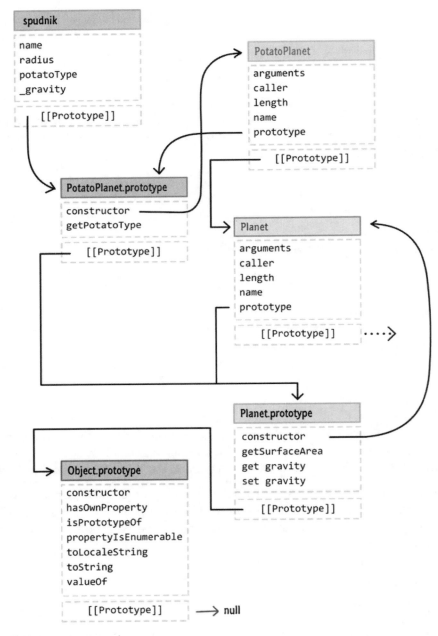

FIGURE 20.4

What extending an object looks like.

If we follow the prototype chain, we go from our `spudnik` object to the `PotatoPlanet.prototype` to `Planet.prototype` to, finally, `Object.prototype`. Our `spudnik` object has access to any property or method defined at any of these prototype stops, which is why it can call things on `Object` or on `Planet` without skipping a beat even though `PotatoPlanet` doesn't define a whole lot on its own. This is the powerful awesomeness of extending objects.

THE ABSOLUTE MINIMUM

The class syntax makes working with objects really easy. You may have caught some glimpses of that here, but you'll start to see more of it later on. The thing about the class syntax is that it allows us to focus more on what we want to do as opposed to fiddling with how exactly to do it. While working with `Object.create` and the `prototype` properties gave us a lot of control, that control was often unnecessary for the majority of our cases. By working with classes, we trade complexity in favor of simplicity. That's not a bad thing when the simple solution also turns out to be the right one...most of the time!

Got a question? Don't wait. Post on **https://forum.kirupa.com**.

IN THIS CHAPTER

- Learn more about what goes on behind *true* and *false*
- Understand what boolean objects and functions do
- Find out the difference between *simple* inequality operators and *strict* inequality operators

21

BOOLEANS AND THE STRICTER === AND !== OPERATORS

While it's polite to say that all types are interesting and fun to be around, you and I both know that is a lie. Some types are just boring. The boolean type is one such example. Here is the reason why. Whenever we initialize a variable using either **true** or **false**, we create a boolean:

```
let sunny = false;
let traffic = true;
```

Congratulations. If you just know this, you are 80% of the way there in fully understanding how booleans operate. Of course, 80% isn't really adequate when you think about it. It's like eating a hot dog without any condiments. It's like watching a live concert and leaving before the encore set. It's like leaving a sentence mid.

What we are going to expand upon a bit here is the other 20% made up of various boolean quirks, the `Boolean` object, the `Boolean` function, and the important === and !== operators.

Onward!

The Boolean Object

Booleans are meant to be used as primitives. I'm going to be extra lazy and just reuse the example you saw a few moments earlier to show you an example of what a Boolean primitive would look like:

```
let sunny = false;
let traffic = true;
```

Like you've seen so many times already, behind every primitive there is an Object based representation lurking in the shadows. The way you create a new Boolean object is by using the new keyword, the Boolean constructor name, and an initial value:

```
let boolObject = new Boolean(false);
let anotherBool = new Boolean(true);
```

The initial value you can pass in to the Boolean constructor is commonly **true** and **false**, but you can pretty much pass anything in there that will result in the final evaluation being **true** or **false**. I will detail what kinds of values will predictably result in a **true** or **false** outcome in a little bit, but here is the obligatory warning from the Surgeon General about this approach: *Unless you really REALLY want a Boolean object, you should stick with primitives.*

The Boolean Function

There is one major advantage the Boolean constructor provides, and that advantage revolves around being able to pass in any arbitrary value or expression as part of creating your Boolean object:

```
let boolObject = new Boolean(< arbitrary expression >);
```

This is really advantageous because you may find yourself wanting to evaluate a Boolean expression where the data you end up with isn't a clean **true** or a **false**. This is especially common when you are dealing with external data or code, and you have no control over which of the various false-y or true-y values you get. Here is a contrived example:

```
let isMovieAvailable = getMovieData()[4];
```

The value for isMovieAvailable is probably a **true** or **false**. When it comes to processing data, you often have no guarantee that something at some point will break or change what gets returned. Just like in real life, simply hoping that things will work is never adequate without you taking some actionable steps. The Boolean function is one such step.

Now, creating your own function to deal with the ambiguity may be overkill, but the downside with the `Boolean` constructor is that you are obviously left with a boolean object—which isn't desirable. Fortunately, there is a way to get the flexibility of the `Boolean` constructor with the lightweightness of a Boolean primitive extremely easily. That way is led by the `Boolean` function:

```
let bool = Boolean(true);
```

The Boolean function allows you to pass in arbitrary values and expressions while still returning a **primitive boolean value of true or false**. The main difference in how you use it compared to the constructor approach is that you don't have the new keyword. W00t! Anyway, let's take a few moments and look at the variety of things you can pass in to the Boolean function, and note that all of this will also apply to what you can pass in to the Boolean constructor you saw in the previous section as well.

The values you can pass in to return **false** are `null`, `undefined`, empty/nothing, **0**, an empty string, and (of course) **false**:

```
let bool;


bool = Boolean(null);
bool = Boolean(undefined);
bool = Boolean();
bool = Boolean(0);
bool = Boolean("");
bool = Boolean(false);
```

In all of these examples, the `bool` variable will return **false**. To return **true**, we can pass in a value of **true** or ANYTHING that results in something other than the various **false** values we saw earlier:

```
let bool;


bool = Boolean(true);
bool = Boolean("hello");
bool = Boolean(new Boolean()); // Inception!!!
bool = Boolean("false"); // "false" is a string
bool = Boolean({});
bool = Boolean(3.14);
bool = Boolean(["a", "b", "c"]);
```

In these examples, the `bool` variable will return a **true**. That may seem bizarre given some of the statements, so let's look at a few of the subtle things in play here. If what we are evaluating is an object, such as `new Boolean(new Boolean())` the evaluation will always be **true**. The reason is that the mere existence of an object will trigger the **true** switch, and calling `new Boolean()` results in a new object. Extending this logic a bit, it means the following `if` statement actually results in a **true** as well:

```
let boolObject = new Boolean(false);

if (boolObject) {
  console.log("Bool, you so crazy!!!");
}
```

It doesn't matter that the object we are evaluating is secretly a **false** in disguise... or a `String` object or an `Array` and so on. The rules for primitives are simpler. If we are passing in a primitive (or something that evaluates to a primitive), anything other than `null`, `undefined`, **0**, an empty string, NaN, or **false** will result in a result of **true**.

Strict Equality and Inequality Operators

The last thing we are going to look at is going to combine what we know about types and booleans to add a twist to the various conditional operators we saw earlier. So, we know about `==` and `!=` and have probably seen them in use a few times. These are the equality and inequality operators that let us know if two things are either equal or unequal. Here is the plot twist. There is a subtle and deviant behavior they exhibit that we may not be aware of.

Here is an example:

```
function theSolution(answer) {
  if (answer == 42) {
    console.log("You have nothing more to learn!");
  }
}


theSolution("42"); //42 is passed in as a string
```

In this example, the expression **answer == 42** will evaluate to `true`. This works despite the 42 we passed in being a string and the 42 we are checking against being a number. What is going on here? In what kind of a world is a string and a number equal? With the == and != operators, this is expected behavior. The value for the two things you are comparing is **42**. To make this work, JavaScript forces the two different yet similar values to be the same under the hood. This is formally known as **type coercion.**

The problem is that this behavior can be undesirable—especially when this is happening without us knowing about it. To avoid situations like this, we have stricter versions of the equality and inequality operators, and they are === and !== respectively. What these operators do is that they check for **both value and type** and do not perform any type coercion. They basically force us to write code where the burden on ensuring true equality or inequality falls squarely on us. That is a good thing.

Let's fix our earlier example by replacing the == operator with the === operator:

```
function theSolution(answer) {

  if (answer === 42) {

    console.log("You have nothing more to learn!");

  }

}


theSolution("42"); //42 is passed in as a string
```

This time around, the conditional expression will evaluate to **false**. In this stricter world, a string and number are of different types despite the values being similar. Because no type coercion takes place, the final result is **false**.

The general word on the street is to *always use the stricter forms of the equality and inequality operators*. If anything, using them will help us to spot errors in our code—errors that might otherwise turn out very difficult to identify.

CAUTION If we are comparing two *different* objects, the strict equality operator (and the not-so-strict equality operator) won't work as we might expect. For example, all of these cases below will be false:

```
console.log(new String("A") == new String("A"));

console.log([1, 2, 3] == [1, 2, 3]);

console.log({ a: 1 } == { a: 1 });
```

Keep that in mind when comparing the equality or inequality of two separate, individual objects.

THE ABSOLUTE MINIMUM

Booleans make up one of the most frequently used types in our code. They play a key role in allowing our code to branch out into different directions despite the simplicity they exhibit on the surface. While I can count on one hand the number of times I had to use the `Boolean` function or even the stricter equality and inequality operators, there aren't enough hands with fingers for me to count the number of times I've encountered these strange things in the wild.

If you have any questions, head on over to **https://forum.kirupa.com** and ask away!

22

NULL AND UNDEFINED

One of the great mysteries of the world revolves around making sense of `null` and `undefined`. Most code you see is littered with them, and you've probably run into them yourself a few times. As mysteries go, making sense of `null` and `undefined` isn't particularly bizarre. It is just dreadfully boring...like the most boring (yet important) thing about JavaScript you'll ever have to learn.

Onward!

Null

Let's start with `null`. The `null` keyword is a primitive that fills a special role in the world of JavaScript. It is an explicit definition that stands for **no value**. If you've ever browsed through code others have written, you'll probably see `null` appear quite a number of times. It is quite popular, for the advantage of `null` lies in its definitiveness. Instead of having variables contain stale values or mystery unde- fined values, setting it to `null` is a clear indication that you **want the value to not exist**.

This advantage is important when you are writing code and want to initialize or clear a variable to something that represents nothing.

Here is an example:

```
let name = null;


if (name === null) {
    name = "Peter Griffin";
} else {
    name = "No name";
}
```

The `null` primitive isn't a naturally occurring resource. It is something you con- sciously assign, so you will often see it used as part of variable declarations or passed in as arguments to function calls. Using `null` is easy. Checking for its exis- tence is pretty easy as well:

```
if (name === null) {
  // do something interesting...or not
}
```

The only thing to note is that you should use the `===` operator instead of the lowly `==` one. While the world won't end if you use `==`, it's good practice to check for both type and value when working with null.

Undefined

Here is where things get a little interesting. To represent something that isn't defined, you have the `undefined` primitive. You see undefined in a few cases. The most common ones are when you try to access a variable that hasn't been initialized or when accessing the value of a function that doesn't actually return anything.

Here is a code snippet that points out `undefined` in a few of its natural habitats:

```
let myVariable;
console.log(myVariable); // undefined

function doNothing() {
   // watch paint dry
   return;
}

let weekendPlans = doNothing();
console.log(weekendPlans); // undefined

let person = {
  firstName: "Isaac",
  lastName: "Newton"
}
console.log(person.title); // undefined
```

In your code, you probably won't be assigning `undefined` to anything. Instead, you will spend time checking to see if the value of something is `undefined`. You have several ways to perform this check. The first is a naive way that usually almost always works:

```
if (myVariable === undefined) {
  // do something
}
```

The downside of this approach has to do with what `undefined` actually is. Brace yourself—`undefined` is a global variable that happens to be automatically defined for us, and this means we can potentially overwrite it to something like **true** or whatever else we want to set it to. If `undefined` ever gets overwritten, it would break our code if we just check with a `===` or `==` even. To avoid any shenanigans around this, the safest way to perform a check for `undefined` involves `typeof` and the `===` operator:

```
let myVariable;

if (typeof myVariable === "undefined") {
    console.log("Define me!!!");
}
```

This ensures that you will perform a check for `undefined` and always return the correct answer.

NULL == UNDEFINED, BUT NULL !== UNDEFINED

Continuing the `==` and `===` weirdness, if you ever check for `null  ==` `undefined`, the answer will be a **true**. If you use `===` and have `null  ===` `undefined`, the answer in this case will be **false**.

The reason is that `==` does type coercion where it arm-twists types to conform to what JavaScript thinks the value should be. Using `===`, you check for both type and value. This is a more comprehensive check that detects that `undefined` and `null` are indeed two different things.

A hat tip to senocular (aka Trevor McCauley) for pointing this out!

THE ABSOLUTE MINIMUM

There is a reason why I saved these built-in types for last. `Null` and `undefined` are the least exciting of the bunch, but they are also often the ones that are the most misunderstood. Knowing how to use `null` and detecting for it and `undefined` are very important skills to get right. Not getting them right will lead to very subtle errors that are going to be hard to pinpoint.

If you have any questions about `null` and `undefined` or just want to talk to some of the friendliest developers on the planet to get unblocked, post on **https://forum.kirupa.com**.

IN THIS CHAPTER

- Understand anonymous functions
- Learn how to invoke a block of code immediately
- Take our knowledge of scope further by creating data that is private

23

ALL ABOUT JSON (AKA JAVASCRIPT OBJECT NOTATION)

When it comes to storing, retrieving, or transmitting data, there are a bunch of file formats and data structures that you can use. You've probably used text files, Word documents, Excel spreadsheets, zip files, and so on to deal with the various kinds of data you handle. On the web front, there is one format that reigns supreme over all others. It runs faster. It jumps higher. It has a shinier (and furrier) coat of fur. That format is known as **JSON**—short for **JavaScript Object Notation**.

In this article, we are going to learn all about what makes JSON objects awesome. We'll look in detail at what goes inside them and how you can read values from them as part of your own implementations.

Onward!

What Is JSON?

In JavaScript, you have a way of defining objects using the object literal syntax:

```
let funnyGuy = {
  firstName: "Conan",
  lastName: "O'Brien",

  getName: function () {
    return "Name is: " + this.firstName + " " + this.lastName;
  }
};

let theDude = {
  firstName: "Jeffrey",
  lastName: "Lebowski",

  getName: function () {
    return "Name is: " + this.firstName + " " + this.lastName;
  }
};

let detective = {
  firstName: "Adrian",
  lastName: "Monk",

  getName: function () {
    return "Name is: " + this.firstName + " " + this.lastName;
  }
};
```

If you aren't familiar with this syntax, I highly recommend you read more about it in the **Deeper Look at Objects article**. It will make understanding and working with JSON objects significantly easier!

On the surface, the object literal syntax looks like a bunch of brackets and colons and weird curly braces that define your object's properties and values. Despite how weird it looks, under the covers, it is fairly descriptive. Many of the common data types you would want to use are available. You can neatly represent their properties and values as key and value pairs separated by a colon. Equally important as all the other stuff I just mentioned, this syntax allows you to have structure and nested values. Overall, it is a pretty sweet way of representing JavaScript objects...in a literal representation!

The JSON format borrows heavily from this object literal syntax. Here is an example of some honest-to-goodness real JSON data returned by the WeatherUnderground API for displaying the weather in my hometown of Seattle:

```
{
  "response": {
    "version": "0.1",
    "termsofService":
"http://www.wunderground.com/weather/api/d/terms.html",
    "features": {
      "conditions": 1
    }
  },
  "current_observation": {
    "image": {
      "url": "http://icons.wxug.com/graphics/wu2/logo_130x80.png",
      "title": "Weather Underground",
      "link": "http://www.wunderground.com"
    },
    "display_location": {
      "full": "Seattle, WA",
      "city": "Seattle",
      "state": "WA",
      "state_name": "Washington",
      "country": "US",
      "country_iso3166": "US",
      "zip": "98101",
      "magic": "1",
      "wmo": "99999",
      "latitude": "47.61167908",
      "longitude": "-122.33325958",
      "elevation": "63.00000000"
    },
```

```
"observation_location": {
  "full": "Herrera, Inc., Seattle, Washington",
  "city": "Herrera, Inc., Seattle",
  "state": "Washington",
  "country": "US",
  "country_iso3166": "US",
  "latitude": "47.616558",
  "longitude": "-122.341240",
  "elevation": "121 ft"
},
"estimated": {},
"station_id": "KWASEATT187",
"observation_time": "Last Updated on August 28, 9:28 PM PDT",
"observation_time_rfc822": "Fri, 28 Aug 2015 21:28:12 -0700",
"observation_epoch": "1440822492",
"local_time_rfc822": "Fri, 28 Aug 2015 21:28:45 -0700",
"local_epoch": "1440822525",
"local_tz_short": "PDT",
"local_tz_long": "America/Los_Angeles",
"local_tz_offset": "-0700",
"weather": "Overcast",
"temperature_string": "68.0 F (20.0 C)",
"temp_f": 68.0,
"temp_c": 20.0,
"relative_humidity": "71%",
"wind_string": "Calm",
"wind_dir": "NNW",
"wind_degrees": 331,
"wind_mph": 0.0,
"wind_gust_mph": "10.0",
"wind_kph": 0,
"wind_gust_kph": "16.1",
"pressure_mb": "1008",
"pressure_in": "29.78",
"pressure_trend": "-",
```

```
    "dewpoint_string": "58 F (15 C)",
    "dewpoint_f": 58,
    "dewpoint_c": 15,
    "heat_index_string": "NA",
    "heat_index_f": "NA",
    "heat_index_c": "NA",
    "windchill_string": "NA",
    "windchill_f": "NA",
    "windchill_c": "NA",
    "feelslike_string": "68.0 F (20.0 C)",
    "feelslike_f": "68.0",
    "feelslike_c": "20.0",
    "visibility_mi": "10.0",
    "visibility_km": "16.1",
    "solarradiation": "--",
    "UV": "0",
    "precip_1hr_string": "0.00 in ( 0 mm)",
    "precip_1hr_in": "0.00",
    "precip_1hr_metric": " 0",
    "precip_today_string": "0.00 in (0 mm)",
    "precip_today_in": "0.00",
    "precip_today_metric": "0",
    "icon": "cloudy",
    "icon_url": "http://icons.wxug.com/i/c/k/nt_cloudy.gif",
    "nowcast": ""
  }
}
```

Ignoring the size of the data returned, there are a lot of similarities between the JSON data you see and the object literal syntax you saw earlier. There are some major differences that you need to be aware of as well, but we'll look at all that boring stuff later. First, let's take a deeper look at what exactly makes up a JSON object.

Looking Inside a JSON Object

A JSON object is nothing more than a combination of property names and their values. That seems pretty simple, but there are some important details that we need to go over in this section.

Property Names

Property names are the identifiers you will use to access a value. Visually, they are the things to the left of the colon character:

```
{
  "firstName": "Kirupa",
  "lastName": "Chinnathambi",
  "special": {
    "admin": true,
    "userID": 203
  },
  "devices": [
    {
      "type": "laptop",
      "model": "Macbook Pro 2015"
    },
    {
      "type": "phone",
      "model": "iPhone 6"
    }
  ]
}
```

In this JSON snippet, the property names are **firstName**, **lastName**, **special**, **admin**, **userID**, **devices**, **type**, and **model**. Notice how the property names are defined. They are string values wrapped in quotation marks. The quotation mark is an important detail that you don't have to specify in the object literal case for property names, so don't forget to include them when working in the JSON world!

The Values

Each property name maps to a value, and the types of values you can have are:

- Numbers
- Strings
- Booleans (**true** or **false**)
- Objects
- Arrays
- Null

Let's map these various types to the example we just looked at earlier.

Strings

The string values are the following highlighted lines:

```
{
  "firstName": "Kirupa",
  "lastName": "Chinnathambi",
  "special": {
    "admin": true,
    "userID": 203
  },
  "devices": [
    {
      "type": "laptop",
      "model": "Macbook Pro"
    },
    {
      "type": "phone",
      "model": "iPhone XS"
    }
  ]
}
```

The double quotation marks are a dead giveaway that these values are strings. Besides your usual letters and numbers and symbols, you can also include **escape characters** like \', \", \\, V, and so on to define characters in your string that would otherwise get parsed as some JSON operation.

Numbers

Our lone representative of the number family is the value for the `userID` property:

```
{
  "firstName": "Kirupa",
  "lastName": "Chinnathambi",
  "special": {
    "admin": true,
    "userID": 203
  },
  "devices": [
    {
      "type": "laptop",
      "model": "Macbook Pro"
    },
    {
      "type": "phone",
      "model": "iPhone XS"
    }
  ]
}
```

You can specify both decimal values (eg: **0.204**, **1200.23**, **45**) as well as exponential values (**2e16**, **3e+4**, **1.5e-2**). There are some quirks you need to be aware of, though. You can't prefix your number with a 0 followed by another number. For example, a value of **03.14** isn't allowed.

Booleans

Boolean values are easy:

```
{
  "firstName": "Kirupa",
  "lastName": "Chinnathambi",
  "special": {
    "admin": true,
    "userID": 203
  },
  "devices": [
```

```
  {
    "type": "laptop",
    "model": "Macbook Pro"
  },
  {
    "type": "phone",
    "model": "iPhone XS"
  }
  ]
}
```

The values can either be **true** or **false**. One thing to note—the capitalization is important. Both **true** and **false** have to be lowercase. Using sentence casing (**True** or **False**) or going with all caps (**TRUE** or **FALSE**) is forbidden.

Objects

This is where things get a little interesting:

```
{
  "firstName": "Kirupa",
  "lastName": "Chinnathambi",
  "special": {
    "admin": true,
    "userID": 203
  },
  "devices": [
    {
      "type": "laptop",
      "model": "Macbook Pro"
    },
    {
      "type": "phone",
      "model": "iPhone XS"
    }
  ]
}
```

Objects contain a collection of property names and values, and they are separated from the rest of your content with curly brackets. See? Wasn't that a *little* interesting?

Arrays

Our `devices` property represents an array:

```
{
  "firstName": "Kirupa",
  "lastName": "Chinnathambi",
  "special": {
    "admin": true,
    "userID": 203
  },
  "devices": [
    {
      "type": "laptop",
      "model": "Macbook Pro"
    },
    {
      "type": "phone",
      "model": "iPhone XS"
    }
  ]
}
```

Arrays store an ordered collection of zero or more values that you can iterate through, and they are separated by the bracket notation. Inside an array, you can use any of the JSON types we've seen so far...including other arrays!

Null

The last data type is also the most boring one:

```
{
  "foo": null
}
```

Your JSON values can be **null**. This represents an empty value.

Reading JSON Data

I admit it. The previous section was extremely dull, but there is some good news! Given how boring what you just saw was, this section is by comparison going to seem a whole lot more exciting than it really is. Yay!

Anyway, almost all your interactions with JSON will revolve around reading data. When it comes to reading JSON data, the main thing to keep in mind is that it is very similar to reading values stored inside a typical JavaScript Object. You can either dot into the value you want (property.propertyFoo) or you can use the array approach (property["propertyFoo"]) and access the value that way.

To help explain all this, let's use the following example:

```
let exampleJSON = {
  "firstName": "Kirupa",
  "lastName": "Chinnathambi",
  "special": {
    "admin": true,
    "userID": 203
  },
  "devices": [
    {
      "type": "laptop",
      "model": "Macbook Pro"
    },
    {
      "type": "phone",
      "model": "iPhone XS"
    }
  ]
};
```

To read the value stored by firstName, you can do either of the following:

```
exampleJSON.firstName;
exampleJSON["firstName"];
```

Both lines will return a value of **Kirupa**. There is no right or wrong answer to whether you want to use the dot notation approach or the array approach to access the value you are interested in. Use whatever you are comfortable with, but my personal preference is to use dot notation. Passing in property names as strings makes me queasy, so I will only highlight the dot notation approach in the code snippets that you will be seeing.

Similar to what you saw earlier, to access the value stored by `lastName`, you can do this:

```
exampleJSON.lastName;
```

For simple properties that store simple values, life is pretty simple. The only very VERY minor complication you'll run into is when working with more complex values made up of Objects and Arrays. To read a value stored inside an Object, just keep dotting into each property until you reach the property that stores the value you are interested in.

Here is what trying to access the value stored by the `userID` property will look like:

```
exampleJSON.special.userID;
```

Arrays are no different, but you will eventually have to switch into array notation once you get to the property that stores your array values. If we wanted to access the `model` value of the first device in the `devices` array, we can type something that looks as follows:

```
exampleJSON.devices[0].model;
```

Because the `devices` property refers to an array, you can also perform stereotypical array-like operations such as the following:

```
let devicesArray = exampleJSON.devices;

for (let i = 0; i < devicesArray.length; i++) {
  let type = devicesArray[i].type;
  let model = devicesArray[i].model;

  // do something interesting with this data!
}
```

To reiterate what you saw in the previous section, your JSON values can be either strings, numbers, objects, arrays, booleans, or nulls. Everything that JavaScript supports for a given data type that you encounter inside your JSON object, you can easily take advantage of.

Parsing JSON-looking Data into Actual JSON

In our example, we had our JSON data defined neatly inside the `exampleJSON` variable. There is no doubt in anybody's mind that what we're dealing with is a real JS object that is represented using JSON semantics.

With real-world scenarios, that won't always be the case. Your JSON data could be coming from a variety of different sources, and not all of them will return the JSON data into this workable format that we saw. Many will return JSON data as **raw text**. You will have something that looks like a JSON object, but you can't interact with the data like you would when you are working with a real JSON object.

To deal with this, you have the `JSON.parse` method that takes your "fake" JSON data as its argument:

```
function processRequest(e) {
  if (xhr.readyState == 4 && xhr.status == 200) {
    let response = JSON.parse(xhr.responseText);
    selectInitialState(response.region);
  }
}
```

As you can see from our highlighted line, this method takes whatever JSON-looking data that you end up with and converts it into a real JSON object that you can work with more easily. Whenever I am working with JSON data from an external source, I always use `JSON.parse` just to be safe.

Writing JSON Data?

We just had a section devoted entirely to reading values from JSON data. It would seem logical to also have a section that is focused on writing JSON data. As it turns out, writing JSON data just isn't all that popular unless you are saving JSON data to a file or doing something with web services. If you are doing either of these tasks, statistically you are doing development on Node or writing code in a programming language other than JavaScript.

For front-end development, I can't think of too many cases where information on writing JSON would be useful. If you run into the rare situation where you need to do something other than reading JSON data, my recommendation is for you to use Google!

THE ABSOLUTE MINIMUM

At one point in time, this article would have been focused on XML. Even today, XML is still widely popular as a file format for storing or communicating information. Only in a world where the web browser is king (aka the world that we live in) is where JSON is extremely popular. Outside of web sites, web applications, and REST-based web services, dealing with data in the JSON format isn't all that popular. You should keep that in mind when running into older, less web-centric situations!

If you have any JSON-related questions, or questions on anything else, head over and post on the forums at **https://forum.kirupa.com**.

24

JS, THE BROWSER, AND THE DOM

So far, we've looked at JavaScript in isolation. We learned a lot about its basic functionality, but we did so with little to no connection with how it ties to the real world—a world that is represented by your browser and swimming with little HTML tags and CSS styles. This chapter will serve as an introduction to this world, and subsequent chapters will dive in much deeper.

In the following sections, you will learn about the mysterious data structure and programming interface known as the **Document Object Model (DOM)**. You'll learn what it is, why it is useful, and how it ties in to everything that you'll be doing in the future.

Onward!

What HTML, CSS, and JavaScript Do

Before we dive in and start answering the meaning of life…err, the DOM, let's quickly look at some things you probably already know. For starters, the stuff you put into your HTML documents revolves around HTML, CSS, and JavaScript. We treat these three things as equal partners in building up what you see in your browser (Figure 24.1).

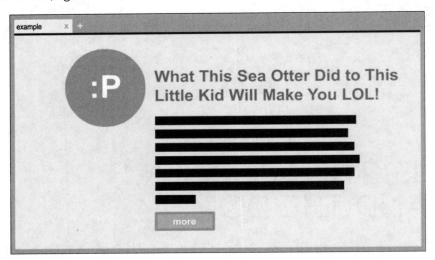

FIGURE 24.1

A typical web page is made up of HTML, CSS, and JavaScript.

Each partner has an important role to play, and the role each one plays is very different.

HTML Defines the Structure

Your HTML defines the structure of your page and typically contains the content that you see:

```
<!DOCTYPE html>
<html>

<head>
  <meta content="sea otter, kid, stuff" name="keywords">
  <meta content="Sometimes, sea otters are awesome!"
name="description">
  <title>Example</title>
```

```
  <link href="foo.css" rel="stylesheet" />
</head>

<body>
  <div id="container">
    <img src="seaOtter.png" />

    <h1>What This Sea Otter Did to This Little Kid Will Make You
LOL!</h1>

    <p class="bodyText">
      Nulla tristique, justo eget semper viverra,
      massa arcu congue tortor, ut vehicula urna mi
      in lorem. Quisque aliquam molestie dui, at tempor
      turpis porttitor nec. Aenean id interdum urna.
      Curabitur mi ligula, hendrerit at semper sed,
      feugiat a nisi.
    </p>

    <div class="submitButton">
      more
    </div>
  </div>
  <script src="stuff.js"></script>
</body>

</html>
```

HTML by itself, kinda like Meg Griffin in *Family Guy*, is pretty boring. If you don't know who Meg is and are too lazy to Google her, Figure 24.2 is an approximation of what she looks like.

A non-copyright infringing interpretation of Meg Griffin!

FIGURE 24.2

An artistic interpretation of Meg Griffin.

Anyway, you don't want your HTML documents to be boring. To transform your content from something plain and drab to something appealing, you have CSS.

Prettify My World, CSS!

CSS is your primary styling language that allows you to give your HTML elements some much-needed aesthetic and layout appeal:

```
body {
  font-family: "Arial";
  background-color: #CCCFFF;
}
#container {
  margin-left: 30%;
}
#container img {
  padding: 20px;
}
```

```
#container h1 {
  font-size: 56px;
  font-weight: 500;
}
#container p.bodyText {
  font-size: 16px;
  line-height: 24px;
}
.submitButton {
  display: inline-block;
  border: 5px solid #669900;
  background-color: #7BB700;
  padding: 10px;
  width: 150px;
  font-weight: 800;
}
```

For the longest time, between HTML and CSS, you had everything you needed to create an awesome-looking and functioning page. You had structure and layout. You had navigation. You even had simple interactions such as mouseovers. Life was good.

It's JavaScript Time!

For all the great things HTML and CSS had going for them, they were both limited in how much interactivity they provided. People wanted to do more on a web document than just passively sit back and observe what is going on. They wanted their web documents to do more. They wanted their documents to help them play with media; remember where they left off; do things with their mouse clicks, keyboard taps, and finger presses; use fancy navigation menus; see spiffy (yes, I used the word spiffy) programmatic animations; interact with their webcams/ microphones; not require a page reload/navigation for any kind of action; and a whole lot more.

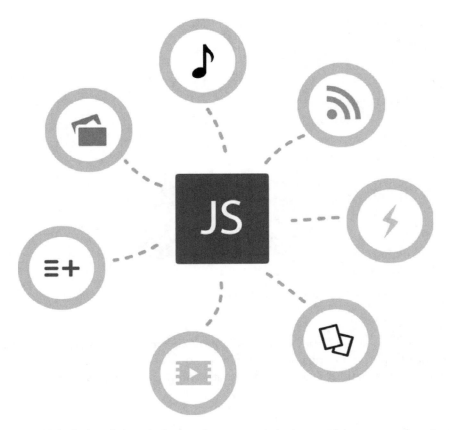

It certainly helped that web developers and designers (aka you and me) were itching for a way to help create these kinds of things as well.

To fill in this gap between what HTML and CSS provided and what people wanted, you had third-party components like Java and Flash that thrived for many years. It wasn't until recently that this trend changed. There were many technical and political reasons for this shift, but one reason was that JavaScript for many years just wasn't ready. It didn't have what it took either in the core language or in what browsers supported to be effective.

That's no longer the case today. JavaScript is now a perfectly capable language that allows you to add the kinds of interactive things that people are looking for. All of these capabilities are accessed by the real star of all this, the DOM.

Meet the Document Object Model

What your browser displays is a web document. More specifically, to summarize the entirety of the previous sections, what you see is a collision of HTML, CSS, and JavaScript working together to create what gets shown. Digging one step deeper, under the covers, there is a hierarchical structure that your browser uses to make sense of everything going on.

This structure is known (again) as the Document Object Model. Friends just call it the DOM. Figure 24.3 shows a very simplified view of what the DOM for our earlier example would look like:

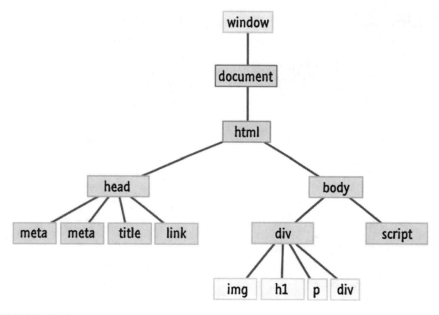

FIGURE 24.3

Our DOM for all the HTML you saw earlier looks sorta like this!

Despite the simplicity, there are several things to drill in on that apply to all DOM structures in general. Your DOM is actually made up many kinds of things beyond just HTML elements. All of those things that make up your DOM are more generically known as **nodes**.

These nodes can be elements (which shouldn't surprise you), attributes, text content, comments, document-related stuff, and various other things you simply never think about. That detail is important to someone, but that "someone" shouldn't be you and me. Almost always, the only kind of node we will care about is the element kind because that is what we will be dealing with 99% of the time. At the boring/technical level, nodes still play a role in our element-centric view.

Every HTML element you want to access has a particular type associated with it, and all of these types extend from the **Node** base that makes up all nodes as shown in Figure 24.4.

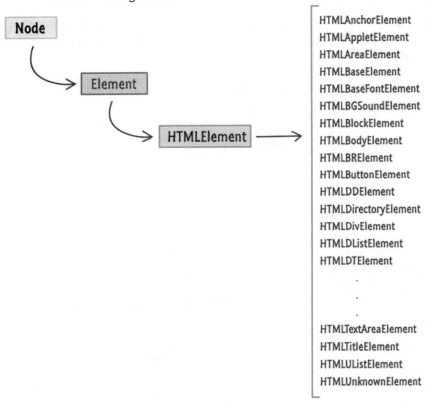

FIGURE 24.4

The arrangement of how the elements we typically see are structured.

Your HTML elements are at the end of a chain that starts with Node and continues with Element and HTMLElement before ending with a type (HTMLDivElement, HTMLHeadingElement, and so on) that matches the HTML element itself. The properties and methods you will see for manipulating HTML elements are introduced at some part of this chain.

Now, before we run toward using the DOM to modify HTML elements, let's first talk about two special objects that get in the way before the road clears up for what we want to do.

The Window Object

In the browser, the root of your hierarchy is the `window` object that contains many properties and methods that help you work with your browser; see Figure 24.5.

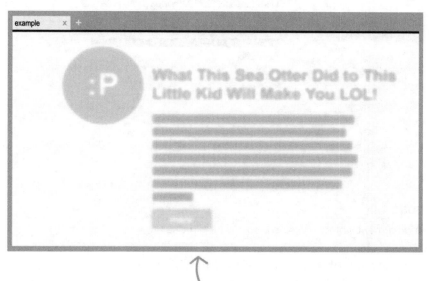

the `window` object deals with your browser window

FIGURE 24.5

The `window` is a pretty big deal up in these here parts.

Some of the things you can do with the help of the `window` object include accessing the current URL, getting information about any frames in the page, using local storage, seeing information about your screen, fiddling with the scrollbar, setting the status bar text, and all sorts of things that are applicable to the container your web page is displayed in.

The Document Object

Now, we get to the `document` object highlighted in Figure 24.6. Here is where things get interesting, and it is also where you and I will be focusing a lot of our time.

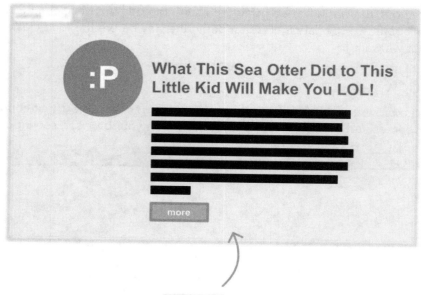

the document object deals with
EVERYTHING that lives in your document

FIGURE 24.6

The document object is also sorta kinda a big deal.

The document object is the gateway to all the HTML elements that make up what gets shown. The thing to keep in mind (and one that makes more sense as we look at future chapters) is that the document object does not simply represent a read-only version of the HTML document. It is a two-way street where you can read as well as manipulate your document at will.

Any change you make to the DOM via JavaScript is reflected in what gets shown in the browser. This means you can dynamically add elements, remove them, move them around, modify attributes on them, set inline CSS styles, and perform all sorts of other shenanigans. Outside of the very basic HTML needed via a script tag to get some JavaScript to run in an HTML document, you can construct a fully functioning page using nothing but JavaScript if you felt like it. Used properly, this is a pretty powerful feature.

Another import aspect of the document object has to do with events. I will go into more detail on this shortly, but if you want to react to a mouse click/hover, checking a check box, detecting when a key was pressed, and so on, you will be relying on functionality the document object provides for listening to and reacting to events.

There are a few more big buckets of functionality the DOM provides, but I'll highlight them as we get to them.

THE ABSOLUTE MINIMUM

The DOM is the single most important piece of functionality you have for working with your HTML documents. It provides the missing link that ties your HTML and CSS with JavaScript. It also provides access one level up to your browser.

Now, knowing about the DOM is just part of the fun. Actually using its functionality to interact with your web document is the much larger and **funner** other part. When you are ready, turn (or flip) on over to the next chapter where we will go further.

If you have any questions about this or any other topic, post on the forums at **https://forum.kirupa.com**.

FINDING ELEMENTS IN THE DOM

As we saw in the previous chapter, our DOM is nothing more than a tree-like structure (see Figure 25.1) made up of all the elements that exist in our HTML document.

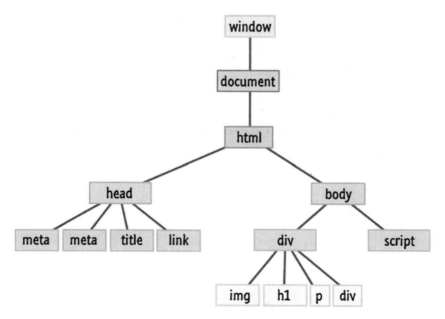

FIGURE 25.1

Yep. Looks like a tree-like structure all right!

That detail is only sort of important. What is important is that you have all of these HTML elements floating around that you want to access and read data from or modify. There are many ways to find these HTML elements. After all, these elements are arranged in a tree-like structure, and if there is one thing computer scientists like to do, it is figuring out crazy ways to run up and down a tree to find something.

I won't subject you to that torture…just yet. In this chapter, you are going to learn how to use two built-in functions called `querySelector` and `querySelectorAll` to solve a good chunk of all your DOM searching needs.

Onward!

Meet the `querySelector` Family

To help explain the awesomeness that `querySelector` and `querySelectorAll` bring to the table, take a look at the following HTML:

```
<div id="main">
  <div class="pictureContainer">
    <img class="theImage" src="smiley.png" height="300" width="150" />
  </div>
  <div class="pictureContainer">
    <img class="theImage" src="tongue.png" height="300" width="150" />
  </div>
  <div class="pictureContainer">
    <img class="theImage" src="meh.png" height="300" width="150" />
  </div>
  <div class="pictureContainer">
    <img class="theImage" src="sad.png" height="300" width="150" />
  </div>
</div>
```

In this example, you have one `div` with an `id` of **main**, and then you have four `div` and `img` elements, each with a class value of **pictureContainer** and **theImage** respectively. In the next few sections, we'll set the `querySelector` and `querySelectorAll` functions loose on this HTML and see what happens.

querySelector

The `querySelector` function basically works as follows:

```
let element = document.querySelector("CSS selector");
```

The `querySelector` function takes an argument, and this argument is a string that represents the CSS selector for the element you wish to find. What gets returned by `querySelector` is the first element it finds—even if other elements exist—that could get targeted by the selector. This function is pretty stubborn like that.

Taking the HTML from our earlier example, if we wanted to access the `div` whose id is **main**, you would write the following:

```
let element = document.querySelector("#main");
```

Because **main** is the `id`, the selector syntax for targeting it would be #main. Similarly, let's specify the selector for the **pictureContainer** class:

```
let element = document.querySelector(".pictureContainer");
```

What gets returned is the first `div` whose class value is **pictureContainer**. The other `div` elements with the class value of **pictureContainer** will simply be ignored.

The selector syntax is not modified or made special because you are in JavaScript. The exact syntax you would use for selectors in your stylesheet or style region can be used!

querySelectorAll

The `querySelectorAll` function returns all elements it finds that match whatever selector you provide:

```
let elements = document.querySelectorAll("CSS selector");
```

With the exception of the number of elements returned, everything I described about `querySelector` above applies to `querySelectorAll` as well. That important detail changes how you end up actually using the `querySelectorAll` function. What gets returned is not a single element. Instead, what gets returned is an array-like container of elements!

Continuing to use the HTML from earlier, here is what our JavaScript would look like if we wanted to use `querySelectorAll` to help us display the `src` attribute of all the `img` elements that contain the class value **theImage**:

```
let images = document.querySelectorAll(".theImage");

for (let i = 0; i < images.length; i++) {
  let image = images[i];
  console.log(image.getAttribute("src"));
}
```

See? This is pretty straightforward. The main thing you need to do is remember how to work with Arrays, which you should be a pro at by now. The other (slightly weirder) thing is the mysterious `getAttribute` function. If you aren't familiar with `getAttribute` and how to read values from elements, that's totally okay. We'll look at all that really soon. For now, just know that it allows you to read the value of any HTML attribute the HTML element in question may be sporting.

It Really Is the CSS Selector Syntax

The thing that surprised me when I first used `querySelector` and `querySelectorAll` is that it actually takes the full range of CSS selector syntax variations as its argument. You don't have to keep it simple like I've shown you so far.

If you wanted to target all of the `img` elements without having to specify the class value, here is what our `querySelectorAll` call could look like:

```
let images = document.querySelectorAll("img");
```

If you wanted to target only the image whose `src` attribute is set to **meh.png**, you can do the following:

```
let images = document.querySelectorAll("img[src='meh.png']");
```

Note that I just specified an **attribute selector**[1] as my argument to `querySelectorAll`. Pretty much any complex expression you can specify for a selector in your CSS document is fair game for specifying as an argument to either `querySelector` or `querySelectorAll`.

There are some caveats that you should be aware of:

Not all pseudo-class selectors are allowed. A selector made up of `:visited`, `:link`, `::before`, and `::after` is ignored and no elements are found.

---

1. http://bit.ly/kirupaAttribute

How crazy you can get with the selectors you provide depends on the browser's CSS support. Internet Explorer 8 supports `querySelector` and `querySelectorAll`. It doesn't support CSS3. Given that situation, using anything more recent than the selectors defined in CSS2 will not work when used with `querySelector` and `querySelectorAll` on IE8. Chances are, this doesn't apply to you because you are probably supporting more recent versions of browsers where this IE8 issue isn't even on the radar.

The selector you specify only applies to the descendants of the starting element you are beginning your search from. The starting element itself is not included. Not all `querySelector` and `querySelectorAll` calls need to be made from a `document`.

THE ABSOLUTE MINIMUM

The `querySelector` and `querySelectorAll` functions are extremely useful in complex documents where targeting a particular element is often not straightforward. By relying on the well-established CSS selector syntax, we can cast as small or as wide a net over the elements that we want. If I want all image elements, I can just say `querySelectorAll("img")`. If I only want the immediate `img` element contained inside its parent `div`, I can say `querySelector("div + img")`. Now, that's pretty awesome.

Before we wrap up, there is one more thing I'd like to chat with you about. Missing in all of this element-finding excitement were the `getElementById`, `getElementsByTagName`, and `getElementsByClassName` functions. Back in the day, these were the functions you would have used to find elements in your DOM. The `querySelector` and `querySelectorAll` functions are the present and future solutions for finding elements, so don't worry about the `getElement*` functions anymore. As of right now, the only slight against the `querySelector` and `querySelectorAll` functions is performance. The `getElementById` function is still pretty fast, and you can see the comparison for yourself here: **https://jsperf.com/getelementbyid-vs-queryselector/11**.

Like a wise person once said, life is too short to spend time learning about old JavaScript functions...even if they are a bit faster!

MODIFYING DOM ELEMENTS

At this point, you kinda sorta know what the DOM is. You also saw how to find elements using `querySelector` and `querySelectorAll`. What's next is for us to learn how to modify the DOM elements you found:

✔ **1. Get a vague overview of the DOM**

✔ **2. Learn to find elements**

3. Modify elements
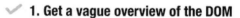

4. ???

We are here!

5. Profit!!!

↑
I have no idea why there is a pizza here.

After all, what's the fun in having a giant lump of clay (or cookie dough) if we can't put our hands on it and make a giant mess? Anyway, besides it being fun and all, we will find ourselves modifying the DOM all the time. Whether we are using JavaScript to change some element's text, swap out an image with a different one, move an element from one part of your document to another, set an inline style, or perform any of the bazillion other changes we will want to do, **we will be modifying the DOM**. This tutorial will teach you the basics of how to go about doing that.

Onward!

DOM Elements Are Objects—Sort of!

Our ability to use JavaScript to modify what gets shown by the browser is made possible because of one major detail. That detail is that every HTML tag, style rule, and other things that go into your page has some sort of a representation in the DOM.

To visualize what I just said, let's say we have an image element defined in markup:

```
<img src="images/lol_panda.png" alt="Sneezing Panda!" width="250"
height="100"/>
```

When our browser parses the document and hits this image element, it creates a node in the DOM that represents it as shown in Figure 26.1.

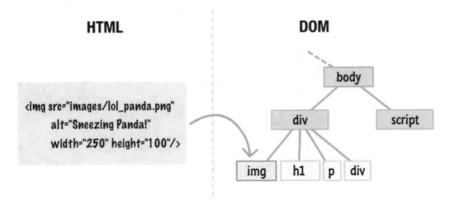

FIGURE 26.1

All of our HTML elements will eventually end up having a DOM representation.

This DOM representation provides us with the ability to do everything we could have done in markup. As it turns out, this DOM representation actually ends up allowing **us to do more with our HTML elements** than we could have done using just plain old markup itself. This is something we'll see a little bit of here and a whole lot of in the future. The reason why our HTML elements are so versatile when viewed via the DOM is because they share a lot of similarities with plain JavaScript objects. Our DOM elements contain properties that allow us to get/set values and call methods. They have a form of inheritance that we saw a little bit about earlier where the functionality each DOM element provides is spread out across the `Node`, `Element`, and `HTMLElement` base types, as seen again in Figure 26.2.

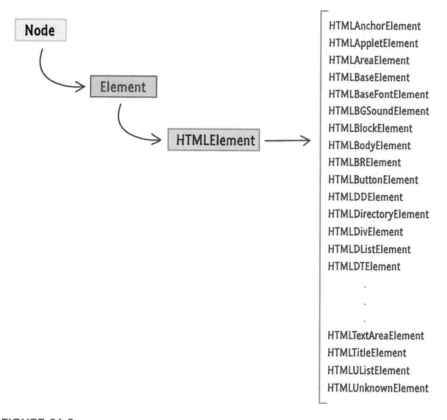

FIGURE 26.2

The hierarchy of the visual elements we'll typically encounter in the HTML.

DOM elements probably even smell like an `Object` when they run inside the house after rolling around in the rain for a bit.

Despite all of the similarities, for legal and...possibly health reasons, I need to provide the following disclaimer: **the DOM was never designed to mimic the way Objects work**. Many of the things we can do with objects we can certainly do with the DOM, but that is because the browser vendors help ensure that. The

W3C specifications don't state that our DOM should behave identically to how we may expect things to behave with plain old Objects. While I wouldn't lose any sleep worrying about this, if you ever decide to extend DOM elements or perform more advanced object-related gymnastics, be sure to test across all browsers just to make sure everything works the way you intended.

Now that we got this awkward conversation out of the way, let's start to actually modify the DOM.

Let's Actually Modify DOM Elements

While we can certainly lean back and passively learn all there is about how to modify elements in the DOM, this is one of those cases where you may have more fun following along with a simple example. If you are interested in following along, we'll be using the following HTML as a sandbox for the techniques we will be covering:

```html
<!DOCTYPE html>
<html>

<head>
  <title>Hello...</title>

  <style>
    .highlight {
      font-family: "Arial";
      padding: 30px;
    }

    .summer {
      font-size: 64px;
      color: #0099FF;
    }
  </style>

</head>

<body>
```

```
<h1 id="bigMessage" class="highlight summer">What's happening?</h1>

<script>

</script>
</body>

</html>
```

Just put all of that into an HTML document and follow along. If you preview this HTML in the browser, you will see something that looks like Figure 26.3.

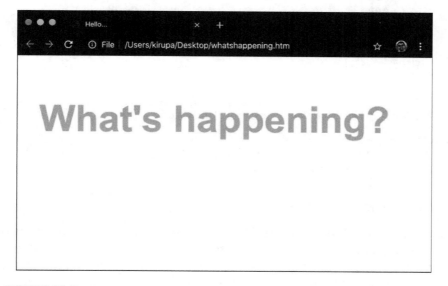

FIGURE 26.3

What's happening?

There isn't really a whole lot going on here. The main piece of content is the h1 tag that displays the **What's happening?** text:

```
<h1 id="bigMessage" class="highlight summer">What's happening?</h1>
```

Now, switching over to the DOM side of things, Figure 26.4 illustrates what this example looks like with all of the HTML elements and nodes like document and window mapped.

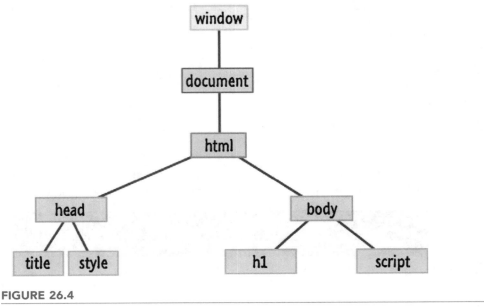

FIGURE 26.4

What our DOM structure for our example looks like.

In the following sections, we'll look at some of the common things you can do in terms of modifying a DOM element.

Changing an Element's Text Value

Let's start off with an easy one. Many HTML elements have the ability to display some text. Examples of such elements are our headings, paragraphs, sections, inputs, buttons, and many more. There is one thing they all have in common. The way you modify the text value is by setting the textContent property.

Let's say we want to change the text that appears in the h1 element from our example. The following snippet shows what that would look like:

```
<body>
  <h1 id="bigMessage" class="highlight summer">What's happening?</h1>

  <script>
    let headingElement = document.querySelector("#bigMessage");
    headingElement.textContent = "Oppa Gangnam Style!";
  </script>
</body>
```

If you make this change and preview in the browser, you will see what is shown in Figure 26.5.

FIGURE 26.5

Changing a heading's text value.

Let's look at what exactly we did to cause this change. The first step to modifying any HTML element in JavaScript is to first get a reference to it:

```
let headingElement = document.querySelector("#bigMessage");
```

Here is where our old friends `querySelector` and `querySelectorAll` come in. As we will see later, we also have indirect ways of referencing an element. The direct approach shown here, though, is what we will use when you have a very specific idea of what element or elements you wish to target.

Once we have the reference to the element, we can just set the `textContent` property on it:

```
headingElement.textContent = "Oppa Gangnam Style!";
```

The `textContent` property can be read like any variable to show the current value. We can also set the property like we are here to change the value that is stored currently. After this line has run, our markup's original value of **What's happening?** will be replaced in the DOM by what we specified in JavaScript.

Attribute Values

One of the primary ways our HTML elements distinguish themselves is through their attributes and the values these attributes store. For example, the `src` and `alt` attributes are what distinguish the following three image elements:

```
<img src="images/lol_panda.png" alt="Sneezing Panda!"/>

<img src="images/cat_cardboard.png" alt="Cat sliding into box!"/>

<img src="images/dog_tail.png" alt="Dog chasing its tail!"/>
```

Every HTML attribute (including custom `data-*` ones) can be accessed via the properties the DOM provides. To help us deal with attributes, our elements expose the somewhat self-explanatory `getAttribute` and `setAttribute` methods.

The `getAttribute` method allows us to specify the name of an attribute on the element it is living on. If the attribute is found, this method will then return the value associated with that attribute. Below is an example:

```
<body>
  <h1 id="bigMessage" class="highlight summer">What's happening?</h1>

  <script>
    let headingElement = document.querySelector("h1");
    console.log(headingElement.getAttribute("id")); // bigMessage
  </script>
</body>
```

In this snippet, notice that we are getting the value of the `id` attribute on our `h1` element. If we specify an attribute name that doesn't exist, we will get a nice value of **null**. The opposite of getting the value of an attribute is to actually set the value. To set the value, we would use the appropriately named `setAttribute` method. We use this method by calling `setAttribute` on the element that we want to affect and specifying both the attribute name as well as the value that attribute will store.

Here is an example of `setAttribute` at work:

```
<body>
  <h1 id="bigMessage" class="highlight summer">What's happening?</h1>

  <script>
    let headingElement = document.querySelector("h1");
```

```
    headingElement.setAttribute("class", "bar foo");
  </script>
</body>
```

We are setting (well...overwriting actually!) the `class` attribute on our `h1` element to **bar foo**. The `setAttribute` function doesn't do any validation to ensure that the attribute we are setting is valid for the element we are setting it on. Nothing prevents us from doing something silly as follows:

```
<body>
  <h1 id="bigMessage" class="highlight summer">What's happening?</h1>

  <script>
    let headingElement = document.querySelector("h1");
    headingElement.setAttribute("src", "http://www.kirupa.com");
  </script>
</body>
```

Our `h1` element doesn't contain a `src` attribute, but we can get away with speci-fying it. When our code runs, our `h1` element will even sport the `src` attribute... probably very uncomfortably.

There is something I need to clarify before we move on. In the examples for how to use `setAttribute` and `getAttribute`, I picked on `id` and `class`. For these two attributes, we do have another way of setting them. Because of how com-mon setting `id` and `class` attributes are, our HTML elements expose the `id` and `className` properties directly:

```
<body>
  <h1 id="bigMessage" class="highlight summer">What's happening?</h1>

  <script>
    let headingElement = document.querySelector("h1");
    console.log(headingElement.id); // bigMessage

    headingElement.className = "bar foo";
  </script>
</body>
```

Getting back to our example, notice that I switched from using `getAttribute` and `setAttribute` to using the `id` and `className` properties instead. The end result is identical. The only difference is that you had a direct way of setting these attribute values without having to use `getAttribute` or `setAttribute`. Now, before we go further, I have to call this strange thing out: yes...we can't use `class` in JavaScript for referring to the class attribute because `class` has a whole different meaning that has to do with dealing with objects. That's why we are using `className` instead.

 TIP There is a much better way of setting class values besides using `className`. That way is via the much more awesome `classList` property that you will learn all about in the next chapter.

THE ABSOLUTE MINIMUM

It may seem a bit odd to end our discussion around modifying DOM elements at this point. While changing an element's text and attribute values is very popular, they are by no means the only major kinds of modifications you will perform. The reason for ending at this cliffhanger is because manipulating the DOM and using an element's properties and methods to accomplish our task is central to everything we are going to be seeing. In subsequent chapters, you are going to see a whole lot more of what you've seen here.

Your main takeaway from this chapter is that the DOM changes you perform will almost always take one of the following two forms:

- Setting a property
- Calling a method

The `textContent`, `setAttribute`, and `getAttribute` methods you saw here cover both of those approaches, and you'll see a lot more of them and their friends shortly.

This is a pretty heavy topic! If you have any questions, don't delay getting an answer. Post on the forums at **https://forum.kirupa.com ASAP**.

IN THIS CHAPTER

- Learn how to change CSS using JavaScript
- Understand the pros and cons of setting styles directly as opposed to adjusting class values
- Use classList to make fiddling with element class values a breeze

STYLING OUR CONTENT

In the previous chapter, we looked at how to modify our DOM's content using JavaScript. The other part of what makes our HTML elements stand out is their appearance, their styling. When it comes to styling some content, the most common way is by creating a style rule and have its selector target an element or elements. A style rule would look as follows:

```
.batman {
  width: 100px;
  height: 100px;
  background-color: #333;
}
```

An element that would be affected by this style rule could look like this:

```
<div class="batman"></div>
```

On any given web page, we'll see anywhere from just a few to many MANY style rules each beautifully stepping over each other to style everything that we see. This isn't the only approach we can use to style content using CSS, though. It wouldn't be HTML if there weren't multiple ways to accomplish the same task!

Ignoring inline styles, the other approach that we can use to introduce elements to the goodness that is CSS styling involves JavaScript. We can use JavaScript to **directly set a style on an element**, and we can also use JavaScript to **add or remove class values on elements** which will alter which style rules get applied.

In this tutorial, we're going to learn about both of these approaches.

Onward!

Why Would We Set Styles Using JavaScript?

Before we go further it is probably useful to explain why we would ever want to use JavaScript to affect the style of an element in the first place. In the common cases where we use style rules or inline styles to affect how an element looks, the styling kicks in when the page is loaded. That's awesome, and that's probably what we want most of the time.

There are many cases, especially as our content gets more interactive, where we want styles to dynamically kick in based on user input, some code having run in the background, and more. In these sorts of scenarios, the CSS model involving style rules or inline styles won't help us. While pseudoselectors like hover provide some support, we are still greatly limited in what we can do.

The solution we will need to employ for all of them is one that involves JavaScript. JavaScript not only lets us style the element we are interacting with, more importantly, it allows us to style elements all over the page. This freedom is very powerful and goes well beyond CSS's limited ability to style content inside (or very close to) itself.

A Tale of Two Styling Approaches

Like we saw in the introduction, we have two ways to alter the style of an element using JavaScript. One way is by setting a CSS property directly on the element. The other way is by adding or removing class values from an element which may result in certain style rules getting applied or ignored. Let's look at both of these cases in greater detail.

Setting the Style Directly

Every HTML element that you access via JavaScript has a `style` object. This object allows you to specify a CSS property and set its value. For example, this is what setting the background color of an HTML element whose id value is **superman** looks like:

```
let myElement = document.querySelector("#superman");
myElement.style.backgroundColor = "#D93600";
```

To affect many elements, you can do something as follows:

```
let myElements = document.querySelectorAll(".bar");

for (let i = 0; i < myElements.length; i++) {
  myElements[i].style.opacity = 0;
}
```

In a nutshell, to style elements directly using JavaScript, the first step is to access the element. Our handy `querySelector` method from earlier is quite helpful here. The second step is just to find the CSS property you care about and give it a value. Remember, many values in CSS are actually strings. Also remember that many values require a unit of measurement like **px** or **em** or something like that to actually get recognized. Also remember...actually, I forgot.

Lastly, some CSS properties require a more complex value to be provided with a bunch of random text followed by the value you care about. One of the more popular ones in this bucket is the transform property. One approach for setting a complex value is to use good old-fashioned string concatenation:

```
myElement.style.transform = "translate3d(" + xPos + ", " + yPos +
"px, 0)";
```

That can get really irritating, for keeping track of the quotation marks and so on is something tedious and error-prone. One less irritating solution is to use the template literal syntax:

```
myElement.style.transform = `translate3d(${xPos}px, ${yPos}px, 0)`;
```

Notice how this approach allows you to still provide custom values while avoiding all of the string concatenation complexity.

TIP   Special Casing Some Names of CSS Properties

JavaScript is very picky about what makes up a valid property name. Most names in CSS would get JavaScript's seal of approval, so you can just use them straight-up from the carton. There are a few things to keep in mind, though.

To specify a CSS property in JavaScript that contains a dash, simply remove the dash. For example, `background-color` becomes `backgroundColor`, the `border-radius` property transforms into `borderRadius`, and so on.

Also, certain words in JavaScript are reserved and can't be used directly. One example of a CSS property that falls into this special category is `float`. In CSS it is a layout property. In JavaScript, it stands for something else. To use a property whose name is entirely reserved, prefix the property with **css** where `float` becomes `cssFloat`.

Adding and Removing Classes Using JavaScript

The second approach involves adding and removing class values that, in turn, change which style rules get applied. For example, let's say we have a style rule that looks as follows:

```
.disableMenu {
  display: none;
}
```

In HTML, we have a menu whose id is **dropDown**:

```
<ul id="dropDown">
  <li>One</li>
  <li>Two</li>
  <li>Three</li>
  <li>Four</li>
  <li>Five</li>
  <li>Six</li>
</ul>
```

Now, if we wanted to apply our `.disableMenu` style rule to this element, all we would need to do is add **disableMenu** as a `class` value to the **dropDown** element:

```
<ul class="disableMenu" id="dropDown">
  <li>One</li>
  <li>Two</li>
  <li>Three</li>
  <li>Four</li>
  <li>Five</li>
  <li>Six</li>
</ul>
```

One way to accomplish this involves setting an element's `className` property, an approach we saw earlier. The trouble with `className` is that we are responsible for maintaining the current list of class values applied. Worse, the list of class values is returned to us as a string. If we have multiple class values we want to add, remove, or just toggle on/off, we have to do a bunch of error-prone string-related trickery that just isn't fun.

To help alleviate some of the inconvenience, we now have a much nicer API that makes adding and removing class values from an element ridiculously easy. This new API is affectionately known as `classList`, and it provides a handful of methods that will make working with class values a piece of cake:

- add
- remove
- toggle
- contains

What these four methods do may be pretty self-explanatory from their names, but let's look at them in further detail.

Adding Class Values

To add a class value to an element, get a reference to the element and call the add method on it via `classList`:

```
let divElement = document.querySelector("#myDiv");
divElement.classList.add("bar");
divElement.classList.add("foo");
divElement.classList.add("zorb");
divElement.classList.add("baz");


console.log(divElement.classList);
```

After this code runs, our `div` element will have the following class values: **bar**, **foo**, **zorb**, **baz**. The `classList` API takes care of ensuring spaces are added between class values. If we specify an invalid class value, the `classList` API will complain and not add it. If we tell the add method to add a class that already exists on the element, our code will still run, but the duplicate class value will not get added.

Removing Class Values

To remove a class value, we can call the `remove` method on `classList`:

```
let divElement = document.querySelector("#myDiv");
divElement.classList.remove("foo");


console.log(divElement.classList);
```

After this code executes, the **foo** class value will be removed. What we will be left with is just **bar** and **zorb**. Pretty simple, right?

Toggling Class Values

For many styling scenarios, there is one very common workflow. First, we check if a class value on an element exists. If the value exists, we remove it from the element. If the value does not exist, we add that class value to the element. To simplify this very common toggling pattern, the `classList` API provides you with the `toggle` method:

```
let divElement = document.querySelector("#myDiv");
divElement.classList.toggle("foo"); // remove foo
divElement.classList.toggle("foo"); // add foo
divElement.classList.toggle("foo"); // remove foo


console.log(divElement.classList);
```

The `toggle` method, as its name implies, adds or removes the specified class value on the element each time it is called. In our case, the **foo** class is removed the first time the `toggle` method is called. The second time, the **foo** class is added. The third time, the **foo** class is removed. You get the picture.

Checking Whether a Class Value Exists

The last thing we are going to look at is the `contains` method:

```
let divElement = document.querySelector("#myDiv");

if (divElement.classList.contains("bar") == true) {
  // do something
}
```

This method checks to see if the specified class value exists on the element. If the value exists, you get **true**. If the value doesn't exist, you get **false**.

Going Further

As you can see, the `classList` API provides you with almost everything you need to add, remove, or inspect class values on an element very easily. The emphasis being on the word almost. For the few things the API doesn't provide by default, you can go online and read my full article on many more things you can do with `classList`: **http://bit.ly/kClassList**.

THE ABSOLUTE MINIMUM

So, there you have it—two perfectly fine JavaScript-based approaches you can use for styling your elements. Of these two choices, if you have the ability to modify your CSS, I would prefer you go style elements by adding and removing classes. The simple reason is that this approach is far more maintainable. It is much easier to add and remove style properties from a style rule in CSS as opposed to adding and removing lines of JavaScript.

Got a question? The friendly people on the forums may have an answer. Head on over to **https://forum.kirupa.com** to ask!

IN THIS CHAPTER

- Learn how to navigate the DOM tree
- Use the various APIs you have for moving and re-parenting elements
- Find an element's sibling, parent, children, and more

28

TRAVERSING THE DOM

As you may have realized by now, our DOM looks like a giant tree—a giant tree with elements dangerously hanging on to branches and trying to avoid the pointy things that litter the place. To get a little more technical, elements in our DOM are arranged in a hierarchy as illustrated in Figure 28.1 that defines what we will eventually see in the browser.

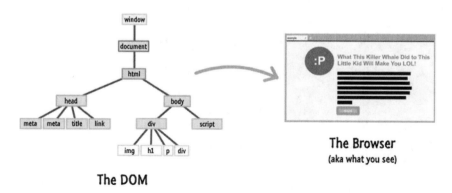

FIGURE 28.1

The DOM and the Browser are like two peas in a pod.

This hierarchy is used to help organize our HTML elements. It is also used to help our CSS style rules make sense of what styles to apply on which things. From the JavaScript angle, this hierarchy does add a bit of complexity. We will spend a fair amount of time trying to figure out where in the DOM we are right now and where we need to be. This is something that will become more apparent when we look into creating new elements or moving elements around. This complexity is something that we need to be comfortable with.

That's where this tutorial comes in. To help you understand how to easily navigate from branch to branch (basically, like a monkey), the DOM provides you with a handful of properties that you can combine with techniques you already know. This tutorial will give you an overview of all that and more.

Onward!

Finding Your Way Around

Before we can find elements and do awesome things with them, we need to first get to where the elements are. The easiest way to tackle this topic is to just start from the top and slide all the way down. That's exactly what we are going to do.

The view from the top of our DOM is made up of our window, document, and html elements as shown in Figure 28.2.

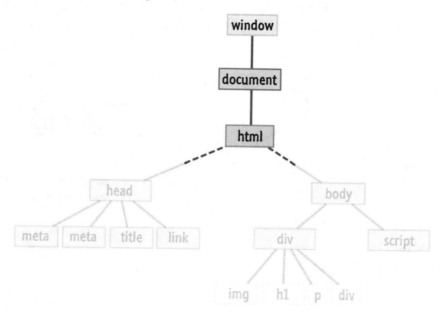

FIGURE 28.2

The view from the top of this tree never changes.

Because of how important these three things are, the DOM provides us with easy access to them via `window`, `document`, and `document.documentElement`:

```
let windowObject = window; // um....
let documentObject = document;  // this is probably unnecessary
let htmlElement = document.documentElement;
```

One thing to note is that both `window` and `document` are global properties. We don't have to explicitly declare them like I did. Just shake and use them straight out of the container.

Once we go below the HTML element level, our DOM will start to branch out and get more interesting. At this point, we have several ways of navigating around. One way that we've seen plenty of is by using `querySelector` and `querySelectorAll` to precisely get at the elements we are interested in. For many practical cases, these two methods are too limiting.

Sometimes, we don't know where we want to go. The `querySelector` and `querySelectorAll` methods won't help us here. We just want to get in the car and drive...and hope we find what we are looking for. When it comes to navigating the DOM, we'll find ourselves in this position all the time. That's where the various built-in properties the DOM provides will help us out, and we are going to look at those properties next.

The thing that will help us out is knowing that all of our elements in the DOM have at least one combination of **parents**, **siblings**, and **children** to rely on. To visualize this, take a look at the row containing the `div` and `script` elements as shown in Figure 28.3.

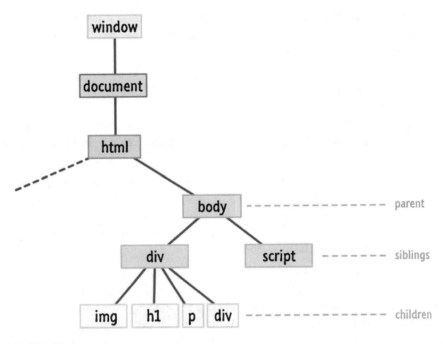

FIGURE 28.3

An example of our tree with some parents, siblings, and children.

Both the `div` and `script` elements are siblings. The reason they are siblings is because they share the `body` element as their parent. The `script` element has no children, but the `div` element does. The `img`, `h1`, `p`, and `div` are children of the `div` element, and all children of the same parent are siblings as well. Just like in real life, the parent, child, and sibling relationship is based on where in the tree we are focusing on. Almost every element, depending on the angle with which we look at them under, can play multiple familial roles.

To help us through all of this, we have a handful of properties that we will rely on. These properties are `firstChild`, `lastChild`, `parentNode`, `children`, `previousSibling`, and `nextSibling`. From just looking at their names, you should be able to infer what role these properties play. The guy in red with the pointed pitchfork is in the details, so we'll look at this in greater detail next.

Dealing with Siblings and Parents

Of these properties, the easiest ones to deal with are the parents and siblings. The relevant properties for this are parentNode, previousSibling, and nextSibling. The following diagram represented by Figure 28.4 gives you an idea of how these three properties work.

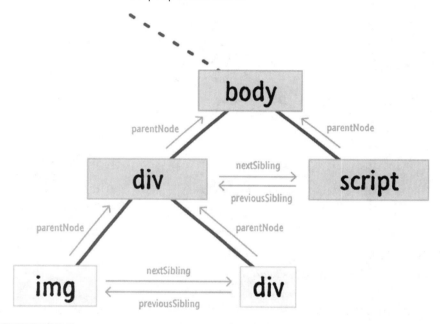

FIGURE 28.4

The relationship between siblings and parents from our DOM's point of view.

This diagram is a little busy, but you can sort of make out what is going on here. The parentNode property points you to the element's parent. The previousSibling and nextSibling properties allow an element to find its previous or next sibling. You can see this visualized in the diagram by just moving in the direction of the arrow. In the last line, our img's nextSibling is the div. Our div's previousSibling is the img. Accessing parentNode on either of these elements will take you to the parent div in the second row. It's all pretty straightforward.

Let's Have Some Kids!

What is a little less straightforward is how the children fit into all of this, so let's take a look at the firstChild, lastChild, and children properties shown in Figure 28.5.

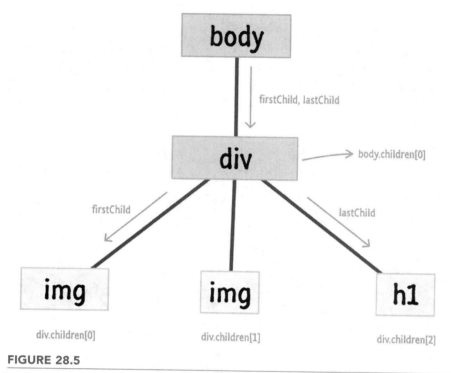

FIGURE 28.5

A view of children and more children!

The `firstChild` and `lastChild` properties refer to a parent's first and last child elements. If the parent only has one child, as is the case with the `body` element in our example, then both `firstChild` and `lastChild` point to the same thing. If an element has no children, then these properties return a **null**.

The tricky one compared to the other properties we've looked at is the `children` property. When you access the `children` property on a parent, you basically get a collection of the child elements the parent has. This collection is not an `Array`, but it does have some `Array`-like powers. Just like with an `Array`, you can iterate through this collection or access the children individually kind of like what you see in the diagram. This collection also has a `length` property that tells you the count of how many children the parent is dealing with. If your head is spinning from this, don't worry. The snippets in the next section will help clarify the vagueness in my explanation.

Putting It All Together

Now that we have a good idea of all the important properties we have for traversing the DOM, let's look at some code snippets that tie in all the diagrams and words into some sweet lines of JavaScript.

Checking If A Child Exists

To check if an element has a child, we can do something like the following:

```
let bodyElement = document.querySelector("body");


if (bodyElement.firstChild) {
  // do something interesting
}
```

This `if` statement will return **null** if there are no children. We could also have used `bodyElement.lastChild` or `bodyElement.children.count` if you enjoy typing, but I prefer to just keep things simple.

Accessing All the Child Elements

If we want to access all of a parent's children, we can always rely on good old uncle `for` loop:

```
let bodyElement = document.body;


for (let i = 0; i < bodyElement.children.length; i++) {
  let childElement = bodyElement.children[i];

  document.writeln(childElement.tagName);
}
```

Notice that we are using the `children` and `length` properties property just like we would an `Array`. The thing to note is that this collection is actually not an `Array`. Almost all of the `Array` methods that we may want to use will not be available in this collection returned by the `children` property.

Walking the DOM

Our last snippet touches upon a little bit of everything we've seen so far. This snippet recursively walks the DOM and touches every HTML element it can find:

```
function theDOMElementWalker(node) {
  if (node.nodeType == Node.ELEMENT_NODE) {

    console.log(node.tagName);
```

```
        node = node.firstChild;

        while (node) {
          theDOMElementWalker(node);
          node = node.nextSibling;
        }
      }
    }
```

To see this function in action, we just call it by passing in a node that we want to start our walk from:

```
let texasRanger = document.querySelector("#texas");
theDOMElementWalker(texasRanger);
```

In this example, we are calling `theDOMElementWalker` function on an element referenced by the `texasRanger` variable. If you want to run some code on the element that this script found, replace the commented out line with whatever you want to do.

THE ABSOLUTE MINIMUM

Finding your way around the DOM is one of those skills that every JavaScript developer should be familiar with. This tutorial provided you an overview of what is technically possible. Applying this in more practical ways falls entirely onto you...or a cool friend who helps you out with these things. With that said, in subsequent tutorials, we will expand upon what we've seen here as part of continuing our deep dive into everything we can do with the DOM. Doesn't that sound exciting?

Got a question? Head on over to **https://forum.kirupa.com** for an answer from friendly developers just like yourself!

29

CREATING AND REMOVING DOM ELEMENTS

This part may blow you away. For the following sentences, I suggest you hold onto something sturdy:

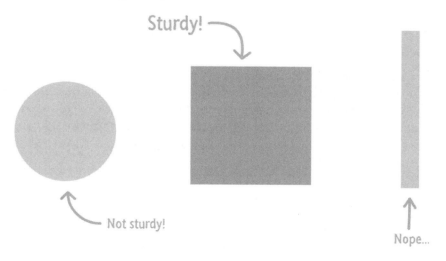

Despite what our earlier discussions about the DOM may have led you to believe, our DOM does not have to be made up of HTML elements that exist in markup. We have the ability to create HTML elements out of thin air and add them to our DOM using just a few lines of JavaScript. We also have the ability to move elements around, remove them, and do all sorts of god-like things. Let's pause for a bit while we let all of that sink in. This is pretty big.

Besides the initial coolness of all this, the ability to dynamically create and modify elements in our DOM is an important detail that makes a lot of our favorite websites and applications tick. When you think about this, this makes sense. Having everything predefined in our HTML is very limiting. We want our content to change and adapt when new data is pulled in, when we interact with the page, when we scroll further, or when we do a billion other things.

In this chapter, we are going to cover the basics of what makes all of this work. We are going to look at how to create elements, remove elements, re-parent elements, and clone elements. This is also the last of our chapters looking directly at DOM-related shenanigans, so call your friends and get the balloons ready!

Onward!

Creating Elements

It is very common for interactive sites and apps to dynamically create HTML elements and have them live in the DOM. If this is the first time you are hearing about something like this being possible, you are going to love this section!

The way we can create elements is by using the `createElement` method. The way `createElement` works is pretty simple. We call it via our `document` object and pass in the HTML tag name of the element we wish to create. In the following snippet, we are creating a paragraph element represented by the letter p:

```
let myElement = document.createElement("p");
```

The `myElement` variable holds a reference to our newly created element.

If we run this line of code as part of a larger app, it will execute and a p element will get created. Creating an element is the simple part. Actually raising it to be a fun and responsible member of the DOM is where we need some extra effort. We need to actually place this element somewhere in the DOM, for our dynamically created p element is just floating around aimlessly right now:

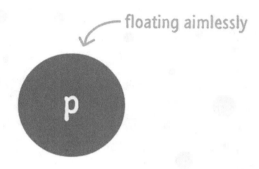

The reason for this aimlessness is because our DOM has no real knowledge that this element exists. In order for an element to be a part of the DOM, there are two things we need to do:

1. Find an element that will act as the parent

2. Use `appendChild` and add the element we want into that parent element

The best way to make sense of all this is to look at an example that ties this all together. If you want to follow along, create a new HTML document and add the following HTML, CSS, and JS into it:

```
<!DOCTYPE html>
<html>

<head>
  <title>Creating Elements</title>

  <style>
    body {
      background-color: #0E454C;
      padding: 30px;
    }
```

```
    h1 {
      color: #14FFF7;
      font-size: 72px;
      font-family: sans-serif;
      text-decoration: underline;
    }

    p {
      color: #14FFF7;
      font-family: sans-serif;
      font-size: 36px;
      font-weight: bold;
    }
  </style>
</head>

<body>
  <h1>Am I real?</h1>
  <script>
    let newElement = document.createElement("p");
    let bodyElement = document.querySelector("body");

    newElement.textContent = "Or do I exist entirely in your
imagination?";

    bodyElement.appendChild(newElement);
  </script>
</body>

</html>
```

Save this file and preview it in your browser. If everything worked out, you should see something that resembles the following screenshot:

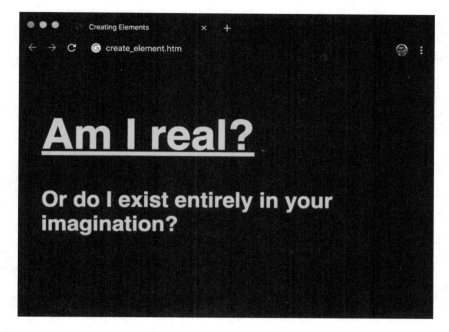

Now, we are going to take a step back and look at what exactly is going on in our example. If we look at our JavaScript, everything we need for creating an element and adding it to our DOM is located in between the `script` tags:

```
let newElement = document.createElement("p");
let bodyElement = document.querySelector("body");


newElement.textContent = "Or do I exist entirely in your
imagination?";


bodyElement.appendChild(newElement);
```

With `newElement`, we are storing a reference to our newly created `p` tag. With `bodyElement`, we are storing a reference to our `body` element. On our newly created element (`newElement`), we set the `textContent` property to what we ultimately end up displaying. The last thing we do is take our aimlessly floating `newElement` and parent it as a child of our `body` element by relying on good old `appendChild`.

Figure 29.1 is a visualization of what the DOM for our simple example looks like.

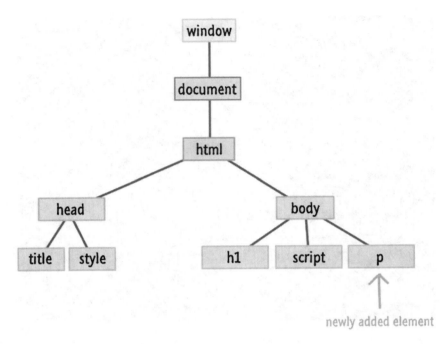

newly added element

FIGURE 29.1

What the DOM looks like after our code has run.

Now, a detail about the `appendChild` function is that it always adds the element to the end of whatever children a parent may have. In our case, our `body` element already has the `h1` and `script` elements as its children. The `p` element gets appended after them as the youngest child. With that said, we do have control over the exact order where under a parent a particular element will live.

If we want to insert `newElement` directly after our `h1` tag, we can do so by calling the `insertBefore` function on the parent. The `insertBefore` function takes two arguments. The first argument is the element you want to insert. The second argument is a reference to the sibling (aka child of a parent) you want to precede. Here is our example modified to have our `newElement` live after our `h1` element (and before our `script` element):

```
let newElement = document.createElement("p");

let bodyElement = document.querySelector("body");

let scriptElement = document.querySelector("script");


newElement.textContent = "I exist entirely in your imagination.";


bodyElement.insertBefore(newElement, scriptElement);
```

Notice that we call `insertBefore` on the `bodyElement` and specify that `newElement` should be inserted before our `script` element. Our DOM in this case would look as shown in Figure 29.2.

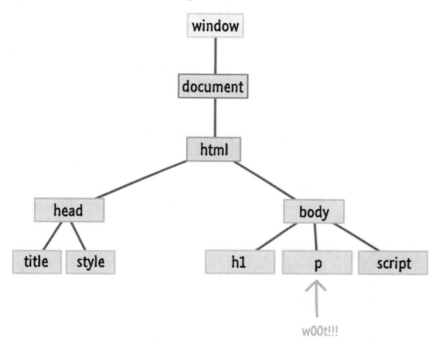

FIGURE 29.2

The newly inserted element is in between the `h1` *and* `script` *elements.*

You might think that if there is an `insertBefore` method, there must be an `insertAfter` method as well. As it turns out, that isn't the case. There isn't a widely supported built-in way of inserting an element AFTER an element instead of before it. What we can do is trick the `insertBefore` function by telling it to insert an element **an extra element ahead**. That probably makes no sense, so let me show you the code first and explain later:

```
let newElement = document.createElement("p");

let bodyElement = document.querySelector("body");

let h1Element = document.querySelector("h1");


newElement.textContent = "I exist entirely in your imagination.";


bodyElement.insertBefore(newElement, h1Element.nextSibling);
```

Pay attention to the highlighted lines, and then take a look at Figure 29.3 that illustrates what is happening before our code runs and after our code runs.

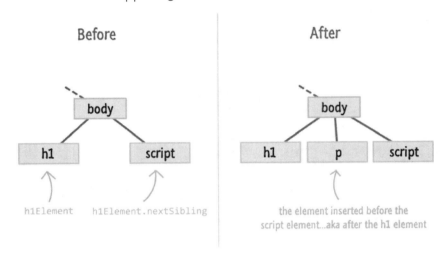

FIGURE 29.3

Our trick we can use to simulate an insertAfter *behavior.*

The h1Element.nextSibling call finds the script element. Inserting our newElement before our script element accomplishes our goal of inserting our element after the h1 element. What if there is no sibling element to target? Well, the insertBefore function in that case is pretty clever and just appends the element you want to the end automatically.

HANDY DANDY FUNCTION

If for some reason you find yourself wanting to insert elements after another sibling all the time, then you may want to use this function to simplify your life a bit:

```
function insertAfter(target, newElement) {
    target.parentNode.insertBefore(newElement, target.nextSibling);
}
```

Yes, I do realize this is a roundabout way of doing this, but it works...really well. Below is an example of this function at work:

```
let newElement = document.createElement("p");
let bodyElement = document.querySelector("body");
let h1Element = document.querySelector("h1");


newElement.textContent = "I exist entirely in your imagination.";


function insertAfter(target, element) {
  target.parentNode.insertBefore(element, target.nextSibling);
}


insertAfter(bodyElement, newElement);
```

You can even go all out and extend `HTMLElement` with this function to provide this functionality more conveniently to all your HTML elements. **Chapter 19, "Extending Built-in Objects,"** covers how to do something like that in greater detail. Note that extending your DOM is frowned upon by some people, so make sure to have some witty banter on the ready to lighten the mood if you ever are accosted by these "some people".

A more generic way of adding children to a parent is by realizing that parent elements treat children like entries in an array. To access this array of children, we have the `children` and `childNodes` properties. The `children` property only returns HTML elements, and the `childNodes` property returns the more generic nodes that represent a lot of things that we don't care about. Yes, I realize I am repeating myself, and you can check out the previous Chapter 28, "Traversing the DOM," for more details on more ways you have for pinpointing an element.

Removing Elements

I think somebody smart once said the following: **That which has the ability to create, also has the ability to remove**. In the previous section, we saw how we can use the createElement method to create an element. In this section, we are going to look at removeChild which, given its slightly unsavory name, is all about removing elements.

Take a look at the following snippet of code that can be made to work with the example we have been looking at for some time:

```
let newElement = document.createElement("p");
let bodyElement = document.querySelector("body");
let h1Element = document.querySelector("h1");


newElement.textContent = "I exist entirely in your imagination.";


bodyElement.appendChild(newElement);


bodyElement.removeChild(newElement);
```

The p element stored by newElement is being added to our body element by the appendChild method. We saw that earlier. To remove this element, we call removeChild on the body element and pass in a pointer to the element we wish to remove. That element is, of course, newElement. Once removeChild has run, it will be as if your DOM never knew that newElement existed.

The main thing to note is that we need to call removeChild from the parent of the child we wish to remove. This method isn't going to traverse up and down our DOM trying to find the element we want to remove. Now, let's say that we don't have direct access to an element's parent and don't want to waste time finding it. We can still remove that element very easily by using the parentNode property as follows:

```
let newElement = document.createElement("p");
let bodyElement = document.querySelector("body");
let h1Element = document.querySelector("h1");


newElement.textContent = "I exist entirely in your imagination.";


bodyElement.appendChild(newElement);


newElement.parentNode.removeChild(newElement);
```

In this variation, we remove `newElement` by calling `removeChild` on its parent by specifying `newElement.parentNode`. This looks roundabout, but it gets the job done.

Now, there is a newer, shinier, and better way to remove an element. In this way, we just call the `remove` method on the element we wish to remove directly. This example looks as follows:

```
let newElement = document.createElement("p");
let bodyElement = document.querySelector("body");
let h1Element = document.querySelector("h1");


newElement.textContent = "I exist entirely in your imagination.";


bodyElement.appendChild(newElement);
```

```
newElement.remove();
```

Now, why am I not beginning and ending this conversation around removing elements with the `remove` method? It has to do with browser support. This approach is still fairly new, so older browsers like Internet Explorer don't have support for it. If supporting Internet Explorer is important for you, then the other approaches we've looked at will work.

If you are looking for a universally accepted approach for removing elements, despite some minor quirks, the `removeChild` function is quite merciless in its efficiency. If you want something direct, `remove` is your friend. Both of these approaches have the ability to remove any DOM element—including ones that were created in markup originally. We aren't limited to removing DOM elements we dynamically added. If the DOM element we are removing has many levels of children and grandchildren, all of them will be removed as well.

Cloning Elements

This chapter just keeps taking a turn for the weirder-er the further we go into it, but fortunately we are at the last section. The one remaining DOM manipulation technique we need to be aware of is one that revolves around cloning elements where we start with one element and create identical replicas of it:

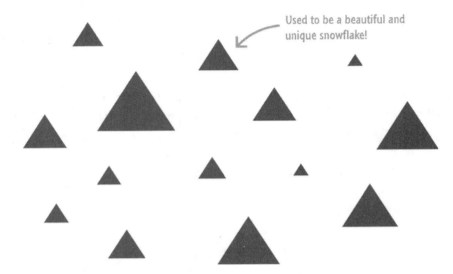

Used to be a beautiful and unique snowflake!

The way we clone an element is by calling the `cloneNode` function on the element we wish to clone along with providing a **true** or **false** argument to specify whether we want to clone just the element or the element and all of its children. Here is what the snippet of code for cloning an element (and adding it to the DOM) will look like:

```
let bodyElement = document.querySelector("body");
let item = document.querySelector("h1");

let clonedItem = item.cloneNode(false);

// add cloned element to the DOM
bodyElement.appendChild(clonedItem);
```

Once our cloned elements have been added to the DOM, we can then use all the tricks we've learned to modify them. Cloning elements is such an important thing for us to get familiar with, let's go beyond this snippet and look at a fuller example:

```
<!DOCTYPE html>
<html>

<head>
  <title>Cloning Elements</title>

  <style>
    body {
      background-color: #60543A;
```

```
      padding: 30px;
    }

    h1 {
      color: #F2D492;
      font-size: 72px;
      font-family: sans-serif;
      text-decoration: underline;
    }

    p {
      color: #F2D492;
      font-family: sans-serif;
      font-size: 36px;
      font-weight: bold;
    }
  </style>
</head>

<body>
  <h1>Am I real?</h1>
  <p class="message">I exist entirely in your imagination.</p>

  <script>
    let bodyElement = document.querySelector("body");
    let textElement = document.querySelector(".message");

    setInterval(sayWhat, 1000);

    function sayWhat() {
      let clonedText = textElement.cloneNode(true);
      bodyElement.appendChild(clonedText);
    }
  </script>
</body>

</html>
```

If you put all of this code into a HTML document and preview it in your browser, you'll see something that resembles our earlier example:

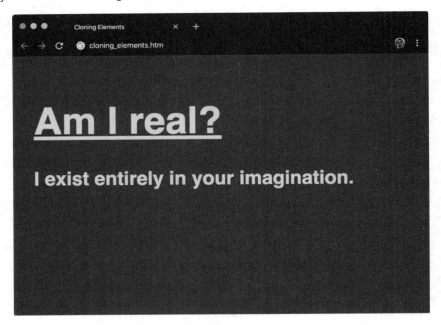

After a few seconds, though, you'll notice that this example is quite a bit different. The message keeps duplicating:

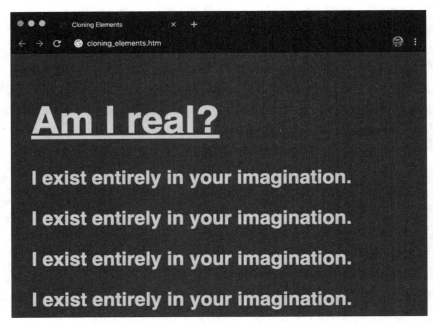

The secret to what is going on here lies in our code. Let's jump back to the code inside the `script` tags and take a moment to understand what is going on:

```
let bodyElement = document.querySelector("body");
let textElement = document.querySelector(".message");
```

At the top, we have our `bodyElement` variable that references the `body` element in our HTML. Similarly, we have our `textElement` variable that references our `p` element with a class value of **message**. Nothing too special here.

Now, here is where things get a little interesting. We have our `setInterval` timer function that calls the `sayWhat` function every 1000 milliseconds (1 second):

```
setInterval(sayWhat, 1000);
```

It is inside this `sayWhat` function where the actual cloning takes place:

```
function sayWhat() {
  let clonedText = textElement.cloneNode(true);
  bodyElement.appendChild(clonedText);
}
```

We call `cloneNode` on our `textElement`. The result of us doing this is that a copy of our `textElement` is now created and stored as part of the `clonedText` variable. The last step is for us to add our newly cloned element to the DOM so that it shows up. Thanks to our `setInterval`, all of the code under `sayWhat` repeats to keep adding our cloned element to the page.

One thing you may have noticed is that what we are cloning is the following paragraph element:

```
<p class="message">I exist entirely in your imagination.</p>
```

What we specified in our code is the following:

```
let clonedText = textElement.cloneNode(true);
```

We are calling `cloneNode` with the **true** flag to indicate we want to clone all of the children as well. Why? Our paragraph element doesn't seem to have any children, right? Well...this is where the distinction between *elements* and *nodes* comes into play. Our paragraph tag doesn't have any child *elements*, but the text wrapped by the `p` tag is a child *node*. This detail is important to keep in mind when you find yourself cloning something and finding that you don't exactly get what you want when you specify that children shouldn't get cloned.

THE ABSOLUTE MINIMUM

If there is anything you walk away from after reading all this, I hope you walk away with the knowledge that our DOM is something you can touch and extensively modify. We sort of talked about how everything in the DOM can be altered earlier, but it is here where we saw first-hand the depth and breadth of the alterations we can easily make using methods like `createElement`, `removeElement`, `remove`, and `cloneNode`.

With everything you've learned here, there is nothing preventing you from starting off with a completely empty page and using just a few lines of JavaScript to populate everything inside it:

```html
<!DOCTYPE html>
<html>

<head>
  <title>Look what I did, ma!</title>
</head>

<body>
  <script>
    let bodyElement = document.querySelector("body");

    let h1Element = document.createElement("h1");
    h1Element.textContent = "Do they speak English in 'What'?";

    bodyElement.appendChild(h1Element);

    let pElement = document.createElement("p");
    pElement.textContent = "I am adding some text here...like a boss!";

    bodyElement.appendChild(pElement);
  </script>
</body>

</html>
```

Just because you can do something like this doesn't mean you always should. The main problem with dynamically creating content is that search engines, screen readers, and other accessibility tools often have difficulty knowing what to do. They are more familiar with content specified in markup than they are with things created using JavaScript. Just be aware of that limitation if you ever decide to get over-enthusiastic with dynamically modifying your DOM.

As always, if you have any questions, ask away at **https://forum.kirupa.com**.

30

IN-BROWSER DEVELOPER TOOLS

All of the major browsers—Google Chrome, Apple Safari, Mozilla Firefox, and Microsoft Edge (formerly Internet Explorer)—do more than just display web pages. For developers, they provide access to a lot of cool functionality for figuring out what is actually going on with the web page that is displayed. They do all of this via what I'll generically just call the **Developer Tools**. These are tools that are built in to the browser, and they give you the ability to fiddle with your HTML, CSS, and JavaScript in a lot of neat and interesting ways.

In this chapter, let's look at these Developer Tools and learn how we can use them to make our lives easier.

Onwards!

I'LL BE USING GOOGLE CHROME

For all of the examples you are about to see, I'll be using Google's Chrome browser. While each browser provides similar functionality for what I'll be describing, the exact UI and steps to get there will vary. Just be aware of that, and also note that the version of Chrome you may be using might be more recent than the one that is used in this chapter.

Meet the Developer Tools

Let's start at the very beginning. When you navigate to a web page, your browser will load whatever document it was told to load:

This should all be very familiar for you, as this part of the browser functionality really hasn't changed much since the very first browser that was released in the 1800s...or therabouts. While using Chrome, *press (Cmd-Opt-I) on the Mac or the F12 key [or Ctrl+Shift+I] in Windows.*

Once you've pressed those key or keys, notice what happens. While you may not hear heavenly music followed by the earth rumbling and laser beams shooting across the sky, you will see your browser's layout change to show something mysterious (usually) toward the bottom or right of the screen as shown in Figure 30.1.

FIGURE 30.1

Your browser with its developer tools displayed right below it.

Your browser will split into two parts. One part is where your browser deals with displaying your web pages. We like this guy and have known him for quite some time. The other part, the new guy whom we eye suspiciously from a distance, provides you with access to information about the currently displayed page that only a developer such as yourself would appreciate. This guy is better known as the Developer Tools.

The Developer Tools provide you with the ability to:

- Inspect the DOM

- Debug JavaScript

- Inspect objects and view messages via the console

- Figure out performance and memory issues

- See the network traffic

- …and a whole lot more!

In the interest of time (**Game of Thrones** is about to start soon, and this is the episode where I believe Ned Stark comes back to life as a dire wolf), what I'm going to do is focus on the first three items that are directly related to what you are learning about in this book.

Inspecting the DOM

The first Developer Tool feature we will look at is how you can inspect and even manipulate the contents of your DOM. With Chrome launched, navigate to **http://bit.ly/kirupaDevTool**.

NO BROWSER? NO PROBLEM!

Now, if you don't have a browser handy or simply can't access that link, don't worry. I'll explain what is going on at each step of the way so that you aren't left out of all the fun.

When you load this page, you will see a colorful background with some text displayed:

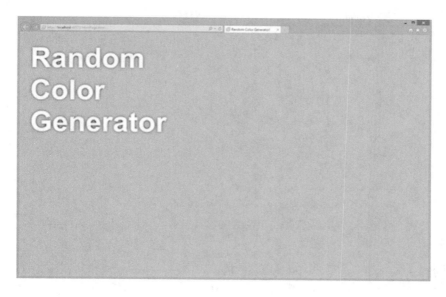

If you reload this page, you'll see this page showing up with a different background color. As you can guess, each page reload will result in a different background color getting generated:

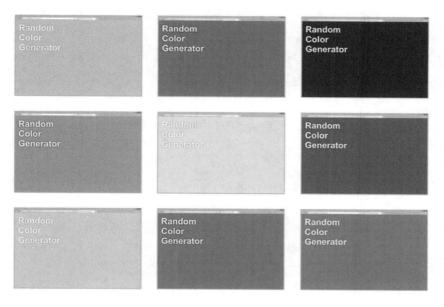

The first thing we'll do with this example is examine the DOM to see what is going on. Make sure your Developer Tools are visible, and ensure the Elements tab is selected:

What you will see is a view of your *live* markup from the page that is currently shown. To be more specific, this is a **view of your DOM**. The importance of this distinction is that this view provides you with a live version of what your page looks like. Any shenanigans JavaScript or your browser may have pulled on the DOM will be shown in this view.

Using our example as an…um…example, using **View Source** will result in something that looks as follows:

```
<!DOCTYPE html>
<html>


<head>
  <title>Random Color Generator!</title>
  <style>
    h2 {
      font-family: Arial, Helvetica;
      font-size: 100px;
      color: #FFF;
      text-shadow: 0px 0px 11px #333333;
      margin: 0;
      padding: 30px;
    }
```

```
      </style>
  </head>

  <body>
    <h2>Random
      <br />Color
      <br />Generator</h2>
    <script src="js/randomColor.js"> </script>
    <script>
      let bodyElement = document.querySelector("body");
      bodyElement.style.backgroundColor = getRandomColor();
    </script>
  </body>

</html>
```

The View Source command simply gives you a view of the markup as stored in the HTML page. Another way of saying this is that View Source gives you a (stale) version of the markup as it lives on the server and not a version of the DOM.

If you use the Developer Tool's DOM view, you will see a *DOM-based representation* of your document based on the *live version of the page*:

```
<!DOCTYPE html>
<html>

<head>
  <title>Random Color Generator!</title>
  <style>
    h2 {
      font-family: Arial, Helvetica;
      font-size: 100px;
      color: #FFF;
      text-shadow: 0px 0px 11px #333333;
      margin: 0;
      padding: 30px;
    }
  </style>
```

```
<body style="background-color: rgb(75, 63, 101);">
  <h2>Random
    <br>Color
    <br>Generator</h2>
  <script src="js/randomColor.js"> </script>
  <script>
    let bodyElement = document.querySelector("body");
    bodyElement.style.backgroundColor = getRandomColor();
  </script>

</body>

</html>
```

If you pay close attention, you'll notice some subtle differences in how some elements look. The biggest difference is the highlighted inline **background-color** style on the **body** element that only exists in the DOM view but not in the traditional View Source view. The reason is that we have some JavaScript that dynamically sets an inline style on the **body** element. The following note expands on why this happens!

THE DIFFERENCE BETWEEN THE DOM VIEW AND VIEW SOURCE

The reason for the discrepancy between the two code views goes back to what the DOM represents. To repeat this one more time, your DOM is the result of your browser and JavaScript having run to completion. It provides you with a fresh-from-the-oven look that mimics what your browser sees.

View Source is just a static representation of your document as it was on the server (or your computer). It doesn't contain any of the liveliness of your running page that the DOM view highlights. If you look at our JavaScript, you'll see that I specified that our **body** element get its **backgroundColor** set dynamically:

```
let bodyElement = document.querySelector("body");
bodyElement.style.backgroundColor = getRandomColor();
```

When this code runs, it modifies the DOM to set the **backgroundColor** property on the **body** element. You would never see this using View Source. Ever. That's why the DOM view the Developer Tools provide is your bestest friend in the whole wide world.

As examples highlighting the differences between the source and DOM go, our example was quite simple. To see the real benefit of the DOM view, you should experiment with some element reparentings, creations, and deletions to really see the divergence between viewing the source and examining the DOM. Some of the examples you saw in the previous chapters around DOM manipulation would be good things to inspect as well.

Debugging JavaScript

Moving along, the other big thing that the Developer Tools bring to the table is **debuggability**. I don't know if that is a really word or not, but the Developer Tools allow you to poke and prod at your code to figure out what is going wrong (or not wrong). The general catch-all phrase for all this is known as **debugging**.

In your Developer tools, click on the **Sources** tab:

```
Q  []   Elements  Network | Sources | Timeline  Profiles  Resources  Audits  Console
Sources  Content scripts  Snippets      [◄] randomColorGenerator.htm ×
▼ ⦿ www.kirupa.com                       1  <!DOCTYPE html>
   ▼ ⬜ html5/examples                    2  <html>
      ► ⬜ js                             3  <head>
      ▣ randomColorGenerator.htm         4      <title>Random Color Generator!</title>
                                         5      <style>
                                         6          h2 {
                                         7              font-family: Arial, Helvetica;
                                         8              font-size: 100px;
                                         9              color: #FFF;
                                        10              text-shadow: 0px 0px 11px #333333;
                                        11              margin: 0;
                                        12              padding: 30px;
                                        13          }
                                        14      </style>
                                        15  </head>
                                        16  <body>
                                    {} Line 1, Column 1
```

The Sources tab gives you access to all the files that are currently being used by your document. As the name implies, you are looking at the raw contents of these files—not the DOM-generated version from earlier that is your **bestest** friend.

From the tree view on the left, ensure the **randomColorGenerator.htm** file is selected. This will ensure that the contents of this file are displayed for you to examine on the right. In the displayed file, scroll all the way down until you see the `script` tag with the two lines of code that you saw earlier. Based on the line counts shown in the left gutter, our lines of JavaScript should be lines 20 and 21.

What we want to do is examine what happens when the code in Line 21 is about to execute. To do this, we need to tell the browser to stop when Line 21 is about to get executed. The way you do that is by setting what is known as a **breakpoint**. To set a breakpoint, click directly on the 21 label on the left gutter.

Once you've done that, you'll see the **21** getting highlighted:

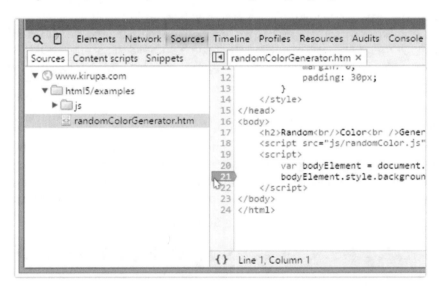

At this point, a breakpoint has been set. The next step is to actually have your browser run into this breakpoint. This is more peacefully known as "hitting the breakpoint." The way a breakpoint is hit is by ensuring your code runs into it. In our case, all we need to do is just hit F5 to refresh the page, as Line 21 will just execute as part your page loading and executing everything inside the `script` tags.

If everything worked as expected, you'll see your page load and suddenly pause with line 21 getting highlighted:

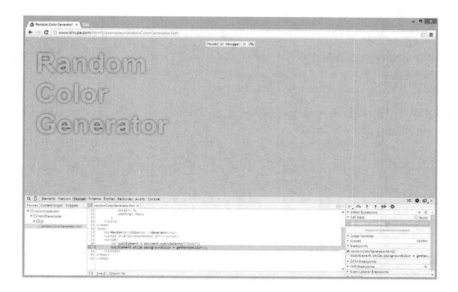

You are currently in **debugging mode**. The breakpoint you set on Line 21 has been hit. This means your entire page ground to a screeching halt the moment the browser hit it. At this point, with your browser being in suspended animation, you have the ability to fiddle with everything going on in your page. Think of this as time having stopped with only you having the ability to move around, inspect, and alter the surroundings. If a movie hasn't been made about this, somebody should get on it!

While in this mode, go back to Line 21, and hover over the `bodyElement` variable. When you hover over it, you'll see a tooltip indicating the various properties and values that this particular object contains:

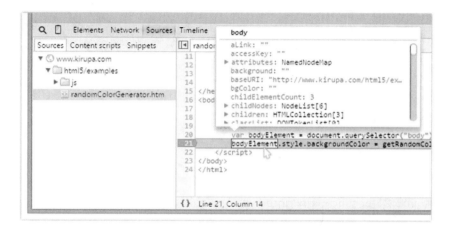

You can then interact with the tooltip, scroll through all the objects, and even dig deeper into complex objects that have more objects inside them. Because `bodyElement` is basically the JavaScript/DOM representation of the `body` element, you'll see a lot of properties that you encountered indirectly from our look at `HTMLElement` a few chapters ago.

On the right side of your source view, you have more angles through which you can inspect your code:

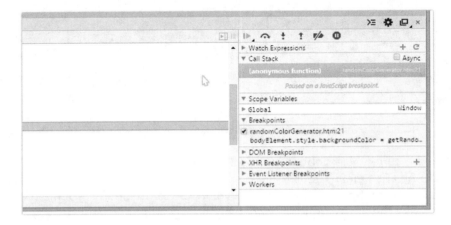

I won't be explaining what all of those categories do, but I am pointing that area out just so you know that you have the ability to examine the current state of all your JavaScript variables and objects in much greater detail if you so wanted to.

The other big advantage a breakpoint provides is the ability for you to step through your code just like your browser would. Right now, we are stuck on Line 21. To step through the code, click on the "Step into function call" button found on the right-hand side:

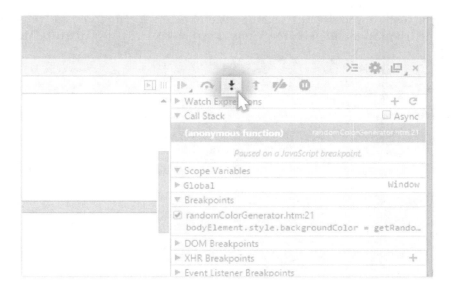

Remember, this is the line of code you are currently broken at:

```
bodyElement.style.backgroundColor = getRandomColor();
```

Once you've clicked that button, notice what happens. You will find yourself inside **randomColor.js** where the `getRandomColor` function has been defined. Keep clicking on the "Step into function call" to continue stepping into your code and going through each line of the `getRandomColor` function. Notice that you now get to see how the objects in your browser's memory update as you go line-by-line and execute the code sequentially. If you are tired of doing that, you can **Step back** by clicking on the **Step out of current function** button (found to the right of your **Step into** button) that exits you out of this function. In our case, that is back to Line 21 in randomColorGenerator.htm.

If you just want to execute your app without stepping through any more of the code, click on the **Play** button found a few pixels to the left of **Step into**:

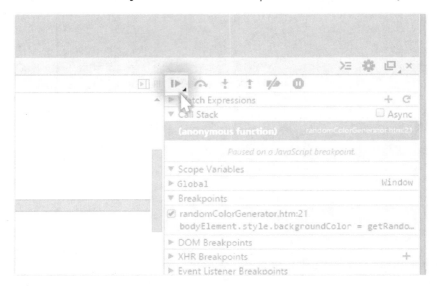

When you hit **Play**, your code will execute. If you happen to have another breakpoint set somewhere in your code's path, that breakpoint will also get hit. When stopped at any breakpoint, you can choose to **Step into**, **Step out**, or just resume execution with **Play**. Because we only set one breakpoint, hitting **Play** will just run the code to completion and have your random color appear as the background for your body element:

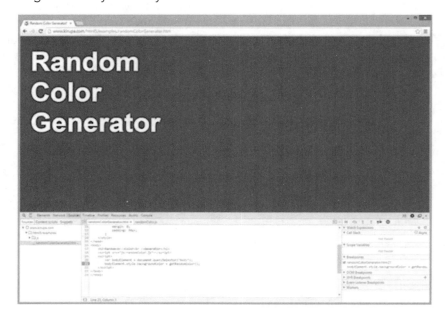

To remove a breakpoint, just click on the line number that you set the breakpoint on. If you click on the Line 21 label again, the breakpoint will toggle itself off and you can just run your application without getting into debugging mode.

So, there you have it. A whirlwind tour of how to use some of the debugging functionality you have at your disposal. To reiterate something I mentioned at the beginning of this chapter, I am only scratching the surface of what is possible. The resources I provide toward the end should help you out further.

Meet the Console

The other OTHER big Debugging Tool functionality we will look at is using what is known as the **Console**. The console provides you with the ability to do several things. It allows you to see messages logged by your code. It also allows you to pass commands and inspect any object that is currently in scope.

To show the Console, navigate to the Console tab by clicking (or tapping) on it:

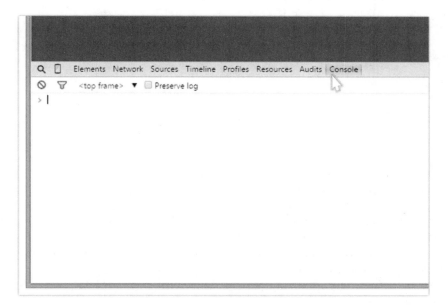

Don't be afraid of the vast emptiness that you see in front of you. Instead, embrace the freedom and fresh air.

Anyway, what the Console provides you with is the ability to inspect or call any object that exists in whatever scope your application is currently running in. With no breakpoints set, launching the console puts you in the global state.

Inspecting Objects

Where your cursor is right now, type in **window** and press Enter:

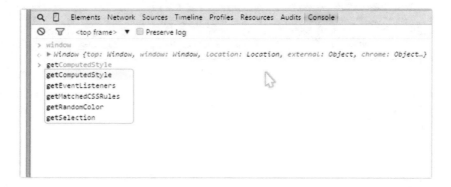

What you will see is an interactive listing of all the things that live in your `window` object. You can start to type in any valid object or property, and if it is in scope, you will be able to access it, inspect its value, or even execute it:

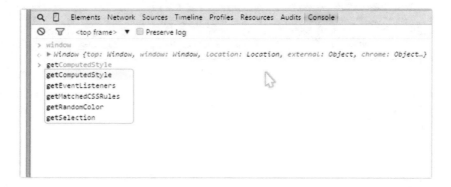

This is by no means a read-only playground. You can cause all sorts of mayhem. For example, if you type in **document.body.remove()** and press Enter, your entire document will just disappear. If you did end up deleting the `body`, just refresh the page to get back to your earlier state. Developer Tools primarily work with the in-memory representation of your page and don't write back to source. Your experimentations will safely stay in the transient realm.

REFRESHER ON THE SCOPE/STATE

On several occasions, I mentioned that your console allows you to inspect the world at whatever scope you are currently in. This is basically just applying what you learned about Variable Scope in Chapter 8, "Variable Scope," to the Console's behavior.

Let's say you have a breakpoint set at the following highlighted line:

```
let oddNumber = false;

function calculateOdd(num) {
  if (num % 2 == 0) {
    oddNumber = false;
  } else {
    oddNumber = true;
  }
}
calculateOdd(3);
```

When you run the code and the breakpoint gets hit, the value of **oddNumber** is still **false**. Your breakpointed line hasn't been executed yet, and you can verify this by testing the value of **oddNumber** in the Console. Next, let's say you run this code, hit this breakpoint, and step through to the next line.

At this point, your **oddNumber** value is set to **true**. Your Console will now reflect the new value, for that is what the in-memory representation of **oddNumber** states. The main takeaway is that your Console's view of the world is directly tied to where in the code you are currently focusing on. This is especially made obvious when you are stepping through code and the scope you are in changes frequently.

Logging Messages

We are almost done with all of this Developer Tools business. The last thing we will look at is the console's ability to log messages from your code. Remember all those times where we did something like this?

```
function doesThisWork() {
    console.log("It works!!!");
}
```

The "this" being where we used an **alert** statement to print some value or prove that the code is being executed. Well, we can stop doing that now. By using the console, you have a far less annoying way of printing messages without interrupting everything with a modal dialog box. You can use the **console.log** function to pass in whatever you want to print into the console:

```
function doesThisWork() {
    console.log("It works!!!")
}
```

When this code executes, you'll see whatever you logged get printed in your Console when you bring it up:

Using the console is, in almost every way, superior to using **alert** for debugging purposes. In future code snippets, you'll start to see me using **console.log** over **alert** in some cases.

THE ABSOLUTE MINIMUM

If you have never used a Developer Tool before, I really REALLY think you should take some time to get familiar with one. JavaScript is one of those languages where things can go wrong even when everything looks right. In the very simple examples you'll encounter in this book, it's easy to spot mistakes. When you start working on larger and more complex applications, having the right tools to diagnose issues will save you many hours of effort.

To learn more about the Developer Tools (aka *Dev Tools* as the cool kids call it) in far greater detail than what I've covered here, check out the following resources:

- **Overview of the Chrome Dev Tools:** http://bit.ly/kirupaChromeDevTools

- **Overview of the IE/Edge F12 Dev Tools:** http://bit.ly/kirupaIEDevTools

- **Overview of the Firefox Dev Tools:** http://bit.ly/kirupaFFDevTools

- **Overview of the Safari Web Inspector** http://bit.ly/kirupaSafariDevTools

EVENTS

In case you haven't noticed, most applications and web sites are pretty boring when left alone. They launch with great fanfare and gusto, but the excitement they bring to the table goes away very quickly if we don't start interacting with them:

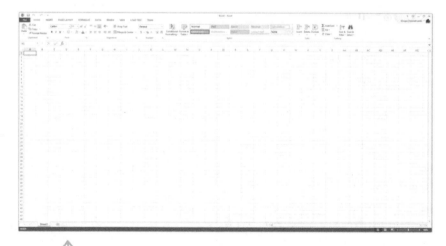

OMG! Just do something...anything!

The reason for this is simple. Our applications exist to react to things that we do to them. They have some built in motivation when we launch them to get themselves out of bed and ready for the day. Everything else that they do afterwards depends largely on what we tell them to do. This is where things get really interesting.

The way we tell our applications what to do is by having them react to what are known as **events**. In this chapter, we will take an introductory look at what events are and how we can use them.

Onward!

What Are Events?

At a high level, everything we create can be modeled by the following statement:

When _____ happens, do _____ .

We can fill in the blanks in this statement in a bajillion different ways. The first blank calls out something that happens. The second blank describes the reaction to that. Here are some examples of this statement filled out:

When **a page load** happens, do **play the video of a cat sliding into cardboard**.

When **a click** happens, do **submit my online purchase**.

When **a mouse release** happens, do **hurl the giant/not-so-happy bird**.

When **a delete key press** happens, do **send this file to the Recycle Bin**.

When **a touch gesture** happens, do **apply this old timey filter to this photo**.

When **a file download** happens, do **update the progress bar**.

This generic model applies to all the code we've written together. This model also applies to all the code our favorite developer/designer friends wrote for their applications. There is no way of escaping this model, so...there is no point in resisting. Instead, we need to learn to embrace the star of this model, the very talented critter known as the **event**.

An event is nothing more than a signal. It communicates that something has just happened. This something could be a mouse click. It could be a key press on our keyboard. It could be our window getting resized. It could just be our document simply getting loaded. The thing to take away is that our signal could be any hundreds of somethings that are built-in to the JavaScript language...or custom somethings that we created just for our app alone.

Getting back to our model, events make up the first half:

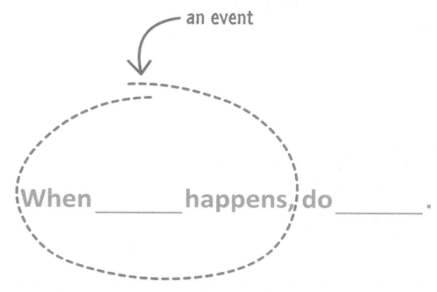

An event defines the thing that happens. **It fires the signal**. The second part of the model is defined by the reaction to the event:

After all, what good is a signal if there isn't someone somewhere that is waiting for it and then takes the appropriate action?! Ok—now that we have a high-level overview of what events are, let's dive into how events live in the nature reserve known as JavaScript.

Events and JavaScript

Given the importance of events, it should be no surprise to you that JavaScript provides us with a lot of great support for working with them. To work with events, there are two things we need to do:

1. Listen for events

2. React to events

These two steps seem pretty simple, but never forget that we are dealing with JavaScript here. The simplicity is just a smokescreen for the depth of the trauma JavaScript will inflict upon us if we take a wrong step. Maybe I am being overly dramatic here, but we'll find out soon enough.

1. Listening for Events

To more bluntly state what I danced around earlier, almost everything we do inside an application results in an event getting fired. Sometimes, our application will fire events automatically...such as when it loads. Sometimes, our application will fire events as a reaction to us actually interacting with it. The thing to note is that our application is bombarded by events constantly whether we intended to have them get fired or not. Our task is to tell our application to listen only to the events we care about.

The thankless job of listening to the right event is handled entirely by a function called `addEventListener`. This function is responsible for being eternally vigilant so that it can notify another part of our application when an interesting event gets fired.

The way we use this function looks as follows:

```
source.addEventListener(eventName, eventHandler, false);
```

That's probably not very helpful, so let's dissect what each part of this function means.

The Source

We call `addEventListener` via an element or object that we want to listen for events on. Typically, that will be a DOM element, but it can also be our `document`, `window`, or any object specially designed to fire events.

The Event Name

The first argument we specify to the `addEventListener` function is the name of the event we are interested in listening to. The full list of events we have at your disposal is simply too large to list here (go **here instead**), but some of the most common events you will encounter are shown in Table 31.1.

TABLE 31.1   Common Events

Event	Event is fired...
Click	...when you press down and release the primary mouse button, trackpad, etc.
Mousemove	...whenever you move the mouse cursor
Mouseover	...when you move the mouse cursor over an element. This is the event you would use for detecting a hover!
Mouseout	...when your mouse cursor moves outside the boundaries of an element.
Dblclick	...when you quickly click twice.
DOMContentLoaded	...when your document's DOM has fully loaded. You can learn more about this event in the following chapter.
Load	...when your entire document (DOM, external stuff like images, scripts, etc.) has fully loaded.
Keydown	...when you press down on a key on your keyboard
Keyup	...when you stop pressing down on a key on your keyboard
Scroll	...when an element is scrolled around
wheel and DOMMouseScroll	...every time you use your mousewheel to scroll up or down

In subsequent chapters, we will look at a lot of these events in greater detail. For now, just take a quick glance at the click event. We will be using that one in a few moments.

The Event Handler

The second argument requires us to specify a function that will get called when the event gets overheard. This function is very affectionately known as the **event handler** by friends and family. We'll learn a whole lot more about this function (and occasionally an object) in a few moments.

To Capture, or Not to Capture, That Is the Question!

The last argument is made up of either a **true** or a **false**. To fully help us understand the implications of specifying either value, we are going to have to wait until the **Event Bubbling and Capturing in JavaScript** chapter. This chapter happens to be next in this series, so we won't be waiting long.

Putting It All Together

Now that we've seen the `addEventListener` function and what it looks like, let's tie it all up with an example of this function fully decked out:

```
document.addEventListener("click", changeColor, false);
```

Our `addEventListener` in this example is attached to the `document` object. When a `click` event is overheard, it calls the `changeColor` function (aka the event handler) to react to the event. This sets us up nicely for the next section which is all about reacting to events.

2. Reacting to Events

As we saw in the previous section, listening to events is handled by `addEventListener`. What to do after an event is overheard is handled by the event handler. I wasn't joking when I mentioned earlier that an event handler is nothing more than a function or object:

```
function normalAndBoring() {
  // I like hiking and puppies and other stuff!
}
```

The only distinction between a typical function and one that is designated as the event handler is that our event handler function is specifically called out by name in an `addEventListener` call (and receives an `Event` object as its argument):

```
document.addEventListener("click", changeColor, false);
```

```
function changeColor(event) {
  // I am important!!!
}
```

Any code we place inside our event handler will execute when the event our `addEventListener` function cares about gets overheard.

A Simple Example

The best way to make sense of what we've learned so far is to see all of this fully working. To play along, add the following markup and code to an HTML document:

```
<!DOCTYPE html>
<html>
```

```
<head>
  <title>Click Anywhere!</title>
</head>

<body>
  <script>
    document.addEventListener("click", changeColor, false);

    function changeColor() {
      document.body.style.backgroundColor = "#FFC926";
    }
  </script>
</body>

</html>
```

If we preview our document in the browser, we will initially just see a blank page as shown in Figure 31.1.

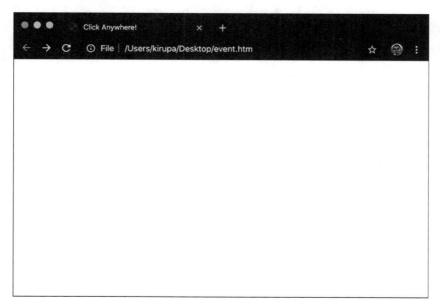

FIGURE 31.1

A blank page is all we see!

Things will change when you click anywhere on the page, though. Once you've completed your click (aka released the mouse press), your page's background will change from being white to a yellow-ish color as seen in Figure 31.2.

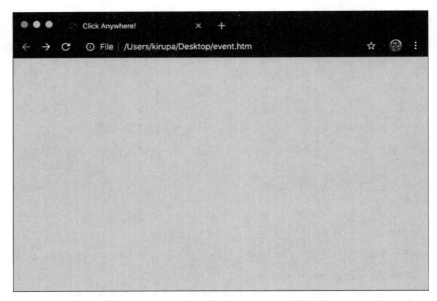

FIGURE 31.2

Our blank page turns yellow when clicked!

The reason why this example does what it does lies in our code:

```
document.addEventListener("click", changeColor, false);


function changeColor() {
  document.body.style.backgroundColor = "#FFC926";
}
```

The addEventListener call is identical to what we saw earlier, so let's skip that one. Instead, let's pay attention to the changeColor event handler.

```
document.addEventListener("click", changeColor, false);


function changeColor() {
  document.body.style.backgroundColor = "#FFC926";
}
```

This function gets called when the **click** event on the document is overheard. When this function gets called, it sets the background color of the body element to a shade of yellow. Tying this back to the very beginning where we generalized how applications work, this is what this example looks like:

When **a click** happens, do **change the background color**.

our click event

the changeColor function

If all of this makes complete sense to you, then that's great! You just learned about one of the most important concepts you'll encounter. We aren't done just yet. We let the event handler off the hook a little too easily, so let's pay it one more visit.

The Event Arguments and the Event Type

Our event handler does more than just get called when an event gets overheard by an event listener. It also provides access to the underlying event object as part of its arguments. To access this event object easily, we need to modify our event handler signature to support this argument.

Here is an example where we specify the event name to refer to our event arguments:

```
function myEventHandler(event) {
  // event handlery stuff
}
```

At this point, our event handler is still a plain old boring function. It just happens to be a function that takes one argument...the event argument! We can go with any valid identifier for the argument, but I tend to go with event or just e because that is what all the cool kids do. There is nothing technically wrong with identifying our event as follows:

```
function myEventHandler(isNyanCatReal) {
  // event handlery stuff
}
```

The important detail is that the event argument points to an event object, and this object is passed in as part of the event firing. There is a reason why we are paying attention to what seems like a typical and boring occurrence. This event object contains properties that are **relevant to the event that was fired**. An event triggered by a mouse click will have different properties when compared to an event triggered by a keyboard key press, a page load, an animation, and a whole lot more. Most events will have their own specialized behavior that we will rely on, and the event object is our window into all of that uniqueness.

Despite the variety of events and resulting event objects we can get, there are certain properties that are common. This commonality is made possible because all event objects are derived from a base `Event` type (technically, an `Interface`). Some of the popular properties from the `Event` type that we will use are:

1. `currentTarget`

2. `target`

3. `preventDefault`

4. `stopPropagation`

5. `type`

To fully understand what these properties do, we need to go a little deeper in our understanding of events. We aren't there yet, so just know that these properties exist. We'll be seeing them real soon in subsequent chapters.

REMOVING AN EVENT LISTENER

Sometimes, we will need to remove an event listener from an element. The way we do that is by using `addEventListener`'s arch-nemesis, the `removeEventListener` function:

```
something.removeEventListener(eventName, eventHandler, false);
```

As we can see, this function takes the exact type of arguments as an `addEventListener` function. The reason for that is simple. When we are listening for an event on an element or object, JavaScript uses the `eventName`, `eventHandler`, and the **true/false** value to uniquely identify that event listener. To remove this event listener, we need to specify the exact same arguments.

Here is an example:

```
document.addEventListener("click", changeColor, false);
document.removeEventListener("click", changeColor, false);

function changeColor() {
  document.body.style.backgroundColor = "#FFC926";
}
```

The event listener we added in the first line is completely neutralized by the removeEventListener call in the highlighted 2nd line. If the removeEventListener call used any argument that was different than what was specified with the corresponding addEventListener call, then its impact would be ignored and the event listening will continue.

THE ABSOLUTE MINIMUM

Well, that's all there is to getting an introduction to events. Just remember that you have your addEventListener function that allows you to register an event handler function. This event handler function will get called when the event your event listener is listening for gets fired. While we touched base on a few other topics, they will make more sense when we view them in the context of more advanced event-related examples that you will see in the following chapters!

IN THIS CHAPTER

- Learn how events travel through the DOM
- Understand the differences between event capturing and event bubbling
- Interrupt events

32

EVENT BUBBLING AND CAPTURING

In the previous chapter, you learned how to use the `addEventListener` function to listen for events that you want to react to. That chapter covered the basics, but it glossed over an important detail about how events actually get fired. An event isn't an isolated disturbance. Like a butterfly flapping its wings, an earthquake, a meteor strike, or a Godzilla visit, many events ripple and affect a bunch of elements that lie in their path.

In this article, I will put on my investigative glasses, a top hat, and a serious British accent to explain what exactly happens when an event gets fired. You will learn about the two phases events live in, why all of this is relevant, and a few other tricks to help you better take control of events.

Event Goes Down. Event Goes Up.

To better help us understand events and their lifestyle, let's frame all of this in the context of a simple example. Here is some HTML we'll refer to.

```html
<!DOCTYPE html>
<html>

<head>
  <title>Events!</title>
</head>

<body id="theBody" class="item">
  <div id="one_a" class="item">
    <div id="two" class="item">
      <div id="three_a" class="item">
        <button id="buttonOne" class="item">one</button>
      </div>
      <div id="three_b" class="item">
        <button id="buttonTwo" class="item">two</button>
        <button id="buttonThree" class="item">three</button>
      </div>
    </div>
  </div>
  <div id="one_b" class="item">

  </div>
  <script>

  </script>
</body>

</html>
```

As we can see, there is nothing really exciting going on here. The HTML should look pretty straightforward (as opposed to being shifty and constantly staring at its phone), and its DOM representation looks as shown in Figure 32.1.

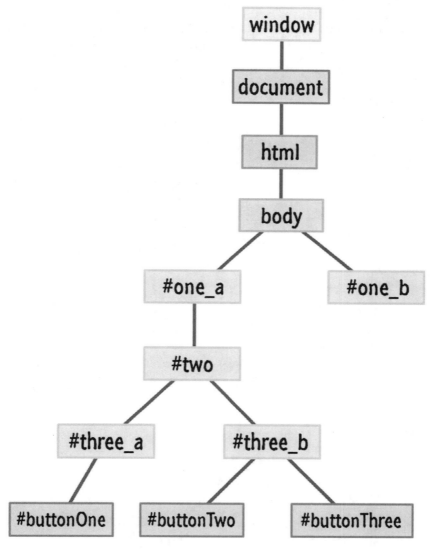

FIGURE 32.1

What the DOM for the markup we saw looks like.

Here is where our investigation is going to begin. Let's say that we click on the **buttonOne** element. From what we saw previously, you know that a click event is going to be fired. The interesting part that I omitted is where exactly the click event is going to get fired from. Your click event (just like almost every other JavaScript event) does not actually originate at the element that you interacted with. That would be too easy and make far too much sense.

Instead, an event starts at the root of your document:

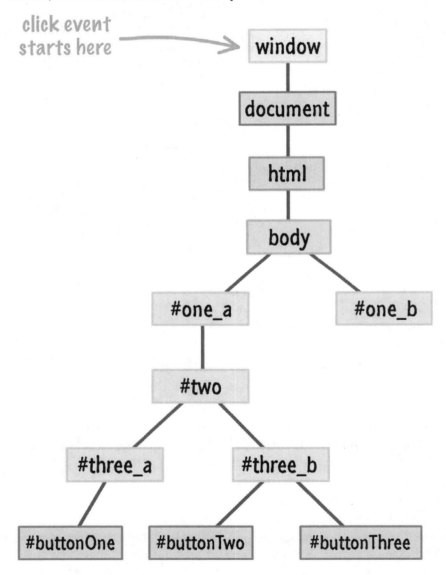

From the root, the event makes its way through the narrow pathways of the DOM and stops at the element that triggered the event, **buttonOne** (also more formally known as the **event target**):

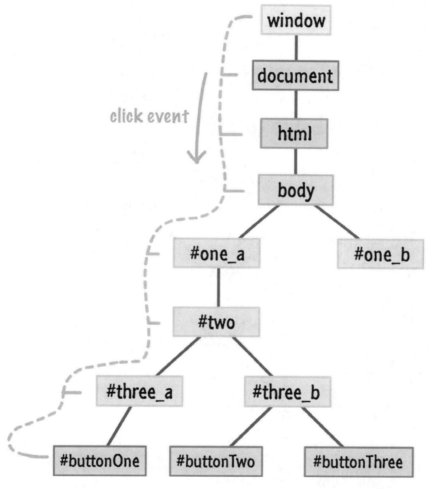

As shown in the diagram, the path your event takes is direct, but it does obnoxiously notify every element along that path. This means that if you were to listen for a click event on **body, one_a, two,** or **three_a**, the associated event handler will get fired. This is an important detail that we will revisit in a little bit.

Now, once our event reaches its target, it doesn't stop. Like some sort of an energetic bunny for a battery company whose trademarked name I probably can't mention here, the event keeps going by retracing its steps and returning back to the root:

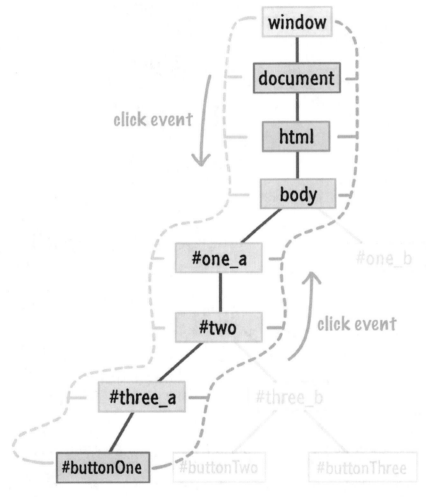

Just like before, every element along the event's path as it is moving on up gets notified about its existence.

Meet the Phases

One of the main things to note is that it doesn't matter where in your DOM you initiate an event. The event always starts at the root, goes down until it hits the target, and then goes back up to the root. This entire journey is very formally defined, so let's look at all of this formalness.

The part where you initiate the event and the event barrels down the DOM from the root is known as the **Event Capturing Phase**:

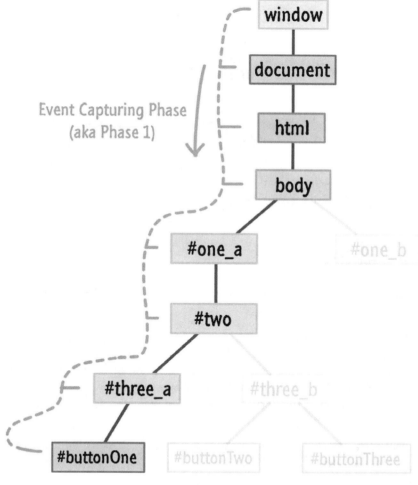

The less learned in the world may just call it **Phase 1**, so be aware that you'll see the proper name and the phase name used interchangeably in event-related content you may encounter in real life. Up next is **Phase 2** where our event bubbles back up to the root:

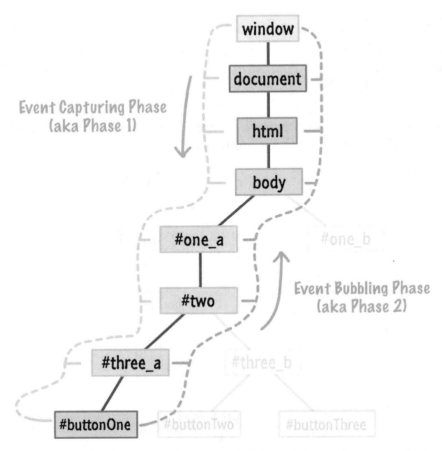

This phase is also known as the **Event Bubbling Phase**. The event "bubbles" back to the top!

Anyway, all of the elements in an event's path are pretty lucky. They have the good fortune of getting notified twice when an event is fired. This kinda sorta maybe affects the code you write, for every time we listen for events, we make a choice on which phase we want to listen for your event on. Do we listen to your event as it is fumbling down in the capture phase? Do we listen to your event as it climbs back up in the bubbling phase?

Choosing the phase is a very subtle detail that you specify with a **true** or **false** as part of your addEventListener call:

```
item.addEventListener("click", doSomething, true);
```

If you remember, I glossed over the third argument to addEventListener in the previous chapter. This third argument specifies whether you want to listen for this event during the capture phase. An argument of **true** means that you want to listen to the event during the capture phase. If you specify **false**, this means you want to listen for the event during the bubbling phase.

To listen to an event across both the capturing and bubbling phases, you can simply do the following:

```
item.addEventListener("click", doSomething, true);
item.addEventListener("click", doSomething, false);
```

I don't know why you would ever want to do this, but if you ever do, you now know what needs to be done.

NOT SPECIFYING A PHASE

Now, you can be rebellious and choose to not specify this third argument for the phase altogether:

```
item.addEventListener("click", doSomething);
```

When you don't specify the third argument, the default behavior is to listen to your event during the bubbling phase. It's equivalent to passing in a **false** value as the argument.

Who Cares?

At this point, you are probably wondering why all of this matters. This is doubly true if you have been happily working with events for a really long time and this is the first time you've ever heard about this. Your choice of listening to an event in the capturing or bubbling phase is mostly irrelevant to what you will be doing. Very rarely will you find yourself scratching your head because your event listening and handling code isn't doing the right thing because you accidentally specified **true** instead of **false** in your addEventListener call.

With all this said…there will come a time in your life when you need to know and deal with a capturing or bubbling situation. This time will sneak up on your code and cause you many hours of painful head scratching. Over the years, these are the situations where I've had to consciously be aware of which phase of my event's life I am watching for:

1. Dragging an element around the screen and ensuring the drag still happens even if the element I am dragging slips out from under the cursor

2. Nested menus that reveal submenus when you hover over them

3. You have multiple event handlers on both phases, and you want to focus only on the capturing or bubbling phase event handlers exclusively

4. A third party component/control library has its own eventing logic and you want to circumvent it for your own custom behavior

5. You want to override some built-in/default browser behavior such as when you click on the scrollbar or give focus to a text field

In my nearly 105 years of working with JavaScript, these five things were all I was able to come up with. Even this is a bit skewed to the last few years, since various browsers didn't work well with the various phases at all.

Event, Interrupted

The last thing I am going to talk about before re-watching Godzilla is how to prevent your event from propagating. An event isn't guaranteed to live a fulfilling life where it starts and ends at the root. Sometimes, it is actually desirable to prevent your event from growing old and happy.

To end the life of an event, you have the stopPropagation method on your Event object:

```
function handleClick(e) {
    e.stopPropagation();


    // do something
}
```

As its name implies, the stopPropagation method prevents your event from continuing through the phases. Continuing with our earlier example, let's say that you are listening for the click event on the **three_a** element and wish to stop the event from propagating. The code for preventing the propagation will look as follows:

```
let theElement = document.querySelector("#three_a");
theElement.addEventListener("click", doSomething, true);


function doSomething(e) {
    e.stopPropagation();
}
```

When you click on **buttonOne**, here is what our event's path will look like:

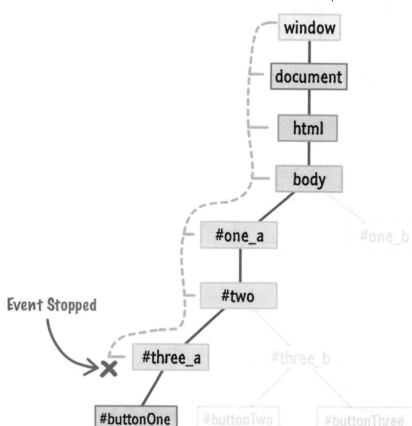

Our `click` event will steadfastly start moving down the DOM tree notifying every element on the path to **buttonOne**. Because the **three_a** element is listening for the `click` event during the capture phase, the event handler associated with it will get called:

```
function doSomething(e) {
   e.stopPropagation();
}
```

In general, events will not continue to propagate until an event handler that gets activated is fully dealt with. Because **three_a** has an event listener specified to react on a `click` event, the doSomething event handler gets called. Your event is in a holding pattern at this point until the doSomething event handler executes and returns.

In this case, the event will not propagate further. The doSomething event handler is its last client, thanks to the stopPropagation function that is hiding in the shadows to kill the event right there and then. The `click` event will never reach the **buttonOne** element nor get a chance to bubble back up. So tragically sad.

TIP Another function that lives on your event object that you may awkwardly run into is `preventDefault`:

```
function overrideScrollBehavior(e) {
  e.preventDefault();

  // do something
}
```

What this function does is a little mysterious. Many HTML elements exhibit a default behavior when you interact with it. For example, clicking in a textbox gives that textbox focus with a little blinking text cursor appearing. Using your mouse wheel in a scrollable area will scroll in the direction you are scrolling. Clicking on a check box will toggle the checked state on or off. All of these are examples of built-in reactions to events your browser instinctively knows how to handle.

If you want to turn off this default behavior, you can call the `preventDefault` function. This function needs to be called when reacting to an event on the element whose default reaction you want to ignore. You can see an example of me using this function in the *Smooth Parallax Scrolling* tutorial online at: **http://bit.ly/kirupaParallax**.

THE ABSOLUTE MINIMUM

So...yeah! How about those events and their bubbling and capturing phases? One of the best ways to learn more about how event capturing and bubbling works is to just write some code and see how your event makes its way around the DOM.

We are done with the technical part of all this, but if you have a few more minutes to spare, then I encourage you watch the somewhat related episode of **Comedians Getting Coffee** aptly titled *It's Bubble Time, Jerry!* In what is probably their *bestest* episode, Michael Richards and Jerry Seinfeld just chat over coffee about events, the bubbling phase, and other very important topics. I think.

IN THIS CHAPTER

- Learn how to listen to the mouse using the various mouse events
- Understand the MouseEvent object
- Deal with the Mouse Wheel

33

MOUSE EVENTS

One of the most common ways people (and possibly cats) interact with their computers is by using a pointing device known as a **mouse** (Figure 33.1).

↖ Aww! Looks sooo cute. Can we keep him?!

FIGURE 33.1

Cats probably like them too.

This magical device allows you to accomplish great things by moving it around with your hands and clicking around with your fingers. Using them as a, um… user is one thing. As a developer, trying to make your code work with a mouse is something else. That's where this chapter comes in.

Meet the Mouse Events

In JavaScript, our primary way of dealing with the mouse is through events. There are a boatload of events that deal with the mouse, but we won't be looking at all of them here. Instead, we'll focus on just the cool and popular ones such as the following:

- `click`
- `dblclick`
- `mouseover`
- `mouseout`
- `mouseenter`
- `mouseleave`
- `mousedown`
- `mouseup`
- `mousemove`
- `contextmenu`
- `mousewheel` and `DOMMouseScroll`

The names of these events should give you a good idea of what they do, but we'll take nothing for granted and look at each of these events in some level of greater detail in the following sections. I should warn you that some events are just dreadfully boring to learn about.

Clicking Once and Clicking Twice

Let's start with probably the most popular of all the mouse events that you will use—the **click** event. This event is fired when you **click** on an element. To state this differently in a way that doesn't involve mentioning the thing you are describing as part of your description, the `click` event is fired when you use your mouse to press down on an element and then release the press while still over that same element.

Here is a totally unnecessary visualization of what I am talking about:

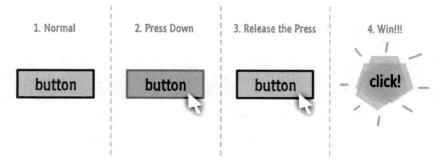

You've seen the code for working with the click event a few times already, but you can never really get enough of it. Here is another example:

```
let button = document.querySelector("#myButton");
button.addEventListener("click", doSomething, false);

function doSomething(e) {
  console.log("Mouse clicked on something!");
}
```

The way you listen to the `click` event is just like almost any other event that you'll encounter, so I won't unnecessarily bore you with that detail and our old friend `addEventListener`. Instead, I will bore you with details about the somewhat related `dblclick` event.

The `dblclick` event is fired when you quickly repeat a click action a double number of times, and the code for using it looks as follows:

```
let button = document.querySelector("#myButton");
button.addEventListener("dblclick", doSomething, false);

function doSomething(e) {
  console.log("Mouse clicked on something...twice!");
}
```

The amount of time between each click that ends up resulting in a `dblclick` event is based on the OS you are running the code in. It's neither browser specific nor something you can define (or read) using JavaScript.

DON'T OVERDO IT

If you happen to listen to both the `click` and `dblclick` event on an element, your event handlers will get called three times when you double-click. You will get two `click` events to correspond to each time you clicked. After your second click, you will also get a `dblclick` event.

Mousing Over and Mousing Out

The classic hover over and hover out scenarios are handled by the appropriately titled `mouseover` and `mouseout` events respectively:

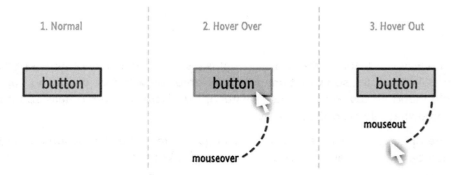

Here is a snippet of these two events in action:

```
let button = document.querySelector("#myButton");
button.addEventListener("mouseover", hovered, false);
button.addEventListener("mouseout", hoveredOut, false);

function hovered(e) {
  console.log("Hovered!");
}

function hoveredOut(e) {
  console.log("Hovered Away!");
}
```

That's all there is to these two events. They are pretty boring overall…which, as you've probably found out by now, is actually a good thing when it comes to programming concepts.

WHAT ABOUT THE OTHER TWO SIMILAR-LOOKING EVENTS?

We just looked at two events (mouseover and mouseout), which are all about hovering over something and hovering away from something. As it turns out, you have two more events that pretty much do the exact same thing. These are your mouseenter and mouseleave events. There is one important detail to know about these events that makes them unique. The mouseenter and mouseleave events do not bubble.

This detail only matters if the element you are interested in hovering over or out from has child elements. All four of these events behave identically when there are no child elements at play. If there are child elements at play:

- mouseover and mouseout will get fired each time you move the mouse over and around a child element. This means that you could be seeing many unnecessary event fires even though it seems like you are moving your mouse within a single region.

- mouseenter and mouseleave will get fired only once. It doesn't matter how many child elements your mouse moves through.

For 90% of what you will do, mouseover and mouseout will be good enough. For the other times, often involving slightly more complex UI scenarios, you'll be happy that the non-bubbling mouseenter and mouseleave events are available.

The Very Click-like Mousing Down and Mousing Up Events

Two events that are almost subcomponents of the `click` event are the `mouse-down` and `mouseup` ones. From the following diagram, you'll see why:

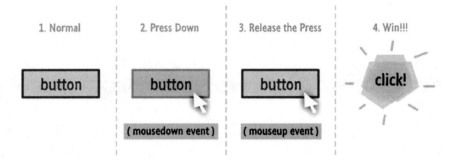

When you press down with your mouse, the `mousedown` event is fired. When you release the press, the `mouseup` event is fired. If the element you pressed down on and released from are the same element, the `click` event will also fire.

You can see all of this from the following snippet:

```
let button = document.querySelector("#myButton");
button.addEventListener("mousedown", mousePressed, false);
button.addEventListener("mouseup", mouseReleased, false);
button.addEventListener("click", mouseClicked, false);

function mousePressed(e) {
  console.log("Mouse is down!");
}

function mouseReleased(e) {
  console.log("Mouse is up!");
}

function mouseClicked(e) {
  console.log("Mouse is clicked!");
}
```

You may be wondering, "Why bother with these two events?" The `click` event seems perfectly suited for most cases where you may want to use `mousedown` and mouseup. If you are spending sleepless nights wondering about this, the answer is…**Yes!** A more helpful (and sensible) answer is that the mousedown and mouseup events simply give you more control in case you need it. Some interactions (such as drags…or awesome moves in video games where you press and hold to charge a lightning bolt of doom!) need you to act only when the mousedown event has happened but the mouseup event hasn't.

The Event Heard Again…and Again…and Again!

One of the most chatty events that you'll ever encounter is the very friendly mousemove event. This event fires a whole lotta times as your mouse moves over the element you are listening for the mousemove event on:

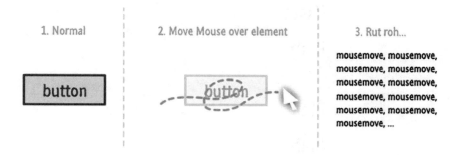

What follows is an example of the mousemove event in code:

```
let button = document.querySelector("#myButton");
button.addEventListener("mousemove", mouseIsMoving, false);

function mouseIsMoving(e) {
  console.log("Mouse is on the run!");
}
```

Your browser controls the rate at which the mousemove event gets fired, and this event gets fired if your mouse moves even a single pixel. This event is great for many interactive scenarios where your mouse's current position is relevant to keep track of, for example.

The Context Menu

The last mouse-related event we are going to look at is affectionately called `contextmenu`. As you probably know very well, when you commonly right-click in various applications, you will see a menu:

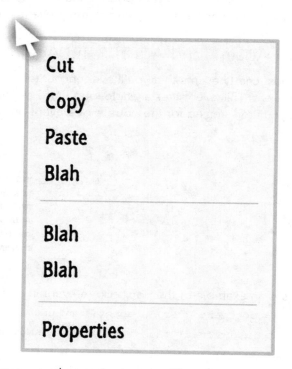

This menu is known as the **context menu**. The `contextmenu` event is fired just before this menu appears.

Now, you may be wondering why anybody would want an event for this situation. To be completely honest with you (as opposed to all of the other times when I've been lying), there is only one primary reason to listen for this event. That reason has to do with preventing this menu from appearing when you right-click or use a context menu keyboard button or shortcut.

Here is an example of how you can **prevent** the **default** behavior where the context menu appears:

```
document.addEventListener("contextmenu", hideMenu, false);

function hideMenu(e) {
  e.preventDefault();
}
```

The preventDefault method on any type of Event stops whatever the default behavior is from actually happening. Because the contextmenu event is fired before the menu appears, calling preventDefault on it ensures the context menu never shows up. The default behavior has been prevented from running. Yes, this is also the second time I'm mentioning this property. As you know, I am being paid by the word (ha ha).

With all of this said, I can think of a billion other ways you could prevent the context menu from appearing without using an event for dealing with all of this, but that's the way things are…for now <insert evil, maniacal laughter>!

The MouseEvent Properties

Let's get a little bit more specific. All of the mouse events we've seen so far are based around MouseEvent. Normally, this is the kind of factoid you keep under your hat for trivia night and ignore. This time around, though, this detail is important because MouseEvent brings with it a number of properties that make working with the mouse easier. Let's look at some of them.

The Global Mouse Position

The screenX and screenY properties return the distance your mouse cursor is from the top-left location of your primary monitor:

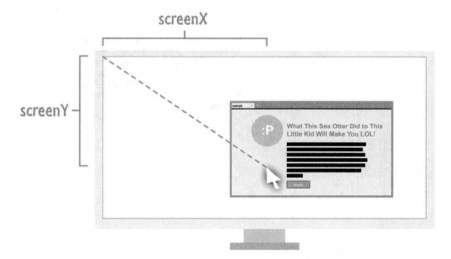

Here is a very simple example of the `screenX` and `screenY` properties at work:

```
document.addEventListener("mousemove", mouseMoving, false);

function mouseMoving(e) {
   console.log(e.screenX + " " + e.screenY);
}
```

It doesn't matter what other margin/padding/offset/layout craziness you may have going on in your page. The values returned are always going to be the distance between where your mouse is now and where the top-left corner of your primary monitor is.

The Mouse Position Inside the Browser

The `clientX` and `clientY` properties return the x and y position of the mouse relative to your browser's (technically, the browser viewport's) top-left corner:

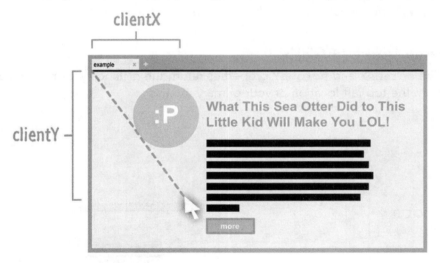

The code for this is nothing exciting:

```
let button = document.querySelector("#myButton");
document.addEventListener("mousemove", mouseMoving, false);

function mouseMoving(e) {
   console.log(e.clientX + " " + e.clientY);
}
```

You just call the `clientX` and `clientY` properties of the event argument that got passed in to our event handler to get the values.

Detecting Which Button Was Clicked

Your mice often have multiple buttons or ways to simulate multiple buttons. The most common button configuration involves a left button, a right button, and a middle button (often a click on your mouse wheel). To figure out which mouse button was pressed, you have the `button` property. This property returns a **0** if the left mouse button was pressed, a **1** if the middle button was pressed, and a **2** if the right mouse button was pressed:

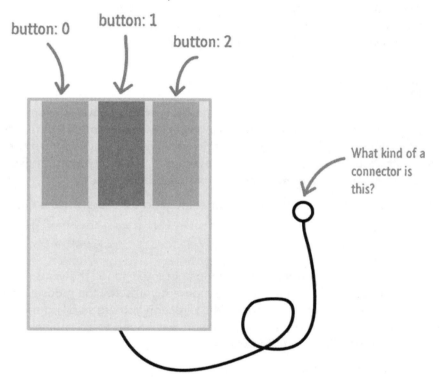

The code for using the button property to check for which button was pressed looks exactly as you would expect:

```
document.addEventListener("mousedown", buttonPress, false);

function buttonPress(e) {
  if (e.button == 0) {
    console.log("Left mouse button pressed!");
```

```
      } else if (e.button == 1) {
        console.log("Middle mouse button pressed!");
      } else if (e.button == 2) {
        console.log("Right mouse button pressed!");
      } else {
        console.log("Things be crazy up in here!!!");
      }
    }
```

In addition to the button property, you also have the buttons and properties that sort of do similar things to help you figure out which button was pressed. I'm not going to talk too much about those two properties, but just know that they exist. You can Google them if you want to know more.

Dealing with the Mouse Wheel

The mouse wheel is special compared to everything else we've seen so far. The obvious difference is that we are dealing with a wheel as opposed to a button. The less obvious, yet probably more relevant, detail is that you have two events to deal with. You have the mousewheel event that is used by Internet Explorer and Chrome and the DOMMouseScroll event used by Firefox.

The way you listen for these mouse wheel-related events is just the usual:

```
document.addEventListener("mousewheel", mouseWheeling, false);

document.addEventListener("DOMMouseScroll", mouseWheeling, false);
```

It's what happens afterwards where things get interesting. The mousewheel and DOMMouseScroll events will fire the moment you scroll the mouse wheel in any direction. For all practical purposes, the direction you are scrolling the mouse-wheel is important. To get that information, we'll need to go spelunking in the event handler to find the event argument.

The event arguments for a mousewheel event contain a property known as wheelDelta. For the DOMMouseScroll event, you have the detail property on the event argument. Both of these properties are similar in that their values change from positive or negative depending on what direction you scroll the mouse wheel. The thing to note is that they are inconsistent in what sign they go with. The wheelDelta property associated with the mousewheel event is positive when you scroll up on the mouse wheel. It is negative when you scroll down. The exact opposite holds true for DOMMouseScroll's detail property. This property is negative when you scroll up, and it is positive when you scroll down.

Handling this `wheelDelta` and `detail` inconsistency is pretty simple…as you can see in the following snippet:

```
function mouseWheeling(e) {
  let scrollDirection;
  let wheelData = e.wheelDelta;

  if (wheelData) {
    scrollDirection = wheelData;
  } else {
    scrollDirection = -1 * e.detail;
  }

  if (scrollDirection > 0) {
    console.log("Scrolling up! " + scrollDirection);
  } else {
    console.log("Scrolling down! " + scrollDirection);
  }
}
```

The `scrollDirection` variable stores the value contained by the `wheelData` property or the `detail` property. Depending on whether this value is positive or negative, you can then special case the behavior.

THE ABSOLUTE MINIMUM

Generally, it is true that if you know how to just work with one event, you pretty much know how to work with all other events. The only thing you need to know is which event corresponds to what you are trying to do. The mouse events are a good introduction to working with events because they are very easy to play with. They aren't very fussy, and the things you learn about them you will use in almost all apps that you build.

Some additional resources and examples that you may want to check out:

- **Move Element to Click Position:** http://bit.ly/kirupaElementClickPosition
- **Are You on a Touch-Enabled Device:** http://bit.ly/kirupaTouchEnabled

If you have any further questions, take a moment and ask away on **https://forum.kirupa.com**.

34

KEYBOARD EVENTS

We spend a lot of time in various applications tapping away at our keyboards. In case you are wondering what a keyboard looks like, Figure 34.1 features a sweet one from I think about a hundred years ago.

This is a keyboard! →

FIGURE 34.1

What a keyboard might look like...in a museum probably.

Anyway, our computers (more specifically, the applications that run on them) just know how to deal with our board of plastic depressible keys. You never really think about it. Sometimes, depending on what you are doing, you will have to think about them. In fact, you'll have to deal with them and make them work properly. Better cancel any plans you have, for this chapter is going to be pretty intense!

By the end of this chapter, you will learn all about how to listen to the keyboard events, what each of those events do, and see a handful of examples that highlight some handy tricks that may come in...um...handy.

Onward!

Meet the Keyboard Events

To work with keyboards in an HTML document, there are three events that you will need to familiarize yourself with. Those events are

- `keydown`
- `keypress`
- `keyup`

Given what these events are called, you probably already have a vague idea of what each event does. The `keydown` event is fired when you press down on a key on your keyboard. The `keyup` event is fired when you release a key that you just pressed. Both of these events work on any key that you interact with.

The `keypress` event is a special bird. At first glance, it seems like this event is fired when you press down on any key. Despite what the name claims, the `keypress` event is fired only when you press down on a key that displays a character (letter, number, and the like). What this means is somewhat confusing, but it makes sense in its own twisted way.

If you press and release a character key such as the letter **y**, you will see the `keydown`, `keypress`, and `keyup` events fired in order. The `keydown` and `keyup` events fire because the **y** key is simply a key to them. The `keypress` event is fired because the **y** key is a character key. If you press and release a key that doesn't display anything on the screen (such as the spacebar, arrow key, or function keys), all you will see are the `keydown` and `keyup` events fired.

This difference is subtle but very important when you want to ensure your key presses are actually overheard by your application.

SAY WHAT?

It is weird that an event called `keypress` doesn't fire when any key is pressed. Maybe this event should be called something else like `characterkeypress`, but that is probably a moo point. (What is a "moo point"? Well… **http://bit.ly/kirupaMoo**)

Using These Events

The way you listen to the `keydown`, `keypress`, and `keyup` events is similar to any other event you may want to listen and react to. You call `addEventListener` on the element that will be dealing with these events, specify the event you want to listen for, specify the event handling function that gets called when the event is overheard, and a **true/false** value indicating whether you want this event to bubble.

Here is an example of me listening to our three keyboard events on the window object:

```
window.addEventListener("keydown", dealWithKeyboard, false);
window.addEventListener("keypress", dealWithKeyboard, false);
window.addEventListener("keyup", dealWithKeyboard, false);

function dealWithKeyboard(e) {
  // gets called when any of the keyboard events are overheard
}
```

If any of these events are overheard, the `dealWithKeyboard` event handler gets called. In fact, this event handler will get called three times if you happen to press down on a character key. This is all pretty straightforward, so let's kick everything up a few notches and go beyond the basics in the next few sections.

The Keyboard Event Properties

When an event handler that reacts to a keyboard event is called, a `Keyboard` event argument is passed in. Let's revisit our `dealWithKeyboard` event handler that you saw earlier. In that event handler, the keyboard event is represented by the `e` argument that is passed in:

```
function dealWithKeyboard(e) {
    // gets called when any of the keyboard events are overheard
}
```

This argument contains a handful of properties:

- `KeyCode`

  Every key you press on your keyboard has a number associated with it. This read-only property returns that number.

- `CharCode`

  This property only exists on event arguments returned by the keypress event, and it contains the ASCII code for whatever character key you pressed.

- `ctrlKey, altKey, shiftKey`

  These three properties return a **true** if the Ctrl key, Alt key, or Shift key is pressed.

- `MetaKey`

- The `metaKey` property is similar to the `ctrlKey`, `altKey`, and `shiftKey` properties in that it returns a **true** if the Meta key is pressed. The Meta key is the Windows key on Windows keyboards and the Command key on Apple keyboards.

The `Keyboard` event contains a few other properties, but the ones you see above are the most interesting ones. With these properties, you can check for which key was pressed and react accordingly. In the next couple of sections, you'll see some examples of this.

 CAUTION The `charCode` and `keyCode` properties are currently marked as deprecated by the web standards people at the W3C. Its replacement might be the mostly unsupported `code` property. Just be aware of this and be ready to update your code in the future when whichever successor to `charCode` and `keyCode` has taken his/her rightful place on the throne.

Some Examples

Now that you've seen the horribly boring basics of how to work with Keyboard events, let's look at some examples that clarify (or potentially confuse!) everything you've seen so far.

Checking That a Particular Key Was Pressed

The following example shows how to use the keyCode property to check if a particular key was pressed:

```
window.addEventListener("keydown", checkKeyPressed, false);


function checkKeyPressed(e) {
  if (e.keyCode == 65) {
    console.log("The 'a' key is pressed.");
  }
}
```

The particular key I check is the **a** key. Internally, this key is mapped to the keyCode value of **65**. In case you never memorized all of them in school, you can find a handy list of all key and character codes at the following link: **http://bit.ly/kirupaKeyCode** Please do not memorize every single code from that list. There are far more interesting things to memorize instead.

Some things to note. The charCode and keyCode values for a particular key are not the same. Also, the charCode is only returned if the event that triggered your event handler was a keypress. In our example, the keydown event would not contain anything useful for the charCode property.

If you wanted to check the charCode and use the keypress event, here is what the above example would look like:

```
window.addEventListener("keypress", checkKeyPressed, false);


function checkKeyPressed(e) {
  if (e.charCode == 97) {
    console.log("The 'a' key is pressed.");
  }
}
```

The charCode for the **a** key is **97**. Again, refer to the table of key and character codes I listed earlier for such details.

Doing Something When the Arrow Keys Are Pressed

We see this most often in games where pressing the arrow keys does something interesting. The following snippet of code shows how that is done:

```
window.addEventListener("keydown", moveSomething, false);


function moveSomething(e) {
  switch (e.keyCode) {
    case 37:
      // left key pressed
      break;
    case 38:
      // up key pressed
      break;
    case 39:
      // right key pressed
      break;
    case 40:
      // down key pressed
      break;
  }
}
```

Again, this should be pretty straightforward as well. And, would you believe it—an actual use for the switch statement that you learned about forever ago in **Chapter 4, "Conditional Statements: if, else, and switch."**

Detecting Multiple Key Presses

Now, this is going to be epic! An interesting case revolves around detecting when we need to react to multiple key presses. What follows is an example of how to do that:

```
window.addEventListener("keydown", keysPressed, false);
window.addEventListener("keyup", keysReleased, false);


let keys = [];


function keysPressed(e) {
  // store an entry for every key pressed
```

```
  keys[e.keyCode] = true;

  // Ctrl + Shift + 5
  if (keys[17] && keys[16] && keys[53]) {
    // do something
  }

  // Ctrl + f
  if (keys[17] && keys[70]) {
    // do something

    // prevent default browser behavior
    e.preventDefault();
  }
}


function keysReleased(e) {
  // mark keys that were released
  keys[e.keyCode] = false;
}
```

Going into great detail about this will require another chapter by itself, but let's just look at how this works very briefly.

First, we have a keys array that stores every single key that you press:

```
let keys = [];
```

As keys get pressed, the `keysPressed` event handler gets called:

```
function keysPressed(e) {
  // store an entry for every key pressed
  keys[e.keyCode] = true;

  // Ctrl + Shift + 5
  if (keys[17] && keys[16] && keys[53]) {
    // do something
  }
```

```
// Ctrl + f
if (keys[17] && keys[70]) {
  // do something

  // prevent default browser behavior
  e.preventDefault();
}
}
```

When a key gets released, the `keysReleased` event handler gets called:

```
function keysReleased(e) {
  // mark keys that were released
  keys[e.keyCode] = false;
}
```

Notice how these two event handlers work with each other. As keys get pressed, an entry gets created for them in the `keys` array with a value of **true**. When keys get released, those same keys are marked with a value of **false**. The existence of the keys you press in the array is superficial. It is the values they store that is actually important.

As long as nothing interrupts your event handlers from getting called properly such as an alert window, you will get a one-to-one mapping between keys pressed and keys released as viewed through the lens of the `keys` array. With all of this said, the checks for seeing which combination of keys have been pressed is handled in the `keysPressed` event handler. The following highlighted lines show how this works:

```
function keysPressed(e) {
  // store an entry for every key pressed
  keys[e.keyCode] = true;

  // Ctrl + Shift + 5
  if (keys[17] && keys[16] && keys[53]) {
    // do something
  }

  // Ctrl + f
  if (keys[17] && keys[70]) {
    // do something
```

```
    // prevent default browser behavior
    e.preventDefault();
  }
}
```

There is one thing you need to keep in mind. Some key combinations result in your browser doing something. To avoid your browser from doing its own thing, use the preventDefault method as highlighted when checking to see if **Ctrl + F** is being used:

```
function keysPressed(e) {
  // store an entry for every key pressed
  keys[e.keyCode] = true;

  // Ctrl + Shift + 5
  if (keys[17] && keys[16] && keys[53]) {
    // do something
  }

  // Ctrl + f
  if (keys[17] && keys[70]) {
    // do something

    // prevent default browser behavior
    e.preventDefault();
  }
}
```

The preventDefault method prevents an event from triggering a default behavior. In this case, it was preventing the browser from showing the Find dialog box. Different key combinations will trigger different reactions by the browser, so keep this method handy to put a stop to those reactions.

Anyway, looking at the code in aggregate, you have a basic blueprint for how to check for multiple key presses easily.

THE ABSOLUTE MINIMUM

The keyboard is pretty important when it comes to how people interact with their computer-like devices. Despite its importance, you often won't have to deal with them directly. Your browser, the various text-related controls/elements, and everything in-between just handle it as you would expect by default. There are certain kinds of applications where you may want to deal with them, though, which is why you have this chapter.

This chapter started off in the most boring way possible by explaining how to work with the Keyboard events and their event arguments. Along the way, things (hopefully) got more interesting as you saw several examples that address common things you would do when dealing with the keyboard in code. If you have any questions about working with the keyboard or anything else, don't hesitate to post on the forums at **https://forum.kirupa.com**.

IN THIS CHAPTER

- Learn about all the events that fire as your page is getting loaded
- Understand what happens behind the scenes during a page load
- Fiddle with the various `script` element attributes that control exactly when your code runs

35

PAGE LOAD EVENTS AND OTHER STUFF

An important part of working with JavaScript is ensuring that your code runs at the right time. Things aren't always as simple as putting your code at the bottom of your page and expecting everything to work once your page has loaded. Yes, we are going to revisit some things we looked at in **Chapter 10, "Where Should Your Code Live?"** Every now and then, you may have to add some extra code to ensure your code doesn't run before the page is ready. Sometimes, you may even have to put your code at the top of your page…like an animal!

There are many factors that affect what the "right time" really is to run your code, and in this chapter, we're going to look at those factors and narrow down what you should do to a handful of guidelines.

Onward!

The Things That Happen During Page Load

Let's start at the very beginning. You click on a link or press Enter after typing in a URL and, if the stars are aligned properly, your page loads. All of that seems pretty simple and takes up a very tiny sliver of time to complete from beginning to end:

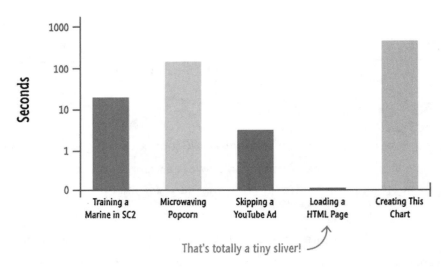

In that short period of time between you wanting to load a page and your page loading, a lot of relevant and interesting stuff happens that you need to know more about. One example of the relevant and interesting stuff that happens is that any code specified on the page will run. When exactly the code runs depends on a combination of the following things that all come alive at some point while your page is getting loaded:

- The `DOMContentLoaded` event
- The `load` Event

- The `async` attribute for script elements
- The `defer` attribute for script elements
- The location your scripts live in the DOM

Don't worry if you don't know what these things are. You'll learn (or re-learn) what all of these things do and the effect they have when your code runs really soon. Before we get there, though, let's take a quick detour and look at the three stages of a page load.

Stage Numero Uno

The first stage is when your browser is about to start loading a new page:

Stage #1: Nothing Much Going On

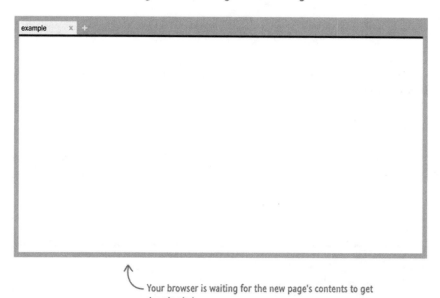

Your browser is waiting for the new page's contents to get downloaded

At this stage, there isn't anything interesting going on. A request has been made to load a page, but nothing has been downloaded yet.

Stage Numero Dos

Things get a bit more exciting with the second stage where the raw markup and DOM of your page has been loaded and parsed:

Stage #2: The DOM is Ready

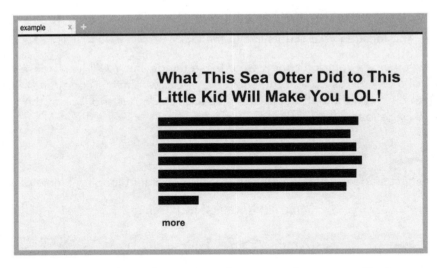

The thing to note about this stage is that external resources like images and linked stylesheets have not been parsed. You only see the raw content specified by your page/document's markup.

Stage Numero Three

The final stage is where your page is fully loaded with any images, stylesheets, scripts, and other external resources making their way into what you see:

Stage #3: Page is Fully Loaded

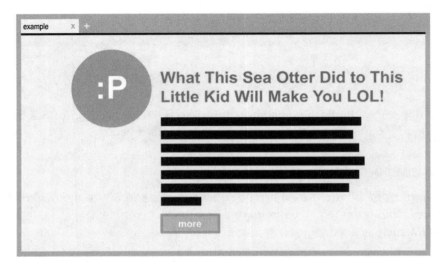

This is the stage where your browser's loading indicators stop animating, and this is also the stage you almost always find yourself in when interacting with your HTML document. That said, sometimes you'll find yourself in an in-between state where 99% of your page has loaded with only some random thing taking forever to load. If you've been to one of those viral/buzz/feedy sites, you'll totally know what I am talking about.

Now that you have a basic idea of the three stages your document goes through when loading content, let's move forward to the more interesting stuff. Keep these three stages at the tip of your fingers (or under your hat if you are wearing one while reading this), as we'll refer back to these stages a few times in the following sections.

The `DOMContentLoaded` and `load` Events

There are two events that represent the two important milestones while your page loads: `DOMContentLoaded` and `load`. The `DOMContentLoaded` event fires at the end of Stage #2 when your page's DOM is fully parsed. The `load` event fires at the end of Stage #3 once your page has fully loaded. You can use these events to time when exactly you want your code to run.

The following is a snippet of these events in action:

```
document.addEventListener("DOMContentLoaded", theDomHasLoaded,
false);

window.addEventListener("load", pageFullyLoaded, false);


function theDomHasLoaded(e) {
  // do something
}


function pageFullyLoaded(e) {
  // do something again
}
```

You use these events just like you would any other event, but the main thing to note about these events is that you need to listen to **DOMContentLoaded** from the `document` element and **load** from the `window` element.

Now that we've got the boring technical details out of the way, why are these events important? Simple. If you have any code that relies on working with the DOM such as anything that uses the `querySelector` or `querySelectorAll` functions, you want to ensure your code runs only after your DOM has been fully loaded. If you try to access your DOM before it has fully loaded, you may get incomplete results or no results at all.

Here is an awesome extreme example from **Kyle Murray** that should help explain this:

```
<!DOCTYPE html>
<html>

<head>
  <script>
      // try to analyze the book's meaning here
  </script>
</head>

<body>
    [INSERT ENTIRE COPY OF /WAR AND PEACE/ HERE]
</body>

</html>
```

A sure-fire way to ensure you never get into a situation where your code runs before your DOM is ready is to listen for the DOMContentLoaded event and let all of the code that relies on the DOM to run only after that event is overheard:

```
document.addEventListener("DOMContentLoaded", theDomHasLoaded, false);

function theDomHasLoaded(e) {
  let headings = document.querySelectorAll("h2");

  // do something with the images
}
```

For cases where you want your code to run only after your page has fully loaded, use the load event. In my years of doing things in JavaScript, I never had too much use for the load event at the document level outside of checking the final dimensions of a loaded image or creating a crude progress bar to indicate progress. Your mileage may vary, but...I doubt it.

Scripts and Their Location in the DOM

In **Chapter 8, "Variable Scope,"** we looked at the various ways in which you can have scripts appear in your document. You saw that your script elements' position in the DOM affects when they run. In this section, we are going to re-emphasize that simple truth and go a few steps further.

To review, a simple script element can be some code stuck inline somewhere:

```
<script>
  let number = Math.random() * 100;
  console.log("A random number is: " + number);
</script>
```

A simple script element can also be something that references some code from an external file:

```
<script src="/foo/something.js"></script>
```

Now, here is the important detail about these elements. Your browser parses your DOM sequentially from the top to the bottom. Any script elements that are found along the way will get parsed in the order they appear in the DOM.

Below is a very simple example where you have many script elements:

```
<!DOCTYPE html>
<html>

<body>
  <h1>Example</h1>
  <script>
    console.log("inline 1");
  </script>
  <script src="external1.js"></script>
  <script>
    console.log("inline 2");
  </script>
  <script src="external2.js"></script>
  <script>
    console.log("inline 3");
  </script>
</body>

</html>
```

It doesn't matter if the script contains inline code or references something external. All scripts are treated the same and run in the order in which they appear in your document. Using the above example, the order in which the scripts will run is as follows: **inline 1**, **external 1**, **inline 2**, **external 2**, and **inline 3**.

Now, here is a really REALLY important detail to be aware of. Because your DOM gets parsed from top to bottom, your script element has access to all of the DOM elements that were already parsed. Your script has no access to any DOM elements that have not yet been parsed. Say, what?!

Let's say you have a script element that is at the bottom of your page just above the closing body element:

```
<!DOCTYPE html>
<html>

<body>
  <h1>Example</h1>

  <p>
    Quisque faucibus, quam sollicitudin pulvinar dignissim, nunc
velit sodales leo, vel vehicula odio lectus vitae
    mauris. Sed sed magna augue. Vestibulum tristique cursus orci,
accumsan posuere nunc congue sed. Ut pretium sit amet
    eros non consectetur. Quisque tincidunt eleifend justo, quis
molestie tellus venenatis non. Vivamus interdum urna ut
    augue rhoncus, eu scelerisque orci dignissim. In commodo purus
id purus tempus commodo.
  </p>

  <button>Click Me</button>

  <script src="something.js"></script>
</body>

</html>
```

When **something.js** runs, it has the ability to access all of the DOM elements that appear just above it such as the h1, p, and button elements. If your script element was at the very top of your document, it wouldn't have any knowledge of the DOM elements that appear below it:

```
<!DOCTYPE html>

<html>


<body>
    <script src="something.js"></script>


  <h1>Example</h1>


  <p>
    Quisque faucibus, quam sollicitudin pulvinar dignissim, nunc
velit sodales leo, vel vehicula odio lectus vitae

    mauris. Sed sed magna augue. Vestibulum tristique cursus orci,
accumsan posuere nunc congue sed. Ut pretium sit amet

    eros non consectetur. Quisque tincidunt eleifend justo, quis
molestie tellus venenatis non. Vivamus interdum urna ut

    augue rhoncus, eu scelerisque orci dignissim. In commodo purus
id purus tempus commodo.
  </p>


  <button>Click Me</button>



</body>


</html>
```

By putting your script element at the bottom of your page as shown earlier, the end behavior is identical to what you would get if you had code that explicitly listened to the DOMContentLoaded event. If you can guarantee that your scripts will appear toward the end of your document after your DOM elements, you can avoid following the whole DOMContentLoaded approach described in the previous section. Now, if you really want to have your script elements at the top of your DOM, ensure that all of the code that relies on the DOM runs after the DOMContentLoaded event gets fired.

Here is the thing. I'm a huge fan of putting your script elements at the bottom of your DOM. There is another reason besides easy DOM access why I recommend having your scripts live toward the bottom of the page. When a script element is being parsed, your browser stops everything else on the page from running while the code is executing. If you have a really long-running script or your external script takes its sweet time in getting downloaded, your HTML page will appear frozen. If your DOM is only partially parsed at this point, your page will also look incomplete in addition to being frozen. Unless you are Facebook, you probably want to avoid having your page look frozen for no reason.

Script Elements—Async and Defer

In the previous section, I explained how a script element's position in the DOM determines when it runs. All of that only applies to what I call **simple** script elements. To be part of the non-simple world, script elements that point to external scripts can have the `defer` and `async` attributes set on them:

```
<script async src="myScript.js"></script>
<script defer src="somethingSomethingDarkSide.js"></script>
```

These attributes alter when your script runs independent of where in the DOM they actually show up, so let's look at how they end up altering your script.

async

The `async` attribute allows a script to run asynchronously:

```
<script async src="someRandomScript.js"></script>
```

If you recall from the previous section, if a script element is being parsed, it could block your browser from being responsive and usable. By setting the `async` attribute on your script element, you avoid that problem altogether. Your script will run whenever it is able to, but it won't block the rest of your browser from doing its thing.

This casualness in running your code is pretty awesome, but you must realize that your scripts marked as `async` will not always run in order. You could have a case where several scripts marked as async will run in an order different from what was specified in your markup. The only guarantee you have is that your scripts marked with `async` will start running at some mysterious point before the `load` event gets fired.

defer

The `defer` attribute is a bit different from `async`:

```
<script defer src="someRandomScript.js"></script>
```

Scripts marked with defer run in the order in which they were defined, but they only get executed at the end just a few moments before the DOMContentLoaded event gets fired. Take a look at the following example:

```
<!DOCTYPE html>
<html>

<body>
  <h1>Example</h1>
  <script defer src="external1.js"></script>
  <script>
    console.log("inline 1");
  </script>
  <script src="external2.js"></script>
  <script>
    console.log("inline 2");
  </script>
  <script defer src="external3.js"></script>
  <script>
    console.log("inline 3");
  </script>
</body>

</html>
```

Take a second and tell the nearest human/pet the order in which these scripts will run. It's okay if you don't provide them with any context. If they love you, they'll understand.

Anyway, your scripts will execute in the following order: **inline 1**, **external 1**, **inline 2**, **inline 3**, **external 3**, and **external 2**. The **external 3** and **external 2** scripts are marked as defer, and that's why they appear at the very end despite being declared in different locations in your markup.

THE ABSOLUTE MINIMUM

In the previous sections, we looked at all sorts of factors that influence when your code will execute. The following diagram summarizes everything you saw into a series of colorful lines and rectangles:

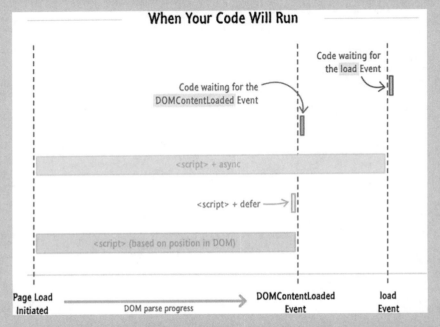

Now, here is probably what you are looking for. When is the right time to load your JavaScript? The answer is...

1. Place your script references below your DOM directly above your closing body element.

2. Unless you are creating a library that others will use, don't complicate your code by listening to the DOMContentLoaded or load events. Instead, see the previous point.

3. Mark your scripts referencing external files with the defer attribute.

4. If you have code that doesn't rely on your DOM being loaded and runs as part of teeing things off for other scripts in your document, you can place this script at the top of your page with the async attribute set on it.

That's it. I think those four steps will cover almost 90% of all your cases to ensure your code runs at the right time. For more advanced scenarios, you should definitely take a look at a third-party library like **require.js**, which gives you greater control over when your code will run. If you have any issues with loading things, post on **https://forum.kirupa.com**.

Some additional resources and examples:

- **Module Loading with RequireJS:** http://bit.ly/kirupaRequireJS
- **Preloading Images:** http://bit.ly/kirupaPreloadImages

36

HANDLING EVENTS FOR MULTIPLE ELEMENTS

In its most basic case, an event listener deals with events fired from a single element:

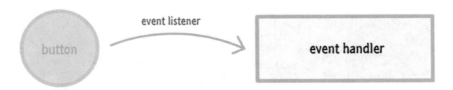

As you build more complicated things, the "one event handler for one element" mapping starts to show its limitation. The most common reason revolves around you creating elements dynamically using JavaScript. These elements you are creating can fire events that you may want to listen and react to, and you can have anywhere from a handful of elements that need eventing support to many MANY elements that need to have their events dealt with.

What you don't want to do is this:

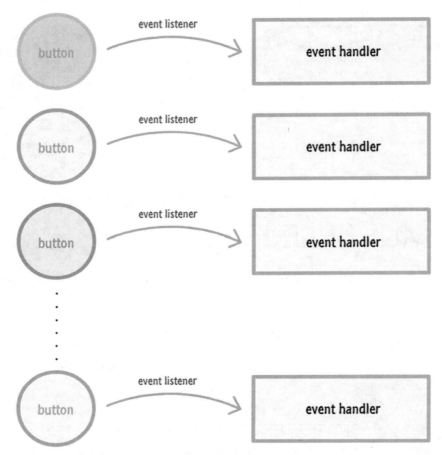

You don't want to create an event listener for each element **IF the event listener is the same for all of them**. The reason is because your parents told you so. The other reason is because it is inefficient. Each of these elements carries around data about the same event listener and its properties that can really start adding up the memory usage when you have a lot of content. Instead, what you want is a clean and fast way of handling events on multiple elements with minimal duplication and unnecessary things. What you want will look a little bit like this:

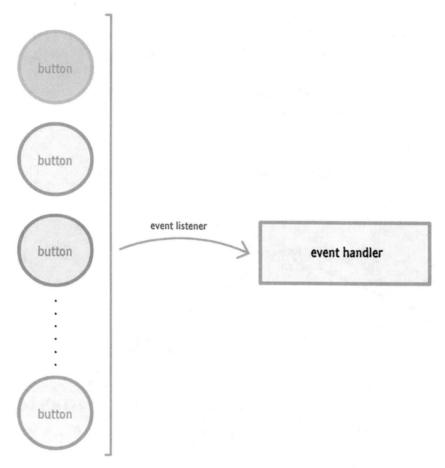

All of this may sound a bit crazy, right? Well, in this chapter, you will learn all about how non-crazy this is and how to implement this using just a few lines of JavaScript.

Onward!

How to Do All of This

Okay—at this point, you know how simple event handling works where you have one element, one event listener, and one event handler. Despite how different the case with multiple elements may seem, by taking advantage of the disruptiveness of events, solving it is actually quite easy.

Imagine we have a case where you want to listen for the click event on any of the sibling elements whose id values are one, two, three, four, and five. Let's complete our imagination by picturing the DOM as follows:

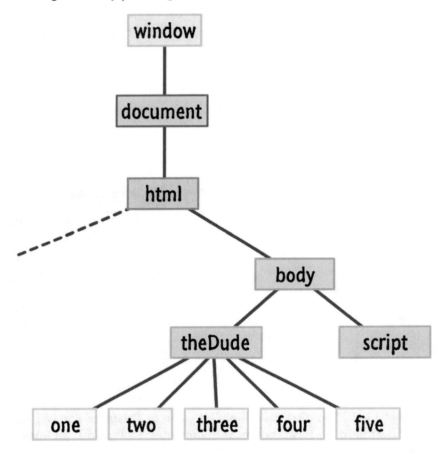

At the very bottom, we have the elements we want to listen for events on. They all share a common parent with an element whose id value is theDude. To solve our event handling problems, let's look at a terrible solution followed by a good solution.

A Terrible Solution

Here is what we don't want to do. We don't want to have five event listeners for each of these buttons:

```
let oneElement = document.querySelector("#one");
let twoElement = document.querySelector("#two");
let threeElement = document.querySelector("#three");
```

```
let fourElement = document.querySelector("#four");
let fiveElement = document.querySelector("#five");

oneElement.addEventListener("click", doSomething, false);
twoElement.addEventListener("click", doSomething, false);
threeElement.addEventListener("click", doSomething, false);
fourElement.addEventListener("click", doSomething, false);
fiveElement.addEventListener("click", doSomething, false);

function doSomething(e) {
  let clickedItem = e.target.id;
  console.log("Hello " + clickedItem);
}
```

To echo what I mentioned in the intro, the obvious reason is that you don't want to duplicate code. The other reason is that each of these elements now has their addEventListener property set. This is not a big deal for five elements. It starts to become a big deal when you have dozens or hundreds of elements each taking up a small amount of memory. The other OTHER reason is that your number of elements, depending on how adaptive or dynamic your UI really is, can vary. Your app may add or remove elements depending on what the user is doing, so it would be difficult to keep track of all the individual event listeners that each object may or may not need. Having one overarching event handler makes this situation much more fun.

A Good Solution

The good solution for this mimics the diagram you saw much earlier where we have just one event listener. I am going to confuse you first by describing how this works. Then I'll hopefully un-confuse you by showing the code and explaining in detail what exactly is going on. The simple and confusing solution to this is:

1. Create a single event listener on the parent **theDude** element.

2. When any of the **one**, **two**, **three**, **four**, or **five** elements are clicked, rely on the propagation behavior that events possess and intercept them when they hit the parent **theDude** element.

3. (Optional) Stop the event propagation at the parent element just to avoid having to deal with the event obnoxiously running up and down the DOM tree.

I don't know about you, but I'm certainly confused after having read those three steps! Let's start to unconfuse ourselves by starting with a diagram that explains those steps more visually:

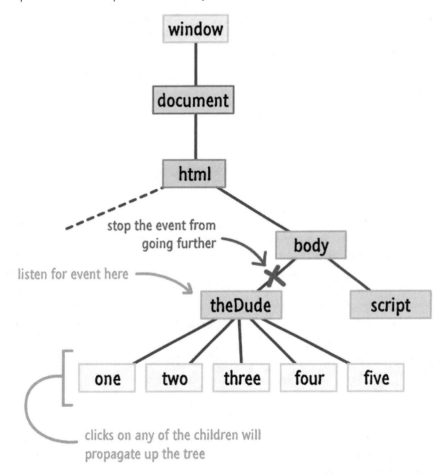

The last step in our quest for complete unconfusedness is the code that translates what the diagram and the three steps represent:

```
let theParent = document.querySelector("#theDude");
theParent.addEventListener("click", doSomething, false);

function doSomething(e) {
  if (e.target != e.currentTarget) {
    let clickedItem = e.target.id;
```

```
      console.log("Hello " + clickedItem);
   }
   e.stopPropagation();
}
```

Take a moment to read and understand the code you see here. After seeing our initial goals and the diagram, we will listen for the event on the parent **theDude** element:

```
let theParent = document.querySelector("#theDude");
theParent.addEventListener("click", doSomething, false);
```

There is only one event listener to handle this event, and that lonely creature is called doSomething:

```
function doSomething(e) {
   if (e.target != e.currentTarget) {
      let clickedItem = e.target.id;
      console.log("Hello " + clickedItem);
   }
   e.stopPropagation();
}
```

This event listener will get called each time **theDude** element is clicked along with any children that get clicked as well. We only care about click events relating to the children, and the proper way to ignore clicks on this parent element is to simply avoid running any code if the element the click is from (aka the event target) is the same as the event listener target (aka **theDude** element):

```
function doSomething(e) {
   if (e.target != e.currentTarget) {
      let clickedItem = e.target.id;
      console.log("Hello " + clickedItem);
   }
   e.stopPropagation();
}
```

The target of the event is represented by e.target, and the target element the event listener is attached to is represented by e.currentTarget. By simply checking that these values not be equal, you can ensure that the event handler doesn't react to events fired from the parent element that you don't care about.

To stop the event's propagation, we simply call the `stopPropagation` method:

```
function doSomething(e) {
  if (e.target != e.currentTarget) {
    let clickedItem = e.target.id;
    console.log("Hello " + clickedItem);
  }
  e.stopPropagation();
}
```

Notice that this code is actually outside of my `if` statement. This is because I want the event to stop traversing the DOM under all situations once it gets overheard.

Putting It All Together

The end result of all of this code running is that you can click on any of `theDude`'s children and listen for the event as it propagates up:

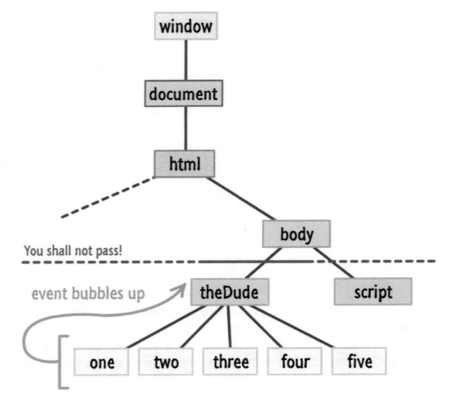

Because all of the event arguments are still unique to the element that we are interacting with (aka the source of the event), we are able to identify and special case the clicked element from inside the event handler despite the `addEventListener` being active only on the parent. The main thing to call out about this solution is that it satisfies the problems we set out to avoid. You only created one event listener. It doesn't matter how many children **theDude** ends up having. This approach is generic enough to accommodate all of them without any extra modification to your code. This also means that you should do some strict filtering if your **theDude** element ends up having children besides buttons and other elements that you care about.

THE ABSOLUTE MINIMUM

For some time, I actually proposed a solution for our Multiple Element Eventing Conundrum (**MEEC** as the cool kids call it!) that was inefficient but didn't require you to duplicate many lines of code. Before many people pointed out the inefficiencies of it, I thought it was a valid solution.

The way this solution worked was by using a `for` loop to attach event listeners to all the children of a parent (or an array containing HTML elements). Here is what that code looked like:

```
let theParent = document.querySelector("#theDude");


for (let i = 0; i < theParent.children.length; i++) {
  let childElement = theParent.children[i];
  childElement.addEventListener('click', doSomething, false);
}


function doSomething(e) {
  let clickedItem = e.target.id;
  console.log("Hello " + clickedItem);
}
```

The end result was that this approach allowed us to listen for the click event directly on the children. The only code I wrote manually was this single event listener call that was parameterized to the appropriate child element based on where in the loop the code was in:

```
childElement.addEventListener('click', doSomething, false);
```

The reason this approach isn't great is because each child element has an event listener associated with it. This goes back to our efficiency argument where this approach unnecessarily wastes memory.

Now, if you do have a situation where your elements are spread throughout the DOM with no nearby common parent, using this approach on an array of HTML elements is not a bad way of solving our MEEC problem.

Anyway, as you start working with larger quantities of UI elements for games, data-visualization apps, and other HTML Element-rich things, you'll end up having to use everything you saw here at least once. I hope. If all else fails, this chapter still served an important purpose. All of the stuff about event tunneling and capturing you saw earlier clearly came in handy here. That's something!

37

CONCLUSION

Well, now you've done it! You just couldn't stop binge reading and now you are nearing the end. How does it feel knowing that you won't have any more new content to look forward to until the next season?

Anyway, if you've been following along from the very beginning, you'll agree that we covered a lot of ground. We started with this:

```
<script>
  console.log("hello, world!");
</script>
```

We ended up with examples and snippets that had many more lines of more complex, useful, and far cooler code.

The thing you should remember is that writing code is easy. Writing **elegant** code that actually solves a problem is hard. This was best captured by one of my favorite lines from **Scarface** where Tony Montana delivered the following line (exact wording may be off a bit...it's hard to understand him sometimes, as you know if you've seen the film):

...you gotta learn the basics first.

Then when you learn the basics, you get to solve interesting problems.

Then when you get to solve interesting problems, then you get the bubble tea.

That's a TOTALLY sweet Al Pacino depiction!

This book is all about the basics. The way you go from the basics to the next step is by continuing to write code, trying out new things, and learning more along the way. This book described all the various tools and provided short examples of how they fit together help you build small things. It's up to you to take this knowledge and apply it towards building all the cooler non-small things that you often see associated with JavaScript. If you are feeling up for it, take a look at some of the more involved tutorials and examples on **https://www.kirupa.com**.

So with that…see you all later, and feel free to drop me a line at **kirupa@kirupa. com** or find me on Facebook and Twitter (**@kirupa**). Like I mentioned in the introduction, I enjoy hearing from readers such as you, so don't be shy about contacting me. If you have any questions (big or small), take a moment and post on **https://forum. kirupa.com**.

Also, I know you have a lot of choices in books for learning JavaScript. Thank you for choosing this book and allowing me to live vicariously through your code editor.

Cheers,

Glossary

A very casual look at the various terms you will encounter in this book and beyond.

A

Arguments The values you provide (or pass in) to a function.

Array A data structure that allows you to store and access a sequence of values.

B

Boolean A data structure that represents true or false.

C

Cascading Style Sheets (CSS) A styling language used primarily for changing how the content in your HTML page looks.

Closure An inner function that has access to an outer function's variables (in addition to its own and any global variables).

Comments Human readable text (often separated by // or /* and */ characters) in your code that is completely ignored by JavaScript.

D

Developer Tools In the context of browsers, they are extensions that help you inspect, debug, and diagnose what is going on inside your web page.

Do...While Loop

Do...While Loop A control statement that executes some code until a condition you specify returns false. (This is great if you don't know how many times you want to loop!)

Document Object Model (DOM) The JavaScript representation (often in a tree-like structure) of your HTML page and all the things inside it.

E

Event Bubbling The phase where an event starts at the element that initiated the event and climbs the DOM back to the root.

Event Capturing The phase where an event starts at the root and traverses down the DOM until it reaches the element that initiated the event.

Event Listener A function that listens for an event and then executes some code when that event is overheard.

Event Target The element that is responsible for having initiated (aka fired) an event.

Event A signal that travels through your DOM to indicate something has happened.

F

For Loop A control statement that executes some code a finite number of times.

Function A reusable block of code that takes arguments, groups statements together, and can be called on to execute the code contained inside it.

G

Global Scope Something declared outside of a function that is accessible to the entire app.

I

If Statement A conditional statement that executes some code if the condition is true.

If/Else Statement A conditional statement that executes different pieces of code depending on whether a condition is true or false.

IIFE (Immediately Invoked Function Expression) A way of writing JavaScript that allows you to execute some code in its own scope without leaving behind any trace of its existence.

Invoke A fancy way of saying the same thing as calling a function.

J

JavaScript A fussy and (often) inconsistent scripting language that, to everyone's surprise over the years, has grown to be quite popular for building apps on the web and the server.

L

Local Scope Something that is accessible only to the enclosing function or block.

Loop A control statement that allows you to execute code repeatedly.

N

Node A generic name for an item in the DOM.

O

Object A very flexible and ubiquitous data structure you can use to store properties and their values and...even other objects.

Operators A built-in function such as your friendly +, -, *, /, `for`, `while`, `if`, `do`, `=`, etc. words.

P

Primitives A basic type that isn't composed of other types.

R

Return A keyword that exits a function or block. In the case of functions, it is often used to return some data back to whatever called the function.

S

Scope A term indicating the visibility of something. In the real world, it is also a brand of mouthwash.

Strict Equality (===) Comparison Checks whether value and type of two things is equal.

Strict Inequality (!==) Comparison Checks whether the value and type of two things is not equal.

String A sequence of characters that make up what we think of as text. It is also the name of a formal type for dealing with text in JavaScript.

Switch Statement A conditional statement that checks a particular condition against a list of cases. If one of the cases matches the condition, the code associated with that case executes.

T

Timer Functions Functions that execute code at a periodic interval. The most common timer functions are `setTimeOut`, `setInterval`, and `requestAnimationFrame`.

Type A classification that helps identify your data and the values you can use.

V

Values The formal name for the various types of data you'll encounter.

Variable Scope The term for describing the visibility of a variable in a section of code.

Variables A named bucket for storing some data.

W

Weak Equality (==) Comparison Checks only whether the value of two things is equal.

Weak Inequality (!=) Comparison Checks only whether the value of two things is unequal.

Web Browser A complex application that, at its bare minimum, helps you browse the Internet and display web pages.

While Loop A control statement that continually executes some code until a condition you specify returns false.

Index

I

J

N

O

P

Q

R

T

text values, changing in DOM, 284–285

textContent property, 284–285

this keyword, 209–211

timers, 77–81
 requestAnimationFrame function, 80–81
 setInterval function, 79–80
 setTimeout function, 78

toggling class values, 294

toLowerCase method, 168

toUpperCase method, 168

trigonometric functions, 183–184

type coercion, 240–241

typeof keyword, 172, 245

types, 133–141. *See also names of specific types*
 list of, 137
 objects, 138, 195–211
  as abstraction, 138–139
  adding properties, 197–200
  constructor functions, 171
  creating, 197, 205–208, 222–224
  extending, 213–220
  list of, 140
  nesting, 199–200
  Object type, 196
  parent/child objects, 206–207
  primitives as, 141, 169–173
  properties, 196
  prototype chain, 201–204
  prototypical inheritance model, 212
  removing properties, 200–201
  this keyword, 209–211
 pizza analogy, 134–136
 primitives, 138
  Object-form of, 141, 169–173

U

UI development with setTimeout function, 78

undefined type, 137, 201, 244–246

undefined variables, 90–92

unshift method, 147–148

uppercase generator example (getters/setters), 191

V

validation example (getters/setters), 192–193

values, 15. *See also* types
 in arrays
  accessing, 145–146
  adding, 147–148
  combining, 155–157
  counting, 146
  filtering, 154–155
  finding, 150
  modifying, 151–153
  removing, 149–150
 changing in variables, 19–20
 in JSON, 253–256
  arrays, 256
  booleans, 254–255
  null, 256
  numbers, 254
  objects, 255–256
  reading, 257–258
  strings, 253
 in log method, 127–128
 null, 244
 undefined, 244–246
 validating, 192–193

var keyword, 90

variable scope, 20, 83–92
 block scope, 87–90
 closures, 98–104

How can we make this index more useful? Email us at indexes@quepublishing.com

W

Photo by Marvent/Shutterstock

VIDEO TRAINING FOR THE **IT PROFESSIONAL**

LEARN QUICKLY
Learn a new technology in just hours. Video training can teach more in less time, and material is generally easier to absorb and remember.

WATCH AND LEARN
Instructors demonstrate concepts so you see technology in action.

TEST YOURSELF
Our Complete Video Courses offer self-assessment quizzes throughout.

CONVENIENT
Most videos are streaming with an option to download lessons for offline viewing.

Learn more, browse our store, and watch free, sample lessons at

informit.com/video

Save 50%* off the list price of video courses with discount code **VIDBOB**

the trusted technology learning source